# INTELLIGENT BIOMATERIALS OUTSMARTING CANCER



## FROM DESIGN TO DELIVERY

MANI SHARMA

Made with ♥ on the Notion Press Platform
www.notionpress.com

*"We dedicate this book, to all the cancer patients who have bravely battled this relentless disease, and to those who have lost their lives in this fight*

*May Lord Shiva bless all who have struggled and continue to struggle"*

# Contents

# Foreword

With over 20 years of experience in drug delivery and oncology, I have come to recognize the invaluable contribution of comprehensive literature in advancing our understanding of cancer treatment. This book, Intelligent Biomaterials Outsmarting Cancer, by Dr. Mani Sharma and Mr. Abhiram Kumar, stands out as a seminal work in this field. It meticulously covers the essential aspects of innovative biomaterials used in cancer drug delivery, offering insights into their transformative potential. It is with great enthusiasm that I endorse this book, confident that it will serve as a vital resource for both researchers and practitioners dedicated to overcoming the challenges of cancer treatment.

"***Dr. Mayank Kumar Singh, Scientist***
*The National Dendrimer & Nanotechnology Center*
*Mt. Pleasant, Michigan, USA*
*mayank89singh@gmail.com*"

# Preface

"One of the greatest collective endeavors is science"

The relationship between society and science is one of mutual benefit and dynamic interaction, with scientists serving as catalysts. Supported by research institutions, libraries, laboratories, and essential resources, scientists devote themselves to enhancing societal conditions. Their work addresses critical needs such as food, water, clean air, and medical advancements through continuous exploration and innovation.

This pursuit of knowledge aims to break free from outdated conventions, fostering new, innovative techniques that benefit humanity and the planet. Science evolves with our beliefs and needs, profoundly impacting education, justice, ethics, and overall human conditions. The complexity and advancement of scientific work increase daily, making it challenging to predict its long-term socio-economic and behavioral impacts. Nonetheless, we aspire to eliminate negative effects on Earth, ensuring a livable planet for future generations. Science systematically explores the universe through experiments, observations, and measurements, offering deep insights into evolution and life improvement. The interdependence of society and science is crucial; societal progress relies on scientific discoveries and inventions, while science thrives on societal support.

India's journey from the Vedic age to modern times showcases numerous scientific champions. Their intellect and dedication have driven revolutionary changes across the nation. Among them, Pt. Jawaharlal Nehru, India's first Prime Minister, played a pivotal role in fostering scientific temper. He once stated, "Science teaches us new ways of doing things. Perhaps, it improves our conditions of industrial life, but the basic thing that science should do is to teach us to think straight, to act straight, and not to be afraid of discarding anything or accepting anything provided there are sufficient reasons for doing so." Science itself is neutral; its impact on society depends on how we choose to apply it.

In developing countries like India, scientific knowledge is crucial for growth and success across various sectors. Medical science, addressing hunger, famine, geographical challenges, astronomy, economic growth, and other areas, highlights the investments needed today for a better tomorrow. Over the past five decades, science has revolutionized education, communication, and travel in India, significantly enhancing human existence.

One of the most valuable contributions of science is in medical advancements, which have greatly reduced human and animal suffering. Increased life expectancy and decreased infant mortality rates are direct results of medical discoveries. Diseases like cancer, smallpox, cholera, tuberculosis, and typhoid are now treatable, and epidemic outbreaks can be prevented.

Therefore, it is imperative to establish a strong foundation ensuring that scientific knowledge and power are harnessed for the benefit of humanity and our planet.

In this book, "***we have endeavored to compile a comprehensive pool of biomaterials and their importanc in cancer science, offering insights and information under one cover***"

Acknowledgements

*"Gain as much knowledge as you can, avoid the word I don't know"*

*- Dr. Vinod Kumar Sharma, Ph.D, History.*

*With deep sense of affection and love I express my heartfelt thanks to all my co-authors who worked tremendously to put up the adequate work in profound deadlines.*

*I also express my sincere thanks and love to my maternal and paternal grandmother and grandfather, my beloved parents Mrs. Kalpana Sharma and Dr. Vinod Kumar Sharma. My loving wife Jyoti Sharma, who have always stood beside me in all my good and bad times sharing her knowledge , love and emotional support due to which it was possible to complete this project. My elder sister Juhi Sharma and younger brother Avi Sharma, for their unconditional love, support and blessings due to which all professional and personal tasks could reach up to a beautiful completion.*

*Let me conclude this by praising Lord Ganesha , for all the blessings that showered on us.*

*Once again I would like to thank all those (friends & family) who were directly or indirectly involved in the completion of this project.*

*Thankful I ever remain.*

*MANI SHARMA*

# Prologue

The battle against cancer has long been one of humanity's most challenging and relentless pursuits. As one of the leading causes of death worldwide, cancer remains a formidable adversary, demanding innovative and effective solutions. This book, "Intelligent Biomaterials Outsmarting Cancer," delves into a revolutionary approach that combines the power of advanced biomaterials with cutting-edge scientific intelligence to outsmart this complex disease.

In recent years, the convergence of materials science, biotechnology, and medical research has given rise to the development of intelligent biomaterials—engineered substances designed to interact with biological systems in sophisticated ways. These materials hold the promise of transforming cancer treatment, diagnosis, and prevention by offering targeted, efficient, and less invasive solutions.

The journey of intelligent biomaterials begins with understanding the intricate landscape of cancer biology. Cancer is not a single entity but a diverse group of diseases characterized by uncontrolled cell growth and spread. Each type of cancer has its own unique set of challenges, making a one-size-fits-all approach ineffective. The advent of intelligent biomaterials marks a significant shift towards personalized medicine, where treatments are tailored to the specific characteristics of a patient's cancer.

This book explores the multifaceted world of intelligent biomaterials, from their foundational principles to their applications in cancer therapy. We will navigate through the synthesis and design of these materials, examining how they are crafted to respond to the dynamic environment of cancerous tissues. Intelligent biomaterials can be engineered to release drugs in a controlled manner, target cancer cells with pinpoint accuracy, and even signal the presence of malignancies at early stages.

Moreover, this book sheds light on the collaborative efforts between scientists, engineers, and clinicians. The development of intelligent biomaterials is a testament to the power of interdisciplinary research and the importance of bridging gaps between various fields of expertise. By fostering a collaborative spirit, researchers are pushing the boundaries of what is possible in cancer treatment.

Throughout these pages, we will showcase groundbreaking research, case studies, and real-world applications of intelligent biomaterials in oncology. From nanoparticles that deliver chemotherapeutic agents directly to tumors, to scaffolds that promote tissue regeneration post-surgery, the potential of these materials is vast and varied.

As we embark on this exploration, it is essential to recognize the ethical considerations and challenges that accompany the development of intelligent biomaterials. Issues such as biocompatibility, long-term effects, and accessibility must be addressed to ensure that these advancements benefit all patients, regardless of socio-economic status.

"Intelligent Biomaterials Outsmarting Cancer" is not just a compilation of scientific achievements; it is a testament to human ingenuity and resilience. It is a narrative of hope, determination, and the relentless pursuit of knowledge. As you delve into the chapters that follow, we invite you to join us in envisioning a future where cancer is no longer a feared adversary, but a conquerable challenge through the brilliance of intelligent biomaterials.

CHAPTER ONE

# Can Biodegradable Biomaterials Enhance Cancer Therapy?

**Anjali Rai[1], Neeraj Sharma[2], Abhiram Kumar[3]***

[1]*Para Medical and Allied Health Sciences, Jagannath University, Jaipur, Rajasthan, 303901, Inida*

[2]*Department of Pharmacy, BanasthaliVidyapith, Jaipur, Rajasthan, 304022, India.*

[3]*Birla Institute of Technology and Sciences Pilani Hyderabad Campus, 500078, India*

**Highlights**

- *Materials like PCL, PLA, and PLGA reduce long-term toxicity and improve patient outcomes in cancer therapy.*
- *Polymeric nanocarriers target cancer through bloodstream extension, endothelial transport, and ligand-mediated targeting, impacting tumor growth and immune responses.*
- *Used in drug delivery, tissue engineering, and medical devices, improving treatment efficacy and reducing side effects.*
- *New materials like SF's, collagen, and gelatin are being explored for cancer therapy, focusing on drug delivery and tissue regeneration.*

**Introduction**

Over the past fifty years, the development of biodegradable polymeric materials has made significant strides in the field of biomedical applications. These materials are particularly valued for use in therapeutic devices such as temporary implants and three-dimensional scaffolds for tissue engineering. Additionally, they have seen advancements in pharmacological applications, serving as delivery vehicles for controlled and sustained drug release. A crucial factor for these materials is their biocompatibility, which refers to the ability of the material to perform with an appropriate response from the host in a given application. Several characteristics of an implant material influence the host tissue response, including molecular weight, solubility, hydrophilicity/hydrophobicity, surface energy, material chemistry, degradation mechanism, lubricity, and the shape and structure of the implant [1,2]. Biodegradable biomaterials must exhibit excellent biocompatibility throughout their lifecycle. As these materials degrade, their physicochemical, mechanical, and biological properties change, and the resulting degradation products must remain biocompatible. Ideally, the degradation products of biodegradable biomaterials should be non-toxic and easily metabolized and cleared from the body [3].

Cancer therapy has long been a pressing concern, driving the need for effective and targeted treatments. Biodegradable biomaterials have emerged as a promising class for cancer therapy due to their natural degradation in the body, reducing long-term toxicity and improving patient outcomes. Among these materials, nanoparticles based on biodegradable polyesters such as polycaprolactone (PCL), polylactic acid (PLA), and polylactic-co-glycolic acid (PLGA) have garnered significant attention securing approval from the U.S. Food and Drug Administration for various clinical applications in DDS[4].

Biodegradable polyesters are ecologically benign and biocompatible, breaking down into small molecule byproducts within the human physiological environment. These biodegradable polyesters show great promise for creating nanoparticles for cancer therapy. These nanoparticles can pass through the spleen and liver's endothelial barriers, allowing them to passively collect at tumor locations. They have high drug loading capacity, promote optimal intracellular uptake, and improve drug stability in the circulation due to their hydrophobic core, which wraps the pharmaceuticals. These nanoparticles can be customized tumors by integrating various functional groups, and modulating their actions within the body.[5].

Researchers exploited cancer cell-specific ligands to increase the delivery system's active targeting capabilities. These ligands, which include peptides, polysaccharides, and antibodies, can easily enter cancer cells via receptor-mediated transcytosis, eliminating reliance only on the EPR effect. Biodegradable polymeric nanocarriers can target cancer through a variety of mechanisms, including bloodstream extension, endothelial transport to the tumour, and ligand-mediated targeting. These nanocarriers can potentially target other cells in the cancer microenvironment, such as neo vasculature and immune cells. Targeting the cancer vasculature is crucial because it provides the tumor with sufficient oxygen and nutrients for growth. Furthermore, controlling the immune response can have a significant effect on whether a cancer goes into remission or expands, emphasizing the importance of targeting immune cells [6].

**Biodegradable Biomaterials**

Biomaterials are essential for the development of drug delivery system (DDS), tissue engineering, implantable medical devices, and drug testing. In DDS, biomaterials such as polymers and lipids can encapsulate and release pharmaceutical molecules in a regulated and targeted manner, improving treatment efficacy, lowering adverse effects, and ensuring long-term release for chronic diseases. For example, biodegradable polymer nanoparticles can be loaded with medications for long-term release at the site of action. Tissue engineering uses biocompatible materials including hydrogels, ceramics, and polymers to create scaffolds that promote cell proliferation and tissue regeneration, resulting in viable replacement tissues and organs. Implantable medical devices such as prosthetic joints, pacemakers, and stents are developed using biomaterials such as titanium alloys and biodegradable polymers to ensure biocompatibility and integration with body tissues, reducing immune responses and improving patient quality of life [7,8].A list of some common biomaterials used is provided below (Table-1)

**Classification**

Biodegradable biomaterials can be classified into two main categories based on their source and composition: natural and synthetic [9].

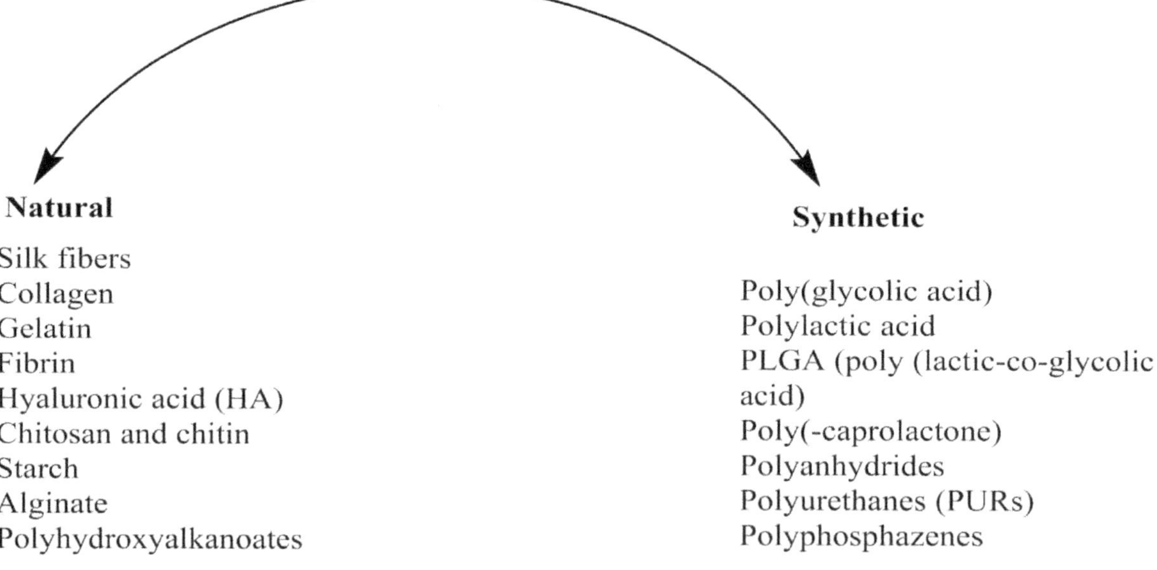

**Natural Biodegradable Biomaterials:**

Include proteins such as collagen, fibrin, and silk, as well as polysaccharides like starch, alginate, and chitin/ chitosan. Native polyesters like polyhydroxyalkanoates (PHA) are also considered natural biodegradable biomaterials [10].

I. **Silk Fibers (SF's)**

Silk is a naturally occurring polymer dating back to the first few millennia BC in China, predominantly used for textiles. It has remained a popular luxury material over the years. Silk has recently discovered new applications in medicine, particularly cancer research [11]. The FDA's approval of silk has resulted in commercializing of various silk-based goods, most notably silk sutures. This approval has also paved the road for silk biomaterial research in the disciplines of tissue engineering, medication delivery, small molecules, gene delivery, and biologics. SF's, derived primarily from the silkworm Bombyx mori, possess high tensile strength, elasticity, and flexibility, making them ideal for various biomedical applications. SF'sis easily processed into gels, films, nanoparticles, scaffolds, and foams, adaptable for tissue engineering, wound repair, and drug delivery. Recent research has highlighted SF's potential in cancer therapy due to its ability to load sensitive drugs, such as proteins and nucleic acids, under mild conditions[12]. For incidence, F. Philipp Seib et. el., demonstrated that doxorubicin-loaded silk films modulating silk crystallinity, specifically the β-sheet content, the release rate of doxorubicin could be finely tuned, spanning from immediate release to sustained release over a period exceeding 4 weeks. The therapeutic efficacy of doxorubicin-loaded silk films was evaluated in mice bearing a humanized orthotopic breast cancer model (adenocarcinoma), assessing both primary tumor growth and metastasis. His findings demonstrated that both soluble and stabilised silk films loaded with doxorubicin had a significantly greater primary tumour response than the equivalent dose of doxorubicin administered intravenously in the absence of the silk film carrier. SF's diverse amino acids facilitate the attachment of biomolecules or antibodies, enhancing its functionality as a drug carrier. Studies are investigating SF's nanoparticles for efficient protein, small-molecule, and anticancer drug delivery, focusing on electrostatic interactions, drug-release kinetics, and compatibility. Although still in early stages, SF's properties, such as tunable biodegradability and biocompatibility, show promise for future advancements in cancer treatment and regenerative medicine [13].

I. **Collagen**

Research subsequently focused on the conformation of the collagen monomer, developing multiple competing models while appropriately addressing the conformation of each peptide chain. In 1955, G. N. Ramachandran proposed the triple-helical "Madras" model, which offered a precise picture of collagen's quaternary structure [14]. Collagen the most prevalent protein in the human body, provides structural support while also altering cellular behaviors and tissue functions. This protein is synthesised from amino acids in cells such as osteoblasts and fibroblasts before being degraded into amino acids by enzymes such as matrix metalloproteinases and collagenases. Because of its distinct mechanical, biological, and physicochemical qualities, collagen is widely used in biomedical applications, including cancer therapy. Collagen-based materials are critical in tissue engineering for reproducing the extracellular matrix and restoring tissue integrity, which is required for cancer-related tissue regeneration. Collagen systems allow sustained local drug delivery with limited systemic exposure, making them useful for treating bone-related malignancies and persistent wounds. Collagen's thrombogenicity makes it a useful hemostatic agent in cancer procedures [15]. According to Liang et al.,2016 indicate that the collagen-binding domain (CBD) was joined to the cetuximabscFv fragment that targets EGFR, resulting in the CBD-scFv construct. This CBD-scFv retained the antigen binding and anti-tumor efficacy of the original cetuximab antibody while also acquiring the ability to attach to collagen. In vitro, tests revealed that the CBD-scFv had higher tumor cell binding and internalization than the unmodified scFv. Furthermore, in vivo investigations showed that CBD-scFv boosted tumor accumulation and retention compared to scFv alone in a xenograft model. Despite its advantages, collagen's immunogenicity, expensive cost, and variable characteristics prevent its widespread clinical application. Advances in recombinant collagen manufacturing aim to address these issues, however they currently lack some key biological activities due to the lack of post-translational modifications. Continued research is required to improve collagen functioning and broaden its applicability in cancer therapy [16].

II. **Gelatin**

Ancient cultures used gelatin-like substances far earlier, but Denis Papin is credited with scientifically identifying and producing gelatin in 1682. His findings paved the way for developing and commercializing gelatin as a biomaterial. Gelatin has been utilized as a biomaterial for thousands of years, including by ancient civilizations such as the Egyptians, who extracted early forms of gelatin from animal skin and bone to manufacture glue. However, the first scientific discovery of gelatin as a biomaterial for tissue engineering applications occurred in the early 2000s[17].

Gelatin, a natural biopolymer generated from collagen via hydrolysis, is highly biodegradable, biocompatible, and inexpensive. It is frequently employed in the medical and pharmaceutical industries, particularly as a drug delivery carrier, due to its water solubility and thermoreversible gel characteristics. Gelatin's varied features can be modified based on its source, extraction method, and degree of cross-linking, making it appropriate for a variety of DDS such as microparticles, nanoparticles, fibers, and hydrogels. Gelatin nanoparticles, for example, are very effective at delivering drugs to the brain or through the vein. Recent research has demonstrated that gelatin-based delivery systems have excellent drug-loading efficiency and regulated release profiles, making them intriguing for cancer treatment [18]. According to Yu Xia et al.,2023, combining several therapy modalities can significantly increase tumor cell death. They created multiresponsive targeted antitumor NPs made of folate-functionalized gelatin NPs under 200 nm in size and encapsulated CuS NPs, $Fe3O4$ NPs, and curcumin (Cur) using cutting-edge microfluidic swirl mixer technology in conjunction with chemotherapy and photothermal-ablation therapy. The optimal production conditions for gelatin NPs with an average particle size of $90 \pm 7$ nm were achieved by analyzing its structure, changing concentration and pH, and fine-tuning fluid dynamics in a microfluidic system. The DDS was tested on lung cancer A549 cells (low level of folate receptors) and breast adenocarcinoma MCF-7 cells (high level of folate receptors). Folic acid aids in the targeting and accurate delivery of nanoparticles to MCF-7 tumour cells. Infrared light irradiation (980 nm) is used to induce synergistic photothermal ablation and curcumin's anticancer effect, while $Fe3O4$ is steered by an external magnetic field to target gelatin NPs and enhance drug uptake, resulting in efficient tumour cell death [19].

Gelatin microparticles have been employed to provide growth factors for bone tissue engineering, while gelatin fibre mats loaded with antifungal drugs have shown improved infection management activity. Additionally, gelatin-based bioadhesives loaded with analgesics such as bupivacaine show promise for pain management in wound care. Despite its benefits, gelatin's weak mechanical qualities and possible immunogenicity from animal sources limit its use in biomedical applications. Recombinant gelatins are being developed to address these concerns. In cancer therapy, gelatin plays an important function as a drug delivery vehicle, providing controlled release and targeted distribution of chemotherapeutic drugs, which can improve treatment efficacy and lessen systemic side effects [20].

IV. **Fibrin**

Marcello Malpighi originally identified fibrin in 1666, describing a clot as "a fibrous texture with a network or nerve-like appearance". Fibrin is made up of the blood proteins fibrinogen and thrombin, both of which contribute to blood clotting. Fibrin glue, also known as fibrin sealant, is a fibrin-based scaffold that has been used to limit surgical bleeding, hasten wound healing, repair hollow body organs, and offer slow-release medicine delivery. In 2001, Joseph Choukron introduced platelet-rich fibrin (PRF) as an autologous biomaterial, ushering in an exciting and promising period in the advancement of tissue healing and regeneration in different medical sectors[21].

Fibrin, which has high mechanical, biodegradable, and biocompatibility qualities, is widely utilized in medical applications. It works particularly well as a fibrin glue for hemostasis and tissue sealing during surgery. Because fibrin is injectable and capable of transporting bioactive molecules, it is an effective delivery route for chemotherapeutic medicines in cancer treatment. Its porous form allows cells to adhere, develop, and differentiate, while growth factors held in fibrin are released in a controlled manner, facilitating tissue regeneration[22]. JunyoungSeo*et al.*,2023 used thrombolytic nanocages containing multivalent clot-targeting peptides and fibrin degradation enzymes, such as micro plasmin, to dissolve fibrin in the tumor microenvironment, naming them fibrinolytic nanocages. These FNCs are very selective and effective at targeting tumor clots. FNCs effectively dissolve fibrin clots inside tumor arteries, suggesting that they can reduce the risk of venous thromboembolism (VTE) in cancer patients. In a syngeneic mouse melanoma model, co-administration of FNC with doxorubicin increased chemotherapy efficacy. Furthermore, FNCs improved the distribution of Doxil/doxorubicin nanoparticles in mouse tumours. These findings indicate that fibrinolytic cotherapy may boost the therapeutic efficacy of anticancer nanomedicines [23]. Even with limitations such as low mechanical strength and rapid deterioration, cross-linking techniques and stronger polymers can help to enhance these properties. Fibrin-based scaffolds, including porous sheets, nanospheres, and microspheres, have been used for cancer treatment and regenerative medicine purposes.

## V. **Hyaluronic acid (HA)**

In 1934, Karl Meyer and John Palmer extracted HA from the vitreous body of a cow's eye. They termed it "hyaluronic acid" because of its clear appearance in water and the possibility of hexuronic acid being one of the components[24]. HA is one type of biomaterial that can help with cancer treatment. It is beneficial for DDS that target cancer cells because to its ability to interact with cell receptors involved in tissue healing and inflammatory control. Formulations based on HA have the potential to reduce systemic toxicity while increasing the delivery of chemotherapeutic medicines and other therapeutic chemicals to cancer cells. Since the 1990s, the number of FDA-approved nanotechnology device-based products and clinical trials has increased dramatically, and about ten years later, HA nanodevices have taken on a prominent role in the cancer therapy field, where they are used to formulate DDS to improve therapeutic efficacy.

HA nanodevices offer several key properties, including minimal immunogenicity, biodegradability, noninflammatory responses, bioavailability, and biocompatibility. Because of its unique properties, HA is the primary component of multifunctional nanodevices used in a variety of cancer therapies [25].To the best of our knowledge, the first example of HA-based nanogels with a size distribution ranging from 200 to 500 nm used for target-specific intracellular siRNA delivery was published in 2007.A few years later, various nanodevices for cancer treatment, such as hydrogel and particle systems, were created. HA-based nanodevices are particularly interesting for drug delivery because, in addition to the qualities listed above, their functional capabilities enable controlled and targeted drug release in response to various triggers, which is appealing in cancer therapy. The devices can be classified into three types based on their physicochemical properties and structures: endogenous stimuli-responsive devices, which include pH, enzyme, and redox responsive materials; exogenous stimuli-responsive devices, which include light, temperature, ultrasound, and magnetic field responsive materials; and multi-stimuli responsive materials. HA-based nanodevices, in particular, have shown promise in terms of active targeting and functional properties [26].

## VI. **Chitosan and chitin**

Chitin was discovered and characterized by Henri Braconnot, a French chemist, in 1811. Braconnot extracted chitin from mushrooms and termed it "chitin," which comes from the Greek word "chiton," meaning "tunic" or "coat of mail."Rouget discovered chitosan in 1859 by heating chitin in an alkaline media. Chitin and chitosan, show considerable promise for usage in biomedicalapplications, particularly cancer treatment [27]. Chitosan, composed of glucosamine and N-acetyl glucosamine, is created by partially deacetylating chitin. Biodegradability and biocompatibility make it suitable for tissue engineering and medicine delivery. Materials based on chitosan have shown promise as drug delivery vehicles in cancer treatment. For example, a pH-responsive magnetic nanocomposite wrapped in chitosan demonstrated high anticancer activity as well as good pH sensitivity, allowing for precise and regulated drug administration. This technique, which delivers chemotherapeutic chemicals precisely to tumour sites, provides a non-toxic and effective way to maximize therapy effectiveness while minimizing systemic side effects [28].

Chitosan and chitin-based biomaterials have demonstrated promise in anticancer therapy via a variety of mechanisms. For example, carboxymethyl chitin (CMC) nanoparticles loaded with the anticancer medication 5-fluorouracil (5-Fu) for cancer treatment. The CMC NPs were created by an emulsion cross-linking technique with FeCl3 as the cross-linking agent. The chemical alteration of chitin to CMC increased its water solubility while retaining biocompatibility and low toxicity.In a mouse model, CMC nanoparticles loaded with 5-Fu shown various promising qualities for anticancer therapy. The nanoparticles released the medication in a controlled and sustained manner, and they were non-toxic to normal fibroblast cells. Furthermore, the nanoparticles demonstrated antimicrobial activity and ferromagnetic characteristics that could be exploited to distribute drugs via tracking systems. This study reveals the efficacy of chitosan and chitin derivatives, such as CMC nanoparticles, as drug delivery methods for targeted cancer therapy with minimal adverse effects. The application of these biomaterials in anticancer therapy is a potential field of research that requires additional examination [29].

### VII. **Starch**

The main polysaccharide used by plants as an energy reserve, starch, is made up of amylose and amylopectin. Because of its biodegradability, biocompatibility, and affordability, it finds usage in biomedical applications like medication delivery and tissue engineering. Its shortcomings, notably low shear and heat resistance, are frequently addressed by mixing it with man-made polymers, such as polycaprolactone (PCL). Starch-based materials have potential as medication delivery systems in cancer therapy. Drugs can be effectively ensnared by starch hydrogels, shielding them from the body's deterioration and enabling precise distribution[30]. Chan Yu et al.,2019 produced Nanocarriers with great safety and efficiency for chemo-photothermal therapy, which is urgently required. In this study, a new type of hydroxyethyl starch (HES) was produced using NPs loaded with doxorubicin (DOX) and indocyanine green (ICG). DOX-loaded HES conjugates with redox-sensitivity (HES-SS-DOX) were initially synthesized before being coupled with ICG to self-assemble into HES-SS-DOX@ICG NPs with regulated compositions and sizes through collaborative interactions. The optimum HES-SS-DOX@ICG NPs were physically and photothermally stable in aqueous conditions, and they demonstrated great photothermal efficiency in vivo. They were able to rapidly release the loaded DOX in response to the redox stimulation and laser irradiation.Based on the H22-tumor-bearing mouse model, these NPs were observed to accumulate more in tumours than in other main organs. During a 14-day therapy period, the HES-SS-DOX@ICG NPs, together with dose-designated laser irradiation, were able to completely eradicate tumours with just one injection and one subsequent laser irradiation on the tumour location. Furthermore, they demonstrated essentially minimal harm to the body. The currently developed HES-SS-DOX@ICG NPs exhibit excellent in vivo safety and anti-tumor efficacy. These nanoparticles, when conjugated with laser irradiation, show promise clinical applications for chemo-photothermal cancer treatment. The potential of starch to be changed for site-specific breakdown in the gastrointestinal system holds promise for future uses in cancer treatment, even though the majority of research on the drug delivery aspect of the technology is theoretical [31].

### VIII. **Alginate**

A British chemist named E.C.C. Stanford discovered and extracted alginate in 1881. He was the first to describe and patent alginate as a biomaterial. Alginate is a non-toxic, biocompatible polymer that is obtained from brown seaweed and some types of bacteria. It is renowned for its inexpensive, simple changes, and gentle gelation conditions [32]. Because of its advantageous qualities, alginate hydrogels are employed in tissue engineering, medication delivery, and wound healing. But alginate's low cell adherence and weak mechanical characteristics are usually improved by mixing it with other biomaterials, such as chitosan. Alginate-based materials offer promise for drug delivery in cancer therapy. Alginate is useful for regulated drug delivery and encapsulation because of its capacity to produce hydrogels that may be cross-linked chemically or physically[33].Alginate-based systems have demonstrated great promise as effective carriers for targeted medication delivery in cancer treatment. One such example is the development of alginate-based nanogels for cancer therapy.Researchers used a microfluidic synthesis process to create manganese-alginate nanogels with self-supplying H2O2 and Mn2+-chelating properties for synergistic chemo/ chemodynamic treatment and improved anticancer immunity. Doxorubicin, a chemotherapy medication, was put into manganese-alginate nanogels. The nanogels were able to produce reactive oxygen species (ROS) in the tumour microenvironment via a Fenton-like reaction, causing immunogenic cell death and boosting the anticancer immune response. This combined chemo/chemodynamic therapy strategy using alginate-based nanogels revealed greater therapeutic efficacy than treatment with doxorubicin alone[34].This is especially helpful for limiting side effects and targeting cancer cells.Subsequent investigations will focus on enhancing the regulation of medication delivery mechanisms, which will facilitate the creation of more potent alginate-based cancer treatments.

## IX. Polyhydroxyalkanoates (PHAs)

Beijerinck identified PHAs as inclusion bodies within bacteria in 1888. In 1927, Lemoigne discovered and isolated the first distinct PHA, poly(3-hydroxybutyrate) (PHB). This laid the groundwork for the discovery and analysis of PHAs as a biomaterial[35].

Microorganisms produce natural, biodegradable polyesters known as PHAs. They are ideal for biomedical applications such as medicine administration, tissue engineering, and implantable devices due to their biodegradability, biocompatibility, and non-toxic breakdown byproducts. However, unmodified PHAs must be changed to improve their function due to limitations such as slow degradation rates, excessive hydrophobicity, and poor mechanical properties. PHAs can be created with a variety of properties by selecting the appropriate production strains, conditions, and carbon sources. Grafting, copolymerization, electrospinning, and blending can all help to improve PHA properties. For example, PHAs can be chemically changed or combined with other biodegradable polymers to improve their hydrophilicity and mechanical properties [36].Pramual S et al.,2016 used PHAs to transport a hydrophobic photosensitizer, 5,10,15,20-Tetrakis(4-hydroxyphenyl)-21H,23H-porphine (pTHPP), for photodynamic treatment (PDT). Three PHA variants, polyhydroxybutyrate, poly(hydroxybutyrate-co-hydroxyvalerate), or P(HB-HV) with 12 and 50% HV, were utilised to create pTHPP-loaded PHA nanoparticles using an emulsification-diffusion process, and we evaluated two different poly(vinyl alcohol) (PVA) stabilisers. Under TEM, the nanoparticles exhibited nano-scale spherical shape with hydrodynamic diameters ranging from 169.0 to 211.2 nm and a narrow size distribution. The amount of drug loaded and drug entrapment efficiency were also studied. In vitro photocytotoxicity was assessed using the human colon adenocarcinoma cell line HT-29, which exhibited time and concentration dependent cell death, similar with pTHPP's progressive release pattern over 24 hours.This is the first work to show that bacterially generated P(HB-HV) copolymers can be used to deliver a hydrophobic photosensitizer medication as nanoparticles, with potential applications in PDT.

PHAs have the potential to serve as pharmaceutical delivery vehicles in cancer therapy. According to a study, a novel alternating block copolymer known as PHB-alt-PEG, which is composed of poly(3-hydroxybutyrate) (PHB) and poly(ethylene glycol) (PEG), has better mechanical and processability properties while remaining cytotoxic. Controlled drug release rates can be accomplished by adjusting the copolymer concentration and PHB-to-PEG ratio in the hydrogel. This approach has been used to treat a mouse model of hepatocellular carcinoma over an extended period of time, indicating significant potential for anticancer applications. PHAs' use in therapeutic biomaterials, including cancer treatment, can be expanded with further research and improvements [37].

**Synthetic Biodegradable Biomaterials:**

Owing to their synthetic flexibility and biocompatibility, polyphosphazenes represent a more recent type of inorganic-organic hybrid polymers that have been investigated for biomedical applications. In order to ensure optimal host tissue response, biodegradable biomaterials, whether natural or synthetic, need to demonstrate superior biocompatibility over an extended period of time [38].

I. **Poly (glycolic acid) (PGA)**

Hydrophilic and extremely crystalline, PGA is renowned for its rapid breakdown, usually losing its mechanical integrity in 2–4 weeks. PGA can be used in tissue engineering, medication delivery, and other biological applications because of its quick breakdown. Its usage is restricted in some regions, nevertheless, by its quick breakdown, acidic byproducts, and limited solubility. To enhance its qualities, PGA has been investigated in combination with other materials for cancer treatment. For example, PGA sheets and fibrin glue have been effectively employed to heal open soft tissue wounds and to rebuild bone surfaces after oral cavity tumor removal[39]. PGA is a biocompatible polymer in the human body. A needle-shaped long-acting anti-cancer preparation (F-PGA needle) was created by combining polyglycolic acid and the anti-cancer medication 5-fluorouracil. The needle released 5-FU for around 10 days before disappearing after a year. A clinical trial with the F-PGA needle was conducted on patients with terminal carcinomas. Tumour shrinkage and necrosis were noted in two patients with metastatic liver carcinomas. The F-PGA needle delivers high-dose 5-FU locally for an extended period of time with fewer side effects by embedding it in tumour tissue. As a result, the F-PGA needle shows promise in the treatment of unresectable cancer as a topical chemotherapeutic application[40].

II. **Polylactic acid (PLA)**

PLA is a commonly utilised biodegradable scaffolding material in biomedical applications. PLA differs from PGA in chemical, physical, and mechanical properties due to the additional methyl group in its repeating units. In contrast to PGA, PLA deteriorates over the course of months to years, which qualifies it for use in load-bearing applications such orthopedic fixation systems. There are currently a number of orthopedic devices on the market that use PLA, demonstrating its usefulness in therapeutic settings. The functional aspects of PLA research have been the focus of recent advances. For example, combining PLA with photoluminescent graphene quantum dots (GQDs) produces a multifunctional nanocomposite with good biocompatibility and minimal cytotoxicity. This composite demonstrates the potential of PLA in biomedical domains, particularly in intracellular molecular investigation and clinical gene treatments [41,42].

III. **PLGA (poly (lactic-co-glycolic acid)**

Robert Langer and his team first develop a biodegradable biomaterial like Poly Lactic-co-Glycolic Acid (PLGA) for controlled-release drug delivery technologies, and further implemented in cancer therapeutics for tumor targeted drug delivery. Accordingly, to his findings Polyester PLGA is a copolymer derived from poly lactic acid (PLA) and poly glycolic acid (PGA). It stands out as the most precisely defined biomaterial for drug delivery in terms of its design and performance. Poly lactic acid contains an asymmetric α-carbon, conventionally denoted in classical stereochemical terms as D or L, and occasionally as R or S. The enantiomeric forms of PLA are poly D-lactic acid (PDLA) and poly L-lactic acid (PLLA). PLGA, or poly D, L-lactic-co-glycolic acid, refers to a copolymer where D- and L- lactic acid components are present in equal proportions[43].When it comes to bone substitute structures, PLGA copolymers are chosen over their constituent homopolymers because of their changeable breakdown rates, which may be adjusted by adjusting the lactide/glycolide ratios. Pure PLGA is not the best material for bone regeneration because of its low osteoinductivity and inadequate mechanical qualities, even though it is biocompatible. To improve its qualities, PLGA is thus frequently mixed with materials such as ceramics or bioactive glass. Notably, in vivo osteoconductivity and strong antimicrobial capabilities have been shown for PLGA composites. AgNP/PLGA-coated stainless steel, for example, demonstrated increased osteoinductivity and antibacterial activity, while PLGA/ hydroxyapatite microsphere composites containing alendronate promoted osteoblast proliferation and suppressed macrophage proliferation. These results demonstrate the potential of PLGA in the creation of orthopedic surgery therapeutic materials [44].

IV. **Poly(ε-caprolactone) (PCL)**

The Carothers group initially synthesized PCL in the early 1930s. PCL is made up of linear aliphatic polyester macrochains that display crystalline properties. Because one of the synthetic polymers can be broken down by microbes, it was quickly brought to market [45].The semi-crystalline, biodegradable polyester PCL has a glass-transition temperature of around −54°C and a melting point of 55°C to 60°C. Since it breaks down gradually over two to four years, it can be used in long-term implants and DDS. Collagen-coated PCL fibers increase the proliferation of human osteoblast cells, suggesting that they could be used as delivery systems for extracellular matrix proteins in tissue healing. Research is still being done on the potential use of PCL in micro- and nanoscale DDS. PCL is useful in entrapping antibiotics for bone regeneration. PCL-calcium phosphate scaffolds have demonstrated the right mechanical characteristics and in vitro cytocompatibility for hard tissue restoration. PCL's characteristics make it a potential material for medication delivery and bone tissue engineering. It can also be used in cancer therapy to help cancer patients' bone regeneration and deliver chemotherapy medicines [46].

V. **Polyanhydrides**

Robert Langer and his group at the Massachusetts Institute of Technology (MIT) were the first to develop polyanhydride biomaterials in the early 1980s. For applications involving controlled drug distribution, Langer and associates created a family of biodegradable synthetic biopolymers called polyanhydrides.In order to overcome the shortcomings of PLA, PGA, and PLGA in drug administration, such as irregular release profiles, polyanhydrides were developed[47]. Surface erosion causes these polymers to break down, maintaining a consistent release profile—especially important for strong medications. Polyanhydrides successfully protect pharmaceuticals because they are biocompatible and degrade into non-toxic metabolites before erosion. Polyanhydrides such as poly [(carboxyphenoxy propane) -(sebacic acid)], which were approved by the FDA in 1996, are utilized for targeted distribution, most notably in the treatment of brain tumors using the chemotherapeutic drug bis-chloroethyl nitrosourea. This polymer drug-delivery method has demonstrated encouraging outcomes in trials involving both humans and animals, underscoring its promise in cancer treatment [48].Because of the high-water liability of the anhydride bonds on the surface and the hydrophobicity that prevents water from penetrating the bulk of the polymer, polyanhydrides are an example of surface eroding polymers. It is anticipated that the drug release for these kinds of chemicals will be directly correlated with the rate of polymer erosion. Experiments conducted in vitro and in vivo demonstrated that polyanhydrides are readily eliminated from the body by the excretion of urine and feces, or in the form of carbon dioxide.Further research was conducted on copolymer as a potential reservoir and delivery method for paclitaxel, 5-fluorouracil, and methotrexate. Polyanhydrides have been used as vaccine antigen delivery systems in addition to drug delivery platforms to promote cellular immune response and produce antitumor immunity. They have also been effectively utilized recently as curcumin nanocarriers and to stop the proliferation of HeLa, osteoblast, and murine breast cancer cells 4T1[49].

VI. **Polyurethanes (PURs)**

In 1937, Otto Bayer is credited with creating polyurethanes (PURs). Wurtz created polyurethanes for the first time in 1849, but Otto Bayer was the one who transformed it into its current form. The flexible polymer family known as polyurethanes is made with long-term use and extreme resistance in mind. They are widely utilized as elastomers, rigid foams, flexible foams, and more and play a significant role in daily life. Because of their toughness, durability, biocompatibility, and biostability, PURs are preferred in medical equipment[50]. Since the late 1990s, biodegradable PURs have gained more attention in tissue engineering and medication delivery because of their adaptable qualities and sensitivity to biodegradation. Biocompatible aliphatic diisocyanates that promote cell adhesion and proliferation, such lysine diisocyanate, are among the recent advancements[51]. Notably, Orthopedic applications are supported by the injectable PolyNova® PUR system, which is based on lysine–diisocyanate and offers greater bonding strength and mechanical support.PURs DDSs with anti-cancer properties are one of the actively researched areas of pharmacy research PURs-DDSs. Stable formulation, enhanced pharmacokinetics, and a certain amount of "passive" or "physiological" targeting to tumor tissue are all provided by PURs-DDSs. Numerous types of PURs-DDSs with anti-cancer properties have been created thus far. Cytostatic medications such doxorubicin (DOX), gefitinib (GEF), gefitinib (5-FU), cyclophosphamide (CYCLOPHO), methotrexate (METX), temozolomide (TMZ), and paclitaxel (PACL) are present in the developed carriers.These developments demonstrate the promise of PURs in cancer treatment, especially in the development of scaffolds for targeted drug delivery and tissue regeneration [52].

VII. **Polyphosphazenes**

In the 1960s, Allcock and colleagues synthesized the first high molecular weight polyphosphazenes, which set the stage for their future development as biomaterials. A novel type of inorganic–organic hybrid polymers known as polyphosphazenes has an inorganic backbone made up of nitrogen and phosphorus atoms. Comparing polyphosphazenes to other polymers, they are more biocompatible, biodegradable, and structurally flexible, which has piqued interest in them as next-generation biomaterials. Numerous biomedical uses, including as drug administration, gene therapy, bioimaging, phototherapy, bone regeneration, and medical devices, have been investigated for polyphosphazenes[53].

They provide for regulated qualities including solubility, hydrophobicity, and degradation rates because of their synthetic flexibility and utility. Polyphosphazenes can undergo erosion on both their surface and bulk, resulting in neutral and non-toxic compounds that can be used for medication administration. Because of their osteoconductivity and biocompatibility, recent research has demonstrated their potential for use as scaffolds in adipose tissue regeneration and bone tissue creation. Notably, by forming porous structures that deteriorate with time, blends containing PLGA may improve their use in osteogenesis[54].Avaji et al. (2016) synthesized the PPZ-docetaxel (DTX) conjugate, typically referred to as "Polytaxel," using cis-aconitic amide bonds that were acid-labile. In a stomach tumor mouse model, the PPZ-DTX self-assembled to form stable micelles (41.8 nm), exhibiting good tumor-targeting capabilities and consequently good anti-cancer action. The same group also created a PPZ-Pt conjugate. Using cis-aconitic acid as a linker, the platinum-based anti-cancer molecule (dach)Pt was conjugated to a PPZ-based carrier polymer to produce a PPZ-Pt conjugate known as "Polyplatin." Nanoparticles having a mean diameter of 55.1 nm were created through the self-assembly of polyplatin. In a gastric tumor model, polyplatin demonstrated strong anti-tumor effectiveness and minimal systemic toxicity.Polyphosphazenes, though still at the research stage, have potential for delivering pharmaceuticals and promoting tissue regeneration in cancer therapy [55].

**Emerging Role of Biomaterial in Anticancer Drug Delivery:**

i. **Biomaterials' current role in anticancer drug delivery.**

**Polymeric nanoparticles:** particularly those made of biodegradable polymers like poly (D, L-lactide) (PLA), poly (D, L-glycolide) (PLG), and its co-polymer poly(lactide-co-glycolide) (PLGA), are gaining importance in anticancer drug administration. These materials provide various advantages, including biological fluid stability, industrial scalability, and surface functionalization. Such functionalization enables tailored degradation rates, making it perfect for regulated medication release[56].

Cisplatin, a commonly used chemotherapeutic drug, was recently encapsulated within PLGA nanoparticles to treat ovarian cancer. This strategy intends to improve the drug's antitumor activity, limit metastasis, lower the required dosage, and lessen adverse effects. Encapsulation allows cisplatin to target cancer cells more efficiently, decreasing its impact on healthy tissues and lowering systemic toxicity[57].According to research findings, polymeric nanoparticles greatly improve anticancer medicines' therapeutic efficacy and pharmacokinetic qualities. These nanoparticles improve medication stability and solubility, control release, and promote accumulation in target tissues. For example, cisplatin encapsulated in PLGA nanoparticles demonstrated improved cytotoxicity against cancer cells while reducing systemic side effects often associated with its treatment[58].

These nanoparticles were developed using carefully selected polymers to provide controlled release and targeted delivery. Researchers adjusted nanoparticle size and surface characteristics to ensure effective drug encapsulation and release at the intended action location. Nanoprecipitation and emulsification-solvent evaporation are likely techniques used to ensure stability and biocompatibility[59].Polymeric nanoparticles serve an important role in anticancer drug delivery by improving solubility, stability, targeted distribution, toxicity, and controlled release. Functionalizing these nanoparticles for particular targeting increases the therapeutic index of anticancer drugs, signifying a big step forward in nanomedicine and a promising technique for improving cancer treatment outcomes. The combination of PLGA nanoparticles with cisplatin, for example, demonstrates these materials‘ potential to improve cancer therapy[60].

In preclinical and clinical studies, developments such as Abraxane (Nab-Paclitaxel) have made substantial progress. Taxanes, such as paclitaxel, which are used to treat breast and other solid cancers, were formerly required in formulations that caused severe toxicity. Abraxane, a cremophor-free, nanoparticulate albumin-bound paclitaxel, was created to enhance medication delivery and targeting[61].

It uses albumin routes to bind to SPARC, increasing tumor penetration and minimizing solvent-related toxicity. Abraxane, which has been approved in several countries, delivers more paclitaxel to tumors while exhibiting different pharmacokinetics, such as greater dispersion and delayed clearance than solvent-based formulations[62].BIND-014, another novel formulation, is a PEGylated polylactic acid nanoparticle encapsulating docetaxel that targets prostate-specific membrane antigen (PSMA) in prostate cancer. Its PEG surface enables regulated release and immune evasion, ensuring that docetaxel solely targets PSMA-expressing cells. Preclinical research revealed superior pharmacokinetics and higher intratumoral concentrations than free docetaxel. Despite initial clinical promise, following trials failed to reach targets, resulting in the discontinuation of research and the company's bankruptcy[63].Livatag, which was created for primary liver cancer, wraps doxorubicin in nanoparticles consisting of polyalkylcyanoacrylate and cyclodextrin to overcome resistance. [64].

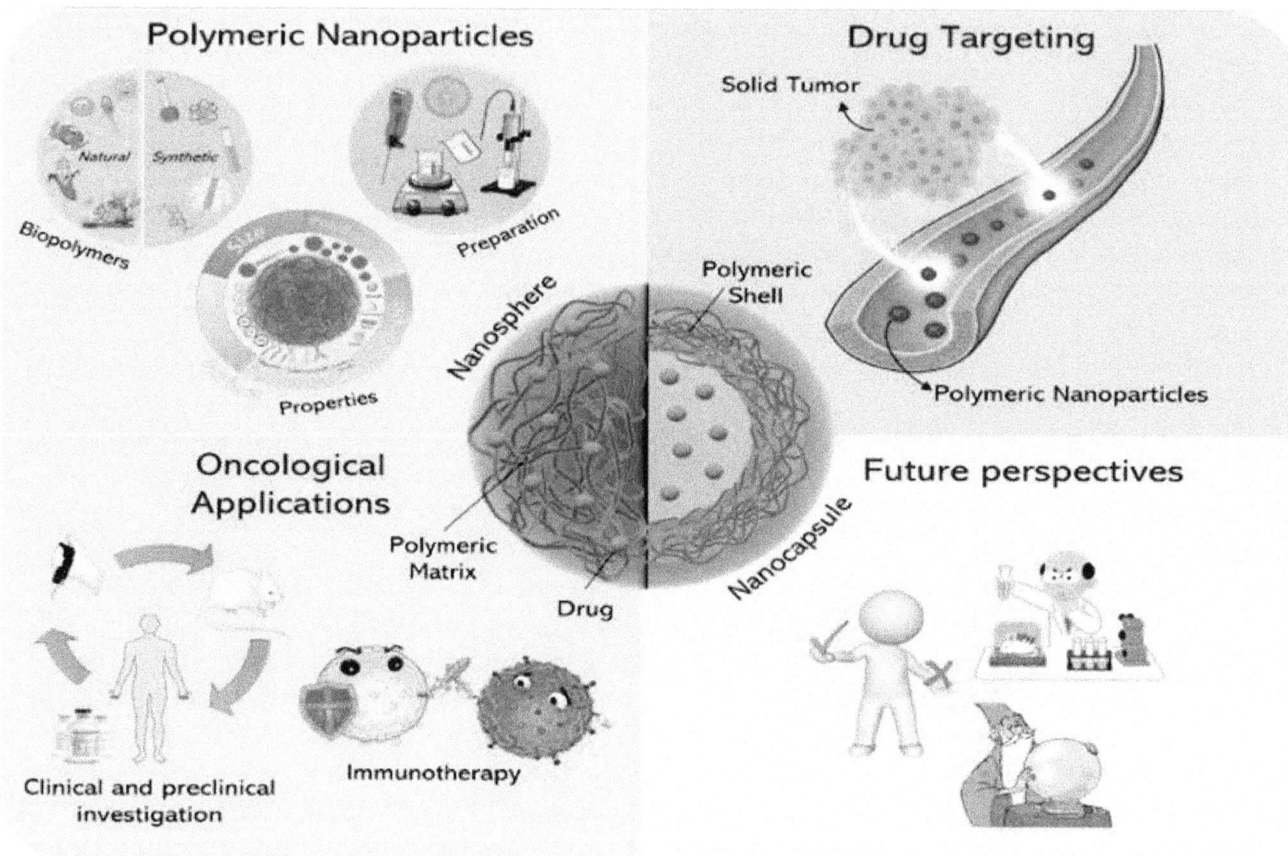


**FIGURE 1**The figure depicts the complexities of NPs DDS in cancer therapy, emphasising the importance of careful design and optimisation. Biodegradable polymeric NPs have a core-shell structure, with a hydrophobic polymer core encapsulating therapeutic drugs and a hydrophilic polymer shell (e.g., PEG) for steric stabilization and extended circulation. Nanoparticles are produced by procedures such as nanoprecipitation and emulsification-solvent evaporation. In the circulation, NPs target tumors using the enhanced permeability and retention (EPR) effect or ligand-receptor interactions, entering tumor cells via endocytosis and escaping endosomes to release their therapeutic payload. Controlled medication release in the tumor microenvironment is initiated by pH changes, redox conditions, or external stimuli such as temperature and light, resulting in cancer cell death, tumor growth suppression, or reduced metastasis, ultimately enhancing patient outcomes in cancer treatment.[65].

ii. **Biomaterial for Cancer Immunotherapy**

The use of the immune system by the body to fight cancer is known as cancer immunotherapy, yet its effectiveness has been limited and it has serious adverse effects. Advanced nanobiomaterials like polymers, silica has become essential tools in addressing these issues. These materials offer a major breakthrough in the treatment of cancer by improving the administration and efficacy of immunotherapeutic drugs while minimizing side effects. Through mechanisms like medication encapsulation by liposomes, which preserve pharmaceuticals from degradation and enable for regulated release to particular tumor areas, nanobiomaterials increase the delivery of anticancer treatments. Long-term medication release is provided by polymer-based scaffolds, and hydrophobic medicines become more stable and soluble when they are dissolved in micelles. These substances can also be used with conventional medications or other nanobiomaterials to further improve treatment results.

Biomaterials play a key role in immunotherapy tactics such as cancer vaccines, modified T cells, checkpoint inhibitors, and cytokines. For example, checkpoint inhibitors administered by biomaterials can achieve targeted delivery, improving efficacy and minimizing toxicity, while cytokines can have their half-lives extended, reducing the need for high doses and mitigating side effects. New developments in cancer treatment, such as injectable systems and implanted scaffolds, appear promising. With the use of these technologies, immunotherapeutic drugs can be precisely and carefully delivered to tumor locations, providing less invasive and more efficient treatment choices.

The incorporation of sophisticated biomaterials into cancer immunotherapy signifies a notable progression in augmenting therapeutic specificity, effectiveness, and security. Utilizing the special qualities of nanobiomaterials, scientists and medical professionals may create more effective treatment plans, which will ultimately improve patient outcomes and lower the incidence of cancer. To completely utilize biomaterials in anticancer medication delivery, more study in this area is necessary [66].

### iii. Biomaterial in Radiation Therapy

Novel treatment approaches including radiation therapy and immunotherapy employ biomaterials. Functionalized polymers have the ability to deliver cytotoxic medications, radiosensitizers, and immune-stimulating radioisotopes directly to the tumor site. The possibility of novel drug delivery methods, such as thermal ablation, ultrasound, X-rays, and near-infrared lasers, to regulate drug release through biomaterials is being investigated.

Additionally crucial to the repair and preservation of radiation-damaged tissues are biomaterials. For instance, spacers made of polymer-based hydrogels are used to shield normal tissues from radiation exposure, reducing side effects and improving patient quality of life [67].Gold nanoparticles (AuNPs) improve radiation therapy because of their high atomic number, which considerably boosts the radiation dose received by tumour cells. This results in the formation of secondary electrons, which cause localised damage to cancer cells. Additionally, gold nanoparticles can be functionalized with targeting ligands, like as antibodies or peptides, allowing them to aggregate selectively in tumour tissue while minimising exposure to healthy cells.

In a study by Hainfeld et al., mice with subcutaneous tumours were given intravenous gold nanoparticles followed by radiation therapy. The findings revealed a significant increase in tumour control and survival rates in mice treated with a combination of gold nanoparticles plus radiation compared to radiation alone. Gold nanoparticles provide various advantages in radiation therapy. They can be tailored to specifically target tumour cells, lowering the risks associated with radiation therapy. Gold nanoparticles enhance tumour cell death by increasing the local radiation dose within the tumour. Furthermore, gold nanoparticles are biocompatible and safe to administer in vivo[68].

### iv. Bio-inspired drugs delivery systems.

Most anticancer medicines have the therapeutic power to eliminate tumour cells; nevertheless, site-specific drug delivery vehicles must be used to direct the compounds to their intended areas. This has prompted the study of several natural particles and biomaterials for the purpose. Bio-inspired platforms that directly replicate natural components in the body have proven to be one of the most adaptable and inventive medication delivery methods in cancer treatment and detection. *RBCs were employed as nanoparticle carriers for anti-cancer medication in one investigation. Through the EPR effect, these altered RBCs targeted tumor locations by efficiently transporting medications through the bloodstream. They did this by taking advantage of their long lifespan and biocompatibility[69].

Drug encapsulation is the process of adding nanoparticles to RBCs by electroporation, hypotonic dilution, or encapsulation during RBC reformation. Without affecting the structure of the RBCs, these nanoparticles fit inside of them. The drug-loaded RBCs had a 120-day half-life after being reintroduced into the bloodstream, which increased the probability that they would reach the tumor site. Because of their inherent immunogenicity and biocompatibility, they were able to elude the immune system and keep a steady level of medication in the blood.Comparing RBC-based nanomedicines to traditional techniques, the study demonstrated a considerable improvement in the accumulation of anti-cancer medications in tumor tissues. This strategy showed the potential of bioinspired DDS to improve outcomes for cancer treatment by increasing therapeutic efficacy and reducing systemic toxicity [70].

**Anticancer Biomarker**

Biomaterials have shown great potential in the development of novel anticancer biomarkers and therapeutic strategies. Recent studies have focused on the use of innovative biomaterials for the targeted delivery of chemotherapeutics to bone cancer sites, such as nanocarrier-based DDS and multifunctional biomaterials. These biomaterials can selectively inhibit bone cancer progression while reducing the loss of healthy bone structural properties.Polymer therapeutics (PTs) provide an exciting approach for cancer treatment by enhancing drug solubility and altering pharmacokinetics. PTs can act as companion diagnostics, with the presence of specific enzymes like cathepsins representing an important biomarker for PT-based therapies. pH-responsive and redox-sensitive nanomaterials are also being investigated as potential biomarkers, as the tumor microenvironment often presents with lower pH and higher reductive potential than normal tissues[71].

Advanced biomaterials can enable cell-specific modulation of cancer immunotherapy, particularly targeting antigen-presenting cells (APCs), T cells, and tumor microenvironment (TME)-resident cells. Functional biomaterials can improve the efficacy of cancer immunotherapies by enhancing antigen delivery to dendritic cells, co-delivering antigens and adjuvants, and promoting anti-tumor immunity[72].

**Nano carrier based Drug Delivery:**

Nanocarrier-mediated DDS can deliver chemotherapeutic drugs to specific areas. Nanocarriers include polymeric nanoparticles, liposomes, micelles, carbon nanotubes, dendrimers, solid lipid nanoparticles, magnetic nanoparticles, and quantum dots [73].

i. **Polymeric nanoparticles**

   Polymeric nanoparticles are made from natural or synthetic polymers and can transport medicines via physical trapping or covalent bonding. These nanoparticles can take the form of capsules, amphiphilic structures, or complicated branching polymers. They provide the benefit of improved medication administration and lower systemic toxicity.

ii. **Liposomes**

   Liposomes are lipid nanocarriers that contain hydrophilic or lipophilic drugs in their aqueous core or lipid bilayer. Because they are both biocompatible and biodegradable, they are ideal for use in clinical settings. Polyethylene glycol (PEG) can be added to liposomes to stabilize them and reduce immunological recognition. Liposomal formulations such as Myocet and Doxil are used in the treatment of breast cancer and Kaposi's sarcoma.

iii. **Polymeric micelles**

   Amphiphilic block copolymers are used to create polymeric micelles, which have a core-shell structure with a hydrophobic core that can retain lipophilic medications and a hydrophilic shell that ensures stability in aqueous environments. It is possible to construct these micelles for more effective therapeutic effects and precise distribution. One example that has completed clinical trials for many cancers is Genexol-PM, a micellar version of paclitaxel.

iv. **Carbon nanotubes**

   Because of their huge surface area and cylindrical shape, CNTs are an ideal medication loading and delivery system. They have the ability to cross cell membranes and enter cells directly to administer medication. However, because to worries regarding toxicity and biocompatibility, their clinical usage is restricted.

v. **Dendrimers**

   Dendrimers are polymers that resemble trees and are very branched. They have several surface functional groups that can be tailored to deliver drugs. Their high degree of functionality and clearly defined structure allow them to provide precise control over medication release and targeting. Drugs can be transported by dendrimers both on their surface and within their interior chambers.

vi. **Solid lipid nanoparticles (SLNs)**

   Solid lipid matrices, or SLNs, are used to encapsulate medications, allowing for more stability and controlled release. Combining the benefits of polymeric nanoparticles and liposomes, they provide a significant pharmacological payload, controlled release, and biocompatibility.

vii. **Magnetic nanoparticles**

An external magnetic field can be used to direct magnetic nanoparticles into tumor regions, enabling more accurate drug administration. In magnetic resonance imaging (MRI), they can also function as contrast agents, enhancing diagnostic potential. Combining therapeutic and diagnostic functions is known as theranostics.

viii. **Quantum Dots**

Semiconductor nanocrystals with distinct optical properties are known as quantum dots. Because they emit light at certain wavelengths when energized, they can be used for targeted drug delivery and imaging. The accuracy of cancer treatments can be increased by using quantum dots to track the transport and accumulation of drugs throughout the body.

**Oxygen-emitting biological materials**

ORBs have the potential to decrease the hypoxic environment of solid tumors, which makes them a significant advancement in anticancer therapy. The high oxygen consumption rate of rapidly proliferating cancer cells causes hypoxia, a characteristic of malignant tumors that reduces the effectiveness of many modern and conventional cancer treatments. By offering a novel method of raising the oxygen tension inside tumors, ORBs may improve treatment outcomes overall and may increase the efficacy of medications like photodynamic therapy (PDT).The way that oxygen is released into the tumor microenvironment by ORBs is regulated. Numerous factors, such as the existence of endogenous hydrogen peroxide (H2O2), which is commonly observed in high concentrations in hypoxic tumors, might cause this release. For instance, some ORBs use nanoparticles of manganese dioxide (MnO2), which reacts with H2O2 to produce oxygen and increase the amount of oxygen in the surrounding area. In addition to reducing hypoxia, this increase in oxygen also increases the production of reactive oxygen species (ROS) during photodynamic therapy (PDT), which is essential for causing cytotoxic effects on cancer cells[74].

Khan MS et al. (2019) developed doxorubicin-loaded oxygen nanobubbles (Dox/ONBs) were created, and the efficiency of drug administration to HeLa and MDA-MB-231 breast cancer cells was assessed. Optical and fluorescent microscopy were used to characterize Dox/ONBs, and nanoparticle tracking analysis (NTA) was used to measure their sizes. Reactive oxygen species (ROS) tests were used to examine Dox's mechanism of action, and confocal imaging was employed to measure cellular penetration. To evaluate the impact of Dox/ONBs under hypoxic conditions relative to normoxic conditions, hypoxic conditions were created. According to our findings, Dox/ONBs are useful for increasing oxygen levels, generating ROS in tumor-derived cell lines, and delivering drugs[75].

**Peroxide-based biomaterials**

Peroxide-based biomaterials, such as calcium peroxide (CaO2), have shown promise as cancer therapies. When exposed to an acidic tumor microenvironment, these metal peroxides can disintegrate and release oxygen and metal ions, which can assist in alleviating tumor hypoxia and trigger oxidative stress in tumor cells.The prolonged release of oxygen from peroxide-based biomaterials can assist overcome hypoxic conditions in solid tumors, which is a significant barrier for oxygen-dependent therapies such as photodynamic therapy. Incorporating peroxides into hydrogels, cryogels, or other biomaterial matrices can offer regulated and extended oxygen release to meet the needs of the tumor tissue.Furthermore, the metal ions generated during peroxide decomposition can improve cancer treatment by boosting other therapeutic methods such as chemodynamic therapy. Researchers are looking into ways to combine peroxide-based biomaterials with photosensitizers, enzymes, or Fenton reagents to enhance the efficacy of cancer treatments.

However, significant obstacles remain in building the perfect peroxide-based system, such as striking the appropriate combination of oxygen release kinetics, mechanical characteristics, and biocompatibility for safe and effective usage in the tumour microenvironment. Ongoing research is aimed at overcoming these limitations in order to improve peroxide-based biomaterials as a possible cancer treatment method[76,77].

**Perfluorocarbons (PFCs) based biomaterials**

Perfluorocarbons (PFCs) are biocompatible substances that are chemically and physiologically inert, with low toxicity, making them ideal for use as oxygen carriers in biomaterials. PFCs have a far better potential to dissolve respiratory gases such as oxygen than water. Researchers created stable PFC nanoemulsions that can be used in a variety of biomedical applications, including blood replacements, cell culture, and tissue engineering. However, including PFCs into biomaterials such as alginate hydrogels has a major impact on their mechanical and transport properties.Researchers created stable PFC nanoemulsions that can be used in a variety of biomedical applications, including blood replacements, cell culture, and tissue engineering. However, including PFCs into biomaterials such as alginate hydrogels has a major impact on their mechanical and transport properties. Specifically, adding a perfluorooctyl bromide (PFOB) PFC emulsion to alginate hydrogels had no significant effect on mechanical properties under mild strains, but did reduce the hydrogels' fracture stress. Furthermore, the effective diffusivity of hydrophobic small molecules decreased in PFC-containing hydrogels[78].

**Current Challenges**

Biodegradable biomaterials, particularly polymeric nanoparticles, hold promise for anticancer therapy because of their capacity to target tumour cells and the tumour microenvironment. However, various problems restrict its efficacy and applicabilitty:

1. **Biological barriers:**
   Nanoparticles must pass into the bloodstream without being filtered, phagocytized, or destroyed by enzymes.Efficient distribution to the tumour site necessitates overcoming obstacles at the cellular and organ levels, such as entering the extracellular matrix and bridging the blood-brain barrier for brain malignancies[79].
2. **Targeted delivery and specificity:**
   Accurately targeting cancer cells while minimising off-target effects remains a serious challenge. Selectively accumulating nanoparticles in tumour tissues is problematic due to their heterogeneity.
   Nanoparticle functionalization for improved targeted specificity is a difficult process. Strategies include altering the surface with ligands or antibodies that recognise cancer-specific markers; however, ensuring these alterations do not damage the nanoparticles' stability or usefulness is problematic.
3. **Biodegradability and toxicology:**
   Despite the fact that biodegradable polymers are intended to break down in physiological conditions, it is imperative that they do so without releasing toxic byproducts. Certain breakdown products may still be harmful or result in unfavourable immune responses. By regulating the rate of degradation, the medicine is released at the right time and location in accordance with the therapeutic schedule [80].
4. **Drug loading and release**

Maintaining the stability and bioactivity of pharmaceuticals within nanoparticles is a challenging task. Certain drugs may become less effective in their formulation or release ineffectively at the site of the tumour. Although systems that respond to pH changes or enzymes are examples of triggered release mechanisms, it is challenging to establish consistent and dependable control over these processes [80].

5. **Scale-up and reproducibility:**
   The manufacture of nanoparticles at an industrial scale is a challenging process to scale up from the lab. Variations in the end product's size, surface properties, and drug loading efficiency can affect its safety and therapeutic performance.
6. **Regulatory and Clinical Translation:**
   It might take a lot of time and money to conduct thorough safety and efficacy testing in order to meet regulatory requirements for approval. Approval of nanoparticle systems could be difficult because of their complexity. Strong preclinical and clinical data are needed to support the advantages of nanoparticle-based treatments, as clinical translation demands proving significant advantages over currently available drugs[80].

**Clinical Significance**

Because biodegradable biomaterials can deliver therapeutic chemicals directly to the tumour site, they have shown great promise in the field of anticancer therapy. It is possible to build these materials so that they break down safely under physiological settings, resulting in reduced toxicity and increased efficacy. For instance, as compared to free paclitaxel, polymeric nanoparticles like NK105, created by Nippon Kayaku Co., have shown improved anti-tumor activities, decreased off-target toxicity, and extended circulation time. Additionally, in vivo research has demonstrated that micelles affixed to PLGA microsphere surfaces can greatly enhance drug accumulation in tumours and the lungs, improving treatment outcomes. Furthermore, implanted devices that can distribute anti-cancer medications in a regulated manner, minimising systemic side effects and enhancing therapeutic efficacy, have been developed using bioabsorbable polymers[81,82].

Additionally, increasing popularity is the use of biomaterials in cancer immunotherapy. Advanced biomaterials can be engineered to load several medications and target certain cancer cells, increasing treatment potency and minimising side effects. Examples of these biomaterials include hydrogels, micelles, and nanoparticles. By offering more specialised and potent medicines, these materials have the potential to completely transform the way cancer is treated. Overall, the potential of biodegradable biomaterials to enhance drug transport, lower toxicity, and promote targeted therapy is what makes them clinically significant in the context of anticancer therapy [83].

**Advantage and Disadvantage**

Biodegradable biomaterials are rapidly being investigated for application in anticancer therapy due to their potential to deliver medications directly to tumor cells while minimizing side effects on healthy tissues. These materials can be designed to regulate medication release, increase drug solubility, and improve targeted specificity. However, despite their tremendous promise, various obstacles and limitations must be overcome before they can be completely utilized in clinical applications.

**Advantage**

1. **Biocompatibility and biodegradability:** Biodegradable materials are intended to decompose under physiological circumstances, thereby mitigating possible toxicity and promoting the release of drugs. This characteristic makes it possible to implant the product without having to take out the carrier after medication administration, improving patient comfort and lowering problems following therapy [84].
2. **Targeted Delivery:** Blood vessels that feed nutrients and oxygen to tumours can be targeted, as can immune cells to support anti-cancer immunotherapy, or biodegradable polymeric nanocarriers can be specifically designed to target cancer cells. This focused strategy reduces adverse effects while increasing the effectiveness of anticancer medications [84].
3. **Improved Stability and Control:** Biodegradable polymers with strong drug-loading capacities, such as poly(lactic acid) (PLA) and poly(lactic-co-glycolic acid) (PLGA), enable the best possible intracellular absorption. Their therapeutic potential can be further enhanced by customising them to modulate their functions within the body [85].
4. **Personalised Therapy:** Several medications can be loaded into a single biomaterial, which is then chosen in accordance with the targets found in the biopsy sample taken from the patient. Future research on cancer immunotherapy is anticipated to take a favourable turn in the direction of this tailored approach [86].

**Disadvantage**

1. **Low drug loading rates:** The FDA has approved nanoparticles that typically have drug loading rates of no more than 20%. This means that in order to obtain a therapeutic effect, extra carrier material may be needed, which could increase the risk of toxicity [87].
2. **High cost and complicated fabrication:** Mass production and clinical use are hampered by the complex and expensive synthesis of biodegradable polyester nanoparticles.

3. **Safety issues:** When nanoparticles enter the bloodstream, they can have harmful effects include DNA damage, oxidative stress, inflammation, and changes in the cell cycle. Another issue is sufficient clearance via the glomerular filtration membrane [88].
4. **Products of acidic degradation:** Certain polyesters can degrade into acidic byproducts, which can cause the body to react inflammatorily.

**Conclusive remark**

The potential of biodegradable biomaterials to improve cancer therapy is significant and encouraging. Over the last few decades, tremendous progress has been made in the creation of biodegradable polymeric materials, which have shown to be extremely useful in biomedical applications, particularly DDS, and temporary implants. These materials provide various benefits, including biocompatibility, controlled breakdown, and the capacity to be metabolized and removed from the body, lowering long-term toxicity and enhancing patient outcomes.

One of the most significant advantages of biodegradable biomaterials is their use in nanoparticle-based medication delivery systems. Biodegradable polyesters, such as polycaprolactone (PCL), polylactic acid (PLA), and polylactic-co-glycolic acid (PLGA), have been used to generate nanoparticles that can aggregate at tumour locations due to their capacity to cross physiological barriers. Nanoparticles can be designed for optimal drug loading, intracellular absorption, and stability, making them particularly effective for targeted cancer therapy.

These biodegradable nanoparticles can be functionalized with a variety of ligands to improve their targeting properties. Active targeting provides for targeted delivery of chemotherapeutic drugs to cancer cells, reducing systemic side effects and boosting therapeutic efficacy. Biodegradable biomaterials can target cancer cells, neovasculature, and immune cells, all of which contribute to tumour growth and progression.Despite the apparent promise, Biodegradable biomaterials have great promise for improving cancer treatment. Their ability to administer treatments in a focused, regulated, and biocompatible manner has the potential to revolutionise cancer treatment, paving the way for more effective and less harmful therapies. Future research should focus on resolving the existing constraints and developing creative techniques to maximise the therapeutic potential of these sophisticated biomaterials.

**References**


1. Zehao, Jia. Application of Degradable Polymers for the Treatment of Wounds and Tumors. Highlights in Science, Engineering and Technology, (2022). doi: 10.54097/hset.v26i.3987
2. Biocompatible and biodegradable materials in medical applications. (2023). doi: 10.1016/b978-0-323-95169-2.00010-9
3. Altun, Buse, Karakullukçu., Emel, Taban., Olatunji, Oladimeji, Ojo. Biocompatibility of biomaterials and test methods: a review. MP MATERIALPRUEFUNG - MP MATERIALS TESTING, (2023). doi: 10.1515/mt-2022-0195
4. Sonal, S., Sonawane., Prashant, Pingale., S., V., Amrutkar. PLGA: A Wow Smart Biodegradable Polymer in Drug Delivery System. Indian Journal of Pharmaceutical Education and Research, (2023). doi: 10.5530/ijper.57.2s.23
5. Katarzyna, Strzelecka., Urszula, Piotrowska., Marcin, Sobczak., Ewa, Oledzka. The Advancement of Biodegradable Polyesters as Delivery Systems for Camptothecin and Its Analogues—A Status Report. International Journal of Molecular Sciences, (2023). doi: 10.3390/ijms24021053
6. Hailong, Tian., Tingting, Zhang., Siyuan, Qin., Zhao, Huang., Li, Zhou., Jia-Zhen, Shi., Edouard, C., Nice., Nancy, Xie., Canhua, Huang., Zhisen, Shen. Enhancing the therapeutic efficacy of nanoparticles for cancer treatment using versatile targeted strategies. Journal of Hematology & Oncology, (2022). doi: 10.1186/s13045-022-01320-5
7. Pires PC, Mascarenhas-Melo F, Pedrosa K, Lopes D, Lopes J, Macário-Soares A, Peixoto D, Giram PS, Veiga F, Paiva-Santos AC. Polymer-based biomaterials for pharmaceutical and biomedical applications: A focus on topical drug administration. European Polymer Journal. 2023 Apr 3;187:111868.
8. Trucillo P. Biomaterials for Drug Delivery and Human Applications. Materials. 2024 Jan 18;17(2):456.

9. Song R, Murphy M, Li C, Ting K, Soo C, Zheng Z. Current development of biodegradable polymeric materials for biomedical applications. Drug design, development and therapy. 2018 Sep 24:3117-45.
10. Lenaghan SC, Serpersu K, Xia L, He W, Zhang M. A naturally occurring nanomaterial from the Sundew (Drosera) for tissue engineering. Bioinspiration & Biomimetics. 2011 Nov 7;6(4):046009.
11. Altman GH, Diaz F, Jakuba C, Calabro T, Horan RL, Chen J, Lu H, Richmond J, Kaplan DL. Silk-based biomaterials. Biomaterials. 2003 Feb 1;24(3):401-16.
12. Vartika, Dhyani., Neetu, Singh., Neetu, Singh. Modifications of silk film for dual delivery.. Biomedical Materials, (2017). doi: 10.1088/1748-605X/AA71BB
13. Anna, Florczak., Tomasz, Deptuch., Kamil, Kucharczyk., Hanna, Dams-Kozlowska. Systemic and Local Silk-Based Drug Delivery Systems for Cancer Therapy. Cancers, (2021). doi: 10.3390/CANCERS13215389
14. Jordi, Bella. Collagen structure: new tricks from a very old dog.. Biochemical Journal, (2016). doi: 10.1042/BJ20151169
15. Lee CH, Singla A, Lee Y. Biomedical applications of collagen. International journal of pharmaceutics. 2001 Jun 19;221(1-2):1-22.
16. Liang H, Li X, Wang B, Chen B, Zhao Y, Sun J, Zhuang Y, Shi J, Shen H, Zhang Z, Dai J. A collagen-binding EGFR antibody fragment targeting tumors with a collagen-rich extracellular matrix. Scientific Reports. 2016 Feb 17;6(1):18205.
17. Kucharov, Sardorbek, Akmalovich. Material Applications of Gelatin. (2023). doi: 10.1007/978-981-19-0710-4_28
18. Xinyue, Zhai., Huaping, Tan. Gelatin-based Targeted Delivery Systems for Tissue Engineering.. Current drug targets, (2023). doi: 10.2174/1389450124666230605150303
19. Xia Y, Xu R, Ye S, Yan J, Kumar P, Zhang P, Zhao X. Microfluidic formulation of curcumin-loaded multiresponsivegelatin nanoparticles for anticancer therapy. ACS Biomaterials Science & Engineering. 2023 May 4;9(6):3402-13.
20. Annalia, Masi., Marta, Madaghiele., Alessandro, Sannino., Luca, Salvatore., Nunzia, Gallo. Current Trends in Gelatin-Based DDS. Pharmaceutics, (2023). doi: 10.3390/pharmaceutics15051499
21. Carlos, Henrique, Bertoni, Reis., Daniela, Vieira, Buchaim., Adriana, de, Cássia, Ortiz., Simone, Ortiz, Moura, Fideles., Jefferson, Aparecido, Dias., Maria, Angélica, Miglino., Daniel, De, Bortoli, Teixeira., Eliana, Pereira., Marcelo, Rodrigues, da, Cunha., Rogério, Leone, Buchaim. Application of Fibrin Associated with Photobiomodulation as a Promising Strategy to Improve Regeneration in Tissue Engineering: A Systematic Review. Polymers, (2022). doi: 10.3390/polym14153150
22. Jannika, Brinkmann., Hanna, Malyaran., Miriam, Aischa, Al, Enezy-Ulbrich., S., Jung., Chloé, Radermacher., Eva, Miriam, Buhl., Andrij, Pich., Sabine, Neuss. Assessment of Fibrin-Based Hydrogels Containing a Fibrin-Binding Peptide to Tune Mechanical Properties and Cell Responses. Macromolecular Materials and Engineering, (2023). doi: 10.1002/mame.202200678
23. Seo J, Do Yoo J, Kim M, Shim G, Oh YK, Park RW, Lee B, Kim IS, Kim S. Fibrinolytic nanocages dissolve clots in the tumor microenvironment, improving the distribution and therapeutic efficacy of anticancer drugs. Experimental & Molecular Medicine. 2021 Oct;53(10):1592-601.
24. Jakub, Kosiński., Jaromir, Jarecki., Joanna, Przepiórka-Kosińska., Magdalena, Ratajczak. Hyaluronic acid in orthopedics..Wiadomościlekarskie (Warsaw Poland), (2020). doi: 10.36740/WLEK202009114
25. Gongming, Qian., Qing, Ye. Hydroxyapatite-based carriers for tumor targeting therapy. RSC Advances, (2023). doi: 10.1039/d3ra01476b
26. Della Sala F, Fabozzi A, di Gennaro M, Nuzzo S, Makvandi P, Solimando N, Pagliuca M, Borzacchiello A. Advances in Hyaluronic-Acid-Based (Nano) Devices for Cancer Therapy. Macromolecular Bioscience. 2022 Jan;22(1):2100304.
27. Extraction of chitin, preparation of chitosan and their structural characterization. (2023). doi: 10.1016/b978-0-323-99853-6.00010-3
28. Digafe, Alemu., Ajoy, Kanti, Mondal. Study on the Physicochemical Properties of Chitosan and their Applications in the Biomedical Sector. International Journal of Polymer Science, (2023). doi: 10.1155/2023/5025341

29. Baharlouei P, Rahman A. Chitin and chitosan: prospective biomedical applications in drug delivery, cancer treatment, and wound healing. Marine Drugs. 2022 Jul 17;20(7):460.
30. Plant polysaccharides-based nanoparticles for drug delivery. (2023). doi: 10.1016/b978-0-323-90780-4.00009-7
31. Yu C, Liu C, Wang S, Li Z, Hu H, Wan Y, Yang X. Hydroxyethyl starch-based nanoparticles featured with redox-sensitivity and chemo-photothermal therapy for synergized tumor eradication. Cancers. 2019 Feb 11;11(2):207.
32. Extraction of alginate from natural resources. (2023). doi: 10.1016/b978-0-323-99853-6.00003-6
33. V., S., Hegde., U.T., Uthappa., Tariq, Altalhi., Ho-Young, Jung., Sung, Soo, Han., Mahaveer, D., Kurkuri. Alginate based polymeric systems for drug delivery, antibacterial/microbial, and wound dressing applications. Materials today communications, (2022). doi: 10.1016/j.mtcomm.2022.104813
34. Iravani S, Varma RS. Alginate-based micro-and nanosystems for targeted cancer therapy. Marine Drugs. 2022 Sep 23;20(10):598.
35. Tania, Palmeiro-Sánchez., Vincent, O'Flaherty., Piet, N.L., Lens. Polyhydroxyalkanoate bio-production and its rise as biomaterial of the future.. Journal of biotechnology, (2022). doi: 10.1016/j.jbiotec.2022.03.001
36. Philippe, Chenaux. Microbial Polyhydroxyalkanoates (PHAs): A Brief Overview of Their Features, Synthesis, and Agro-Industrial Applications. (2022). doi: 10.1007/978-981-16-8918-5_12
37. Pramual S, Assavanig A, Bergkvist M, Batt CA, Sunintaboon P, Lirdprapamongkol K, Svasti J, Niamsiri N. Development and characterization of bio-derived polyhydroxyalkanoate nanoparticles as a delivery system for hydrophobic photodynamic therapy agents. Journal of Materials Science: Materials in Medicine. 2016 Feb;27:1-1.
38. Pradeep, Ilayaperumal., Praveena, Chelladurai., Karthik, Vairan., Pooja, Avinipully, Anilkumar., Balajothi, Balagurusamy. Polyphosphazenes—A Promising Candidate for Drug Delivery, Bioimaging, and Tissue Engineering: A Review. Macromolecular Materials and Engineering, (2023). doi: 10.1002/mame.202200553
39. Vildan, Sanko., Vildan, Sanko., Isa, Sahin., Umran, Aydemir, Sezer., Serdar, Sezer. A versatile method for the synthesis of poly(glycolic acid): high solubility and tunable molecular weights. Polymer Journal, (2019). doi: 10.1038/S41428-019-0182-7
40. Hirano M, Sakatoku M, Yamashita R, Iwa T. Studies on the new long-acting anti-cancer preparation, 5-fluorouracil-polyglycolic acid composite. Gan to Kagaku ryoho. Cancer & Chemotherapy. 1984 Aug 1;11(8):1569-72.
41. Xing, Gao., Tongxi, Zhou., Tat, Thang, Nguyen. Biodegradable Polylactic Acid and Its Composites: Characteristics, Processing, and Sustainable Applications in Sports. Polymers, (2023). doi: 10.3390/polym15143096
42. Hyun, Lee., Da, Young, Shin., Gi-Yeon, Han., Joodeok, Kim., Nahyun, Kim., Hyeong, Seok, Kang., SeKwon, Oh., Chang-Bun, Yoon., Jung, Mi, Park., Hyoun-Ee, Kim., Hyun-Do, Jung., Min, Ho, Kang. Antibacterial PLA/Mg composite with enhanced mechanical and biological performance for biodegradable orthopedic implants.. Biomaterials advances, (2023). doi: 10.1016/j.bioadv.2023.213523
43. Lu X, Miao L, Gao W, Chen Z, McHugh KJ, Sun Y, Tochka Z, Tomasic S, Sadtler K, Hyacinthe A, Huang Y. Engineered PLGA microparticles for long-term, pulsatile release of STING agonist for cancer immunotherapy. Science translational medicine. 2020 Aug 12;12(556):eaaz6606.
44. Makadia HK, Siegel SJ. Poly lactic-co-glycolic acid (PLGA) as biodegradable controlled drug delivery carrier. Polymers. 2011 Aug 26;3(3):1377-97.
45. Blázquez-Blázquez E, Pérez E, Lorenzo V, Cerrada ML. Crystalline characteristics and their influence in the Mechanical Performance in Poly (ε-caprolactone)/High Density Polyethylene Blends. Polymers. 2019 Nov 13;11(11):1874.
46. Konopnicki S, Sharaf B, Resnick C, Patenaude A, Pogal-Sussman T, Hwang KG, Abukawa H, Troulis MJ. Tissue-engineered bone with 3-dimensionally printed β-tricalcium phosphate and polycaprolactone scaffolds and early implantation: an in vivo pilot study in a porcine mandible model. Journal of Oral and Maxillofacial Surgery. 2015 May 1;73(5):1016-e1.
47. Radhakanta, Ghosh., Yuvaraj, Arun., Peter, Siman., Abraham, J., Domb. Synthesis of Aliphatic Polyanhydrides with Controllable and Reproducible Molecular Weight. Pharmaceutics, (2022). doi: 10.3390/pharmaceutics14071403

48. Jain JP, Chitkara D, Kumar N. Polyanhydrides as localized drug delivery carrier: an update. Expert opinion on drug delivery. 2008 Aug 1;5(8):889-907.
49. Krukiewicz K, Zak JK. Biomaterial-based regional chemotherapy: Local anticancer drug delivery to enhance chemotherapy and minimize its side-effects. Materials Science and Engineering: C. 2016 May 1;62:927-42.
50. M.A., Sawpan. Bio-polyurethane and Others. (2020). doi: 10.1201/9781315154190-12
51. Santerre JP, Woodhouse K, Laroche G, Labow RS. Understanding the biodegradation of polyurethanes: from classical implants to tissue engineering materials. Biomaterials. 2005 Dec 1;26(35):7457-70.
52. Marcin, Sobczak., Karolina, Kędra. (2022). Biomedical Polyurethanes for Anti-Cancer Drug Delivery Systems: A Brief, Comprehensive Review. International Journal of Molecular Sciences, doi: 10.3390/ijms23158181
53. Fei-Peng, Chen., Oyindamola, R., Teniola., Cato, T., Laurencin. Biodegradable polyphosphazenes for regenerative engineering. Journal of Materials Research, (2022). doi: 10.1557/s43578-022-00551-z
54. Ambrosio AM, Allcock HR, Katti DS, Laurencin CT. Degradable polyphosphazene/poly (α-hydroxyester) blends: degradation studies. Biomaterials. 2002 Apr 1;23(7):1667-72.
55. Avaji PG, Park JH, Lee HJ, Jun YJ, Park KS, Lee KE, Choi SJ, Lee HJ, Sohn YS. Design of a novel theranostic nanomedicine: synthesis and physicochemical properties of a biocompatible polyphosphazene–platinum (II) conjugate. International Journal of Nanomedicine. 2016 Mar 2:837-51.
56. Palma E, Pasqua A, Gagliardi A, Britti D, Fresta M, Cosco D. Antileishmanial activity of amphotericin B-loaded-PLGA nanoparticles: an overview. Materials. 2018 Jul 9;11(7):1167.
57. Xiao, Ma., Yangjia, Liu., Han, Mei, Wu., J., Tan., Wenying, Yi., Zhenjie, Wang., Zhi-hu, Yu., Xuefeng, Wang. Self-assembly nanoplatform of platinum (Ⅳ) prodrug for enhanced ovarian cancer therapy. Materials today bio, (2023). doi: 10.1016/j.mtbio.2023.100698
58. Haiyan, Zhang., Youlin, Yang., Yi, Chen., Xiahui, Zhang., Xiaopei, Chen. A convergent fabrication of programmed pH/reduction-responsive nanoparticles for efficient dual anticancer drugs delivery for ovarian cancer treatment. Journal of Experimental Nanoscience, (2023). doi: 10.1080/17458080.2023.2193400
59. Srivastava S, Kumar A, Yadav PK, Kumar M, Mathew J, Pandey AC, Chourasia MK. Formulation and performance evaluation of polymeric mixed micelles encapsulated with baicalein for breast cancer treatment. Drug Development and Industrial Pharmacy. 2021 Sep 2;47(9):1512-22.
60. Kumar A, Rana R, Saklani R, Kumar M, Yadav PK, Tiwari A, Chourasia MK. Technology transfer of a validated RP-HPLC method for the simultaneous estimation of andrographolide and paclitaxel in application to pharmaceutical nanoformulation. Journal of Chromatographic Science. 2024 Apr;62(4):356-63.
61. Sharma M, Chouhan NK, Vaidya S, Talati MN. Lipids, peptides, and polymers as targeted drug delivery vectors in cancer therapy. InHandbook of research on advancements in cancer therapeutics 2021 (pp. 255-275). IGI Global.
62. Zhu L, Chen L. Progress in research on paclitaxel and tumor immunotherapy. Cellular & molecular biology letters. 2019 Dec;24(1):40.
63. Von Hoff DD, Mita MM, Ramanathan RK, Weiss GJ, Mita AC, LoRusso PM, Burris III HA, Hart LL, Low SC, Parsons DM, Zale SE. Phase I study of PSMA-targeted docetaxel-containing nanoparticle BIND-014 in patients with advanced solid tumors. Clinical Cancer Research. 2016 Jul 1;22(13):3157-63.
64. Merle P, Camus P, Abergel A, Pageaux GP, Masliah C, Bronowicki JP, Zarski JP, Pelletier G, Bouattour M, Farloux L, Dorval E. Safety and efficacy of intra-arterial hepatic chemotherapy with doxorubicin-loaded nanoparticles in hepatocellular carcinoma. ESMO open. 2017 Jan 1;2(4):e000238.
65. Gagliardi A, Giuliano E, Venkateswararao E, Fresta M, Bulotta S, Awasthi V, Cosco D. Biodegradable polymeric nanoparticles for drug delivery to solid tumors. Frontiers in pharmacology. 2021 Feb 3;12:601626.
66. Yang F, Shi K, Jia YP, Hao Y, Peng JR, Qian ZY. Advanced biomaterials for cancer immunotherapy. ActaPharmacologicaSinica. 2020 Jul;41(7):911-27.
67. Dong Q, Xue T, Yan H, Liu F, Liu R, Zhang K, Chong Y, Du J, Zhang H. Radiotherapy combined with nano-biomaterials for cancer radio-immunotherapy. Journal of Nanobiotechnology. 2023 Oct 30;21(1):395.
68. Milborne B, Arafat A, Layfield R, Thompson A, Ahmed I. The Use of Biomaterials in Internal Radiation Therapy. Recent Progress in Materials. 2020 May;2(2):1-34.

69. Neubi GM, Opoku-Damoah Y, Gu X, Han Y, Zhou J, Ding Y. Bio-inspired DDS: an emerging platform for targeted cancer therapy. Biomaterials science. 2018;6(5):958-73.
70. Xu X, Li T, Jin K. Bioinspired and biomimetic nanomedicines for targeted cancer therapy. Pharmaceutics. 2022 May 23;14(5):1109.
71. Sun L, Liu H, Ye Y, Lei Y, Islam R, Tan S, Tong R, Miao YB, Cai L. Smart nanoparticles for cancer therapy. Signal transduction and targeted therapy. 2023 Nov 3;8(1):418.
72. Ambrosio L, Raucci MG, Vadalà G, Ambrosio L, Papalia R, Denaro V. Innovative biomaterials for the treatment of bone cancer. International journal of molecular sciences. 2021 Jul 30;22(15):8214.
73. Edis Z, Wang J, Waqas MK, Ijaz M, Ijaz M. Nanocarriers-mediated DDS for anticancer agents: an overview and perspectives. International journal of nanomedicine. 2021 Feb 17:1313-30.
74. Willemen NG, Hassan S, Gurian M, Li J, Allijn IE, Shin SR, Leijten J. Oxygen-releasing biomaterials: current challenges and future applications. Trends in biotechnology. 2021 Nov 1;39(11):1144-59.
75. Khan MS, Hwang J, Lee K, Choi Y, Seo Y, Jeon H, Hong JW, Choi J. Anti-tumor drug-loaded oxygen nanobubbles for the degradation of HIF-1α and the upregulation of reactive oxygen species in tumor cells. Cancers. 2019 Sep 29;11(10):1464.
76. Wu X, Han X, Guo Y, Liu Q, Sun R, Wen Z, Dai C. Application prospect of calcium peroxide nanoparticles in biomedical field. Reviews on Advanced Materials Science. 2023 Mar 10;62(1):20220308.
77. Suvarnapathaki S, Nguyen MA, Goulopoulos AA, Lantigua D, Camci-Unal G. Engineering calcium peroxide based oxygen generating scaffolds for tissue survival. Biomaterials Science. 2021;9(7):2519-32.
78. Yong, Wang., Jiaqi, Guo., Sumita, Sumita., Changjie, Shi., Qijia, Zhu., Cong, Li., Weihai, Pang. A Review of Recent Advances in Detection and Treatment Technology for Perfluorinated Compounds. Water, (2022). doi: 10.3390/w14233919
79. Karlsson J, Vaughan HJ, Green JJ. Biodegradable polymeric nanoparticles for therapeutic cancer treatments. Annual review of chemical and biomolecular engineering. 2018 Jun 7;9:105-27.
80. Wang Z, Xiao M, Guo F, Yan Y, Tian H, Zhang Q, Ren S, Yang L. Biodegradable polyester-based nano DDS in cancer chemotherapy: a review of recent progress (2021–2023). Frontiers in Bioengineering and Biotechnology. 2023;11.
81. Sharma M, Ambadipudi SS, Chouhan NK, Nayak VL, Pabbaraja S, Andugulapati SB, Sistla R. Design, synthesis and biological evaluation of novel cationic liposomes loaded with melphalan for the treatment of cancer. Bioorganic & Medicinal Chemistry Letters. 2024 Jan 1;97:129549.
82. Kumar A, Kumar M, Singh R, Upadhyay P, Mukherjee A. Quality by Design (QbD) Aided Formulation Optimization of Amlodipine Besylate Oral Thin Film. Indian Journal of Pharmaceutical Education and Research. 2024 May 27;58(2s):s444-52.
83. Yang F, Shi K, Jia YP, Hao Y, Peng JR, Qian ZY. Advanced biomaterials for cancer immunotherapy. ActaPharmacologicaSinica. 2020 Jul;41(7):911-27.
84. Xinlin, Li., Xinyi, Xu., Mengfei, Xu., Zhaoli, Geng., Ping, Ji., Yi, Liu. Hydrogel systems for targeted cancer therapy. Frontiers in Bioengineering and Biotechnology, (2023). doi: 10.3389/fbioe.2023.1140436
85. Martin, Schulze, Wessel. Enhancement of Immunotherapies in Head and Neck Cancers Using Biomaterial-Based Treatment Strategies. Tissue Engineering Part C-methods, (2023). doi: 10.1089/ten.tec.2023.0090
86. Dennis, Horvath., Michael, Basler. PLGA Particles in Immunotherapy. Pharmaceutics, (2023). doi: 10.3390/pharmaceutics15020615
87. Engineered Nanoparticles Adversely Impact Glucose Energy Metabolism. (2023). doi: 10.1002/9781119896258.ch11
88. Biodegradable polymeric nanoparticle drug for oral delivery applications. (2023). doi: 10.1016/b978-0-323-91376-8.00017-3

CHAPTER TWO

# Biomaterial Based Green Chemical Synthesis

**Aamir Anwar[1], Aquib Rehanullah Siddiqui[2]**
[1]*Amity Institute of Pharmacy, Amity University, Lucknow, Uttar Pradesh, 241001, India*
[2]*Harsha institute of pharmacy, Lucknow, Uttar Pradesh, 226203, India*

**Highlights**

- ***Principles and role of green chemistry:*** *This chapter highlights the principles of green chemistry in reducing hazardous substances and emphasizes strategic design for sustainability at the molecular level.*
- ***Biomaterials as environmentally friendly catalysts:*** *Biomaterials possess significant applications in pharmaceuticals and tissue engineering because of their biodegradability and low toxicity. Also, the significance of enzymes and biopolymers as catalysts in green synthesis is highlighted.*
- ***Nanocatalysts and biomaterial matrices:*** *Immobilization of nanocatalysts on biomaterial matrices to enhance stability and facilitate reuse is explored.*
- ***Biomass-derived chemical precursors:*** *For the production of bio-based chemicals and materials bio-mass derived precursors must be extracted and modified.*
- ***Biomedical application and biocompatibility:*** *Biocompatible biomaterials are significantly used in drug synthesis, tissue engineering and regenerative medicine.*

## 1. Introduction

### Overview of Green Chemistry

Green chemistry (GC) is the method of developing products and processes that reduce or eliminate the use and manufacture of hazardous compounds(1).The rapid increase in the world's population and the improvement in living conditions have caused increased worry about the discharge of harmful compounds into the environment and the exhaustion of natural resources(2).Therefore GC implies a fundamental transformation of the conventional chemical process, which prioritizes producing a high product yield, to a process that seeks to reduce the presence of toxic and/ or hazardous substances in the production and manufacturing of chemical products(3).

The essential element of GC revolves around the notion of design. Design is a deliberate expression of human intention and it cannot be achieved accidentally. It encompasses originality, strategic thinking, and methodical design. The Twelve Principles of GC (Fig. 1) serve as guidelines for chemists to effectively pursue the objective of sustainability through purposeful design. GC is defined by meticulous strategic planning of chemical synthesis and molecular design in order to minimize negative repercussions(4).The GC approach aims to attain sustainability by focusing on the molecular level. Due to the achievement of this objective, it is not surprising that it has been implemented throughout all industry sectors(4).In the past two decades, there has been a significant increase in teaching programs, governmental financing, and the construction of GC Research Centers, all driven by the growing scientific interest for GC. A growing number of universities currently provide courses on GC and Green Engineering.

Several institutions provide academic programs in this particular topic. Government funding has experienced a notable boost in several countries worldwide(5).

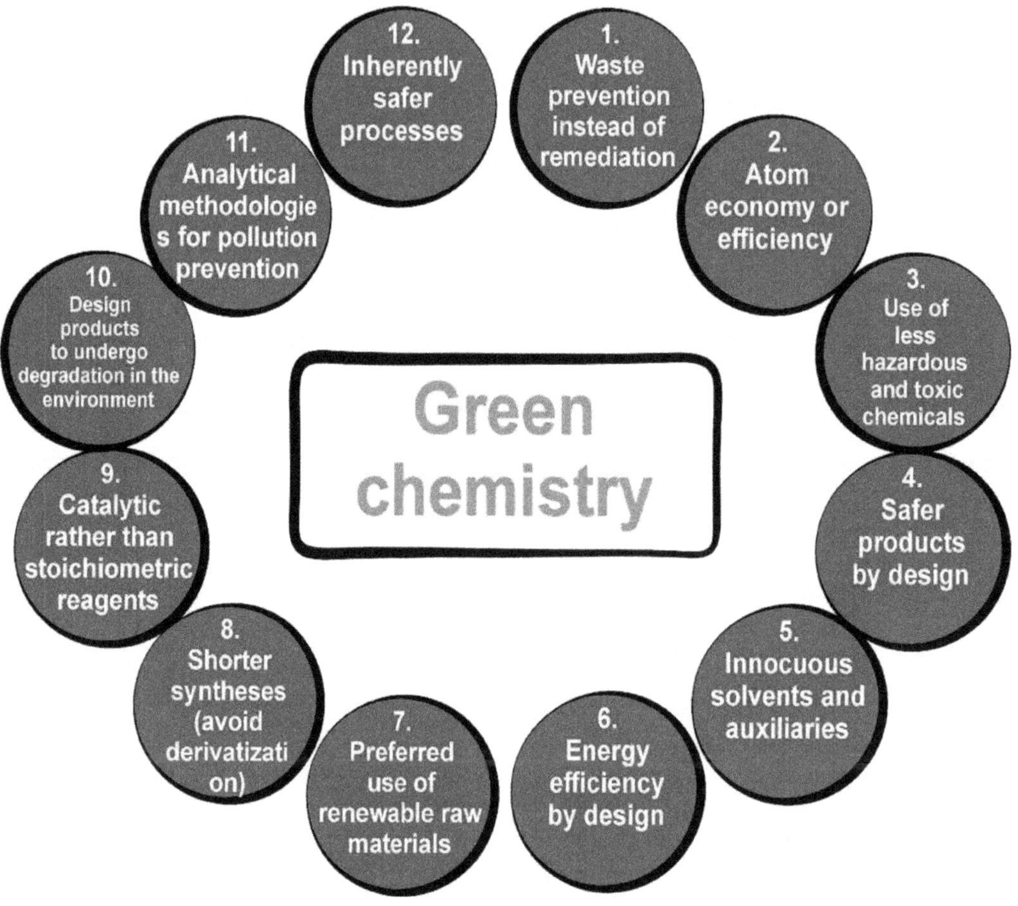


**Fig. 1- Twelve principles of green chemistry**

**Some reactions showing principles of green chemistry**

- **Rearrangement reaction of Allyl phenyl ether on heating at 200°C gives o-allyl phenol(100% atom economical).**

The concept of enhancing atomic usability was established in 1991 by Barry Trost, a professor at Stanford University. Trost argues that the introduction of usability atoms is simply a means of preventing waste at the molecular level.

The notion introduced by Barry Trost led to the re-evaluation and modification of current synthetic reactions, which were previously based on the principle of producing a product without considering its cost. These adjustments are beneficial as they typically result in higher yields(6).

Allyl phenols serve as a fundamental substance for the production of various organic compounds. They are used in the synthesis of biologically active chemicals, as well as in the manufacturing of rubber vulcanization accelerators, explosives, lubrication oils, and gasoline anticorrosive additives(7).

200 °C

(Allyloxy)benzene

2-allylphenol

Enter Caption

- **Polycarbonate (PC) synthesis: Solid-state Process is less hazardous as compare to Phosgene process.**

PCs are very adaptable thermoplastic polymers that find uses in a wide range of fields, including high-end engineering and biomaterials. The primary structures of personal computers consist of a recurring carbonate [–O–C(=O)–O–] bond, and the main component is composed of aromatic and/or aliphatic units(8).

The PC manufactured using the new non-phosgene technique exhibits excellent performance in the following aspects:

(1) Excellent clarity and transparency. (2) The PC produced by the phosgene procedures contains impurities, such as Cl-containing compounds. However, high-purity PC does not include any of these impurities. There is no evidence of corrosion on the metal mold, the stamper used for disk molding, or the recording layer of disks. (3) Oligomers with a molecular weight below about 1000 are present in low quantities(9).

**Polycarbonate Synthesis: Phosgene Process -**

HO, OH, +, O, Cl, Cl, NaOH, O, O, O

4,4'-(propane-2,2-diyl)diphenol

phosgene

4-(2-(4-methoxyphenyl)propan-2-yl)phenyl acetate

**Polycarbonate Synthesis: Solid-State Process -**

HO, OH

4,4'-(propane-2,2-diyl)diphenol

+

O, O, O

diphenyl carbonate

O, O, O

4-(2-(4-methoxyphenyl)propan-2-yl)phenyl acetate

- **Selection of solvents**

The selection of appropriate organic solvent replacements is guided by the principles of green chemistry and takes into account worker safety, process safety, environmental safety, and process sustainability. The solvent should have low volatility, be simple to use, quick to recycle, and stable both chemically and physically. Conventional solvents are preferred, usable, and undesirable depending on the purpose (Table 1)(6).

| Preferred | Useable | Undesirable |
|---|---|---|
| Water | Cyclohexane | Pentane |
| Acetone | Heptane | Hexane |
| Ethanol | Toluene | Di-isopropyl ether |
| 2-Propanol | Methyl cyclohexane | Diethyl ether |
| 1-Propanol | Methyl t-butyl ether | Dichloromethane |
| Ethyl acetate | Isooctane | Dichloromethane |
| Isopropyl acetate | Acetonitrile | Chloroform |
| Methanol | 2-MethylTHF | Dimethyl formamide |
| Methyl ethyl ketone | Tetrahydrofuran | N-Methylpyrrolidinone |
| 1-Butanol | Xylenes | Pyridine |
| t-Butanol | Acetic acid | Dimethyl acetate |

**Table 1: Solvents in Green Chemistry**

**Importance of Biomaterials in Green Chemical Synthesis**

Biomaterials refer to the materials that are specifically created and manufactured to interact with biological systems. These materials are bioactive and can be easily compressed to fit human tissue. They have a high level of biodegradability. They are frequently employed in pharmaceuticals, tissue engineering, the production of human body components, and various manufacturing applications. Sustainability and biomaterials are mutually supportive, enabling the production and development of novel sustainable materials by implementing modern technological methods. The biomaterials possess environmentally favourable characteristics. They are derived from various biological sources or produced utilizing environmentally friendly technology. Several biomaterials have been conceived and developed to serve as prospective alternatives to existing materials in various biomedical disciplines. They are effectively utilized in medical treatments such as cancer therapy, ligament and tendon repair, orthopaedic applications, ophthalmic applications for contact lens design, wound healing, nerve regeneration therapy, breast implants, and the production of various surgical devices (10).

Biomaterials provide a viable and environmentally friendly substitute for conventional chemical materials. Biomaterials have multiple functions in chemical synthesis, such as acting as catalysts, providing nanoparticle support matrices, and serving as precursors for high-value compounds. Because of their biodegradability, low toxicity, and wide availability, they are well-suited for the development of environmentally benign chemical processes(11).

Lichen extracts provide a greener and more eco-friendly alternative to conventional procedures for synthesizing nanoparticles. Lichens, which are recognized for their therapeutic qualities, can decrease and stabilize metallic salts efficiently. This offers an environmentally friendly method for creating nanomaterials that might potentially be used for antibacterial purposes (12).

The production of carbon dots (CDs) from renewable biomass sources such as agro-waste and medicinal plants is a notable advancement in achieving sustainability. These green CDs are cost-effective and possess exceptional characteristics, such as strong durability and compatibility with living organisms, making them well-suited for various biomedical uses. This approach starkly contrasts conventional physicochemical approaches, which frequently incur more costs and have a lesser degree of environmental friendliness (13).

1. **Biomaterials as Catalysts in Green Synthesis**

The academic and industrial sectors have shown growing interest in the development of new catalysts that can minimize or completely remove the use of dangerous substances commonly employed in the chemical industry. This focus on GC aims to find alternative products and processes that can reduce or eliminate the need for hazardous substances. The demand for this becomes even more significant when it pertains to the production and alteration of biopolymers that have extensive usefulness in the biomedical sector, such as poly(lactic acid) (PLA), poly(glycolic acid) (PGA), poly(caprolactone) (PCL), as well as acrylate-based polymers(14).

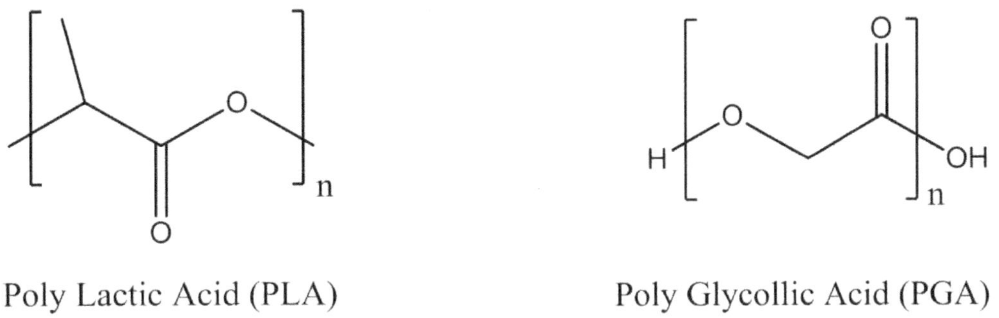

O n O H O OH n O

Poly Lactic Acid (PLA) Poly Glycollic Acid (PGA)

Enter Caption

- **Enzymatic catalysis**

Enzymes are being increasingly favored as catalysts for organic synthesis instead of traditional chemical catalysis. Enzymes possess numerous benefits, such as exceptional selectivity, the capacity to function in gentle environments, the ability to be reused as catalysts, and compatibility with living organisms (15). Enzymes have a wider range of applications in industrial processes because they may be designed to function in non-natural settings(16).

Currently, there are over 3000 commercially available enzymes, with certain ones being genetically altered for use in industrial settings. Oxidoreductases, hydrolases, and isomerases are commonly employed as catalysts in biotransformations due to their inherent stability and widespread usage. Out of them, certain enzymes that are separated from others are commonly employed as catalysts in practical applications. Conversely, lyases and ligases are found in less quantities within living cells and are less resistant to being isolated or separated from living organisms.The breakdown of triglyceride substrates into fatty acids and glycerol is catalyzed by Lipases at the interface between lipids and water in living organisms. These compounds are extensively employed in organic solvents for esterification, transesterification, aminolysis, and Michael addition processes(17).

The lipases most advantageous for organic synthesis include *Porcine pancreatic lipase*, lipase from *Pseudomonascepacia*, lipase from *Candida rugosa*, and lipase B from *Candida antarctica*(18). Amino acid dehydrogenases are primarily used to enzymatically produce pure enantiomers of both natural and synthetic amino acids. Furthermore, these enzymes have been utilized in the synthesis of medicinal substances, such as drugs use for the management of diabetes.Glycosylation reactionsuses glycosyltransferases to connect glycosyl donors to nonprotected acceptors in aqueous environments in order to create pure oligosaccharide preparations (19).

**The interconversion between alcohols and aldehydes or ketones is catalysed by alcoholdehydrogenases, ketoreductases (KREDs) and alcohol oxidases**

O
R1 R2
Alcohol dehydrogenase (ADH)
Ketoredeuctase (KRED)
Oxidase (alcohol to aldehyde / ketrone)
OH
R1 R2

**Baeyer–Villiger monooxygenases oxidize ketones to esters.**

O
R1 R2
Baeyer-Villiger monooxygenase
O
R1 O R2

Enter Caption

**Biopolymer-Based Catalysts**

Biopolymers, including chitosan, cellulose, and alginate, are a type of biomaterials that are used as catalysts in green synthesis. These natural polymers can be modified with catalytic sites, providing a mix of biodegradability, renewability, and catalytic activity. Chitosan-based catalysts have been employed in diverse organic transformations, showcasing both effectiveness and the potential to be reused. Biopolymer-based catalysts offer significant benefits in water-based environments, which aligns with the objective of GC to minimize the use of organic solvents(20).

Chitosan, which is available for purchase, is known to function as a solid base catalyst in the Knoevenagel condensation reaction. This reaction involves the combination of carbonyl compounds with malononitrile, and it occurs under mild reaction conditions. Chitosan is identified through the use of powder X-ray diffraction (XRD), infrared spectroscopy (IR), and elemental analysis. The catalytic efficacy of chitosan is assessed in the Knoevenagel condensation process involving benzaldehyde and malononitrile as representative substrates. The refined reaction conditions are subsequently employed to broaden its catalytic potential with diverse substrates(21).

O
Benzaldehyde
+
N N
Malononitrile
Ethanol,40°C
Chitosan
CN
CN
2-benzylidenemalononitrile

**Knoevenagel condensation**

Evonik Degussa GmbH described a whole-cell cascade to produce diamines — which are valuable building blocks in the polymer industry — from renewably sourced dicarboxylic acids(22).

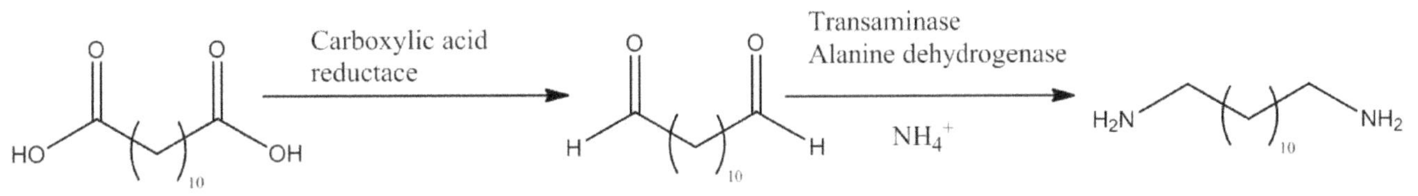

Carboxylic acid reductace

Transaminase
Alanine dehydrogenase
$NH_4^+$

Enter Caption

### 3. Biomaterial-Supported Nanoparticles for Green Synthesis

- **Nanocatalysts Immobilized on Biomaterial Matrices**

Nanocatalysts possess a large surface area and certain characteristics that augment their catalytic efficiency. By immobilizing these nanoparticles on biomaterial matrices, it is possible to avoid their aggregation, enhance their stability, and make it easier to recover and reuse them. Cellulose, starch, and proteins have been utilized as support matrices for metal nanoparticles in green synthesis, serving as biomaterials. These hybrid materials merge the catalytic effectiveness of nanocatalysts with the ecological advantages of biomaterials (23).

- **Applications in Sustainable Synthesis Reactions**

Nanocatalysts assisted by biomaterials have demonstrated encouraging outcomes in several sustainable synthesis reactions, such as hydrogenation, oxidation, and coupling reactions. These catalysts facilitate effective chemical reactions at low temperatures, hence minimizing energy usage and waste production. Gold nanoparticles supported on cellulose have been utilized in the aerobic oxidation of alcohols to aldehydes, demonstrating notable efficacy and specificity(24).

### 4. Biomaterial-Derived Precursors for Green Synthesis

**Extraction and Modification of Biomass-Derived Precursors**

Biomass, a plentiful and renewable resource, can be transformed into useful chemical precursors using several extraction and modification methods. Methods such as hydrolysis, pyrolysis, and fermentation are used to extract sugars, lignin, and other substances from biomass. These initial substances can undergo chemical alterations to generate bio-based building blocks, solvents, and fuels, hence promoting the advancement of environmentally-friendly chemical procedures(25).

**Synthesis of High-Value Chemicals and Materials**

Biomass-derived precursors have the ability to undergo conversion into a diverse array of valuable chemicals and materials, such as bioplastics, biofuels, and medicinal intermediates. An example of this is the process of catalytic conversion, where lignocellulosic biomass is transformed into platform chemicals such as furfural and levulinic acid. This method offers a sustainable pathway for the production of synthetic polymers and resins(26). These procedures not only decrease reliance on fossil fuels but also limit the ecological consequences of chemical manufacture.

### 5. Biomaterials for Green Synthesis in Biomedical Applications

**Biocompatible Biomaterials for Drug Synthesis**

Choosing no solvents or green solvents (preferably water), alternative reaction media, one-pot synthesis, multicomponent reactions (MCRs), continuous processing, and process intensification approaches for atom economy and final waste reduction are just a few ways that the principles of green chemistry (GC) can be fully applied to the green synthesis of drugs(27).

Biocompatibility is an essential factor to take into account in biomedical applications. Biomaterials utilized in the production and administration of drugs must possess the qualities of being non-toxic, non-immunogenic, and capable of interacting safely with biological systems. Polysaccharides, proteins, and lipids are often employed biomaterials in this domain. They can be manipulated to administer medications in a regulated fashion, so improving the effectiveness of treatment and minimizing adverse reactions(28).

**Biomaterial-Based Platforms for Tissue Engineering**

Tissue engineering seeks to create biological replacements that can restore, sustain, or enhance tissue function. Biomaterials are essential in this discipline as they provide structures that facilitate cell adhesion, growth, and specialization. Collagen, gelatin, and hyaluronic acid, which are natural polymers, are commonly employed in many applications because of their biocompatibility and capacity to replicate the extracellular matrix (29). These platforms made from biomaterials play a crucial role in the development of regenerative therapies and the progress of customized medicine.

Ceramic-polymer composites are viewed as a highly promising blend of materials for the purpose of tissue engineering and regenerative medicine methods. In order to address the concerns of low fracture resistance and brittleness in bioceramics, it is suggested to combine them with polymeric matrices. This approach aims to overcome these limits and enable their application in the regeneration of hard tissues like bone.

In addition, bioceramic-polymer composites are frequently used for drug administration. One example is the creation of stimulus-responsive composites using diatom biosilica microcapsules and copolymers of oligo(ethylene glycol) methacrylates, which are used for delivering antibiotics(30).

Polysaccharides, among other biomaterials, have been employed as an environmentally friendly source for skin tissue regeneration. Recently, electrospinning was used to create a remarkable beta vulgaris nanofibrous (obtained from the beetroot [Chenopodiaceae or Amaranthaceae]). The monotone surface of the nylon polymer and B. vulgaris extract nanocomposite was validated by scanning electron microscopy. The composites‘ mechanical strength and immunocytochemistry are on par with those of the original skin tissues. These findings suggested that the green composite scaffolds barely preserved the keratinocytes' natural functionalities(31).

**6. Advantages and Disadvantages**

Biomaterials possess numerous benefits in the field of green synthesis, such as their ability to be renewed, their capacity for biodegradation, and their low levels of toxicity. They facilitate the creation of sustainable chemical processes and products, thereby diminishing environmental repercussions. Nevertheless, it is important to tackle obstacles such as fluctuations in the composition of raw materials, difficulties in achieving scalability, and the possibility of incurring substantial expenses. In order to promote the extensive use of biomaterials in green synthesis, it is crucial to enhance extraction and modification procedures, devise cost-efficient manufacturing methods, and maintain a constant level of quality(32).

**7. Challenges and Future Directions**

**Scalability and Cost-Effectiveness**

Expanding the utilization of biomaterials for industrial purposes continues to be a major obstacle. In order to make biomaterials competitive with traditional materials, it is necessary to develop production processes that are both efficient and cost-effective. Biotechnological advancements, including genetic engineering and bioprocess optimization, offer potential for enhancing the productivity and decreasing the expenses associated with biomaterial manufacturing (33).

**Integration of Biomaterials into Industrial Processes**

In order to effectively incorporate biomaterials into pre-existing industrial procedures, it is essential to surmount technological and economic limitations. Hybrid systems that amalgamate biomaterials with conventional materials and technologies have the potential to ease this incorporation, thereby enabling a seamless transition and broader acceptance within industrial settings. The collaboration among academia, industry, and governmental entities plays a pivotal role in promoting the utilization of biomaterials by stimulating innovation, facilitating the exchange of knowledge, and providing regulatory backing, ultimately propelling the adoption of sustainable materials across diverse industries. Through collective efforts, these key stakeholders can tackle obstacles, advance research and development initiatives, and establish a supportive environment conducive to the successful integration of biomaterials into industrial operations (34).

**Emerging Trends and Opportunities in Biomaterial-Based Green Synthesis**

The domain of biomaterial-based green synthesis is undeniably progressing swiftly, with a specific emphasis on sustainable material advancement. The utilization of natural reagents such as fungi in green synthesis methodologies is on the rise due to their environmental advantages and distinctive material characteristics. The transition towards eco-friendly synthetic pathways for sustainable materials holds significant importance in mitigating environmental contamination and financial setbacks linked to traditional approaches. Additionally, the enhancement of material performance and sustainability through the creation of innovative biomaterials and bio-based nanocomposites is paving the way for a myriad of applications including energy storage and conversion. Techniques for characterization like UV-vis spectroscopy and bioimaging are currently being utilized for the examination of the properties of nanoscale materials produced using green techniques, consequently propelling the domain of biomaterial-based green synthesis further(35).

**8. Clinical Significance**

**Biocompatibility and Safety**

The biocompatibility and safety of biomaterials are of utmost importance in therapeutic applications. Medical devices, implants, and drug delivery systems require biomaterials that adhere to strict regulatory criteria in order to guarantee the safety of patients. Consistent investigation and meticulous experimentation are important in order to create biomaterials that are both efficacious and secure for therapeutic use (36).

**Reduced Environmental Impact**

Biomaterials play a role in mitigating the ecological consequences of chemical and biological procedures. Their inherent renewability and ability to biodegrade effectively reduce both waste and pollution, hence adhering to the fundamental tenets of GC. Advancements in the production of eco-friendly biomaterials have the potential to promote sustainable healthcare practices and diminish the environmental impact of the medical sector(37).

**Improved Drug Delivery Systems**

Biomaterials are essential for the advancement of medication delivery systems. They can be manipulated to deliver medications at precise locations and rates, enhancing the effectiveness of treatment and minimizing adverse reactions. Advancements in drug delivery using biomaterials involve the development of targeted delivery systems, carriers that can degrade naturally, and materials that respond to specific stimuli(38).

**Personalized Medicine**

Personalized medicine seeks to customize medical therapy for individual patients by considering their genetic, environmental, and lifestyle characteristics. Biomaterials facilitate personalized medicine by facilitating the creation of tailored implants, pharmaceutical compositions, and diagnostic instruments. The progress in biomaterials technology is causing a change towards healthcare that is more tailored to each individual and more efficient(39).

**Regenerative Medicine**

Regenerative medicine is a field that specifically targets the repair or replacement of injured tissues and organs by utilizing biological alternatives. Biomaterials play a crucial role in this domain by offering scaffolds and matrices that facilitate cell proliferation and tissue rejuvenation. Advancements in the field of biomaterials for regenerative medicine are resulting in significant progress in the managing ailments such as heart disease, osteoarthritis, and spinal cord injuries (40).

**Affordability and Accessibility**

Ensuring that biomaterials are both affordable and accessible is crucial for their widespread implementation in healthcare. Implementing tactics aimed at decreasing manufacturing expenses, optimizing supply chains, and encouraging the utilization of materials obtained from nearby sources can significantly increase the availability of biomaterials, especially in economically disadvantaged nations(41).

**Clinical Translation and Regulatory Compliance**

Moving biomaterial discoveries from the lab to clinical practice requires understanding and manoeuvring through many regulatory processes. Complying with regulatory norms and securing appropriate permissions are crucial prerequisites for introducing innovative biomaterials to the market. The clinical translation of biomaterial-based innovations can be facilitated through collaboration among researchers, physicians, and regulatory bodies(42).

**9. Conclusion**

Integrating biomaterials into GC shows potential for creating sustainable and eco-friendly chemical processes. Biomaterials possess distinct benefits such as renewable, biodegradable, and biocompatible properties, rendering them highly suitable for a range of applications in chemical synthesis, biomedical engineering, and environmental protection. Despite the obstacles, continuous research and technical progress are facilitating the wider implementation of biomaterials in the fields of industry and healthcare. Biomaterials can have a significant impact on promoting sustainable development and enhancing human health by resolving issues of scalability, cost-effectiveness, and regulatory compliance.

**References**


1.Voigt K, Scherb H, Bruggemann R, Schramm KW. Discrete mathematical data analysis approach: A valuable assessment method for sustainable chemistry. Science of The Total Environment. 2013 Jun;454–455:149–53.

2.Silvestri C, Silvestri L, Forcina A, Di Bona G, Falcone D. Green chemistry contribution towards more equitable global sustainability and greater circular economy: A systematic literature review. J Clean Prod. 2021 Apr;294:126137.

3. Anastas PT, Warner JC. Green Chemistry. Oxford University PressOxford; 2000.

4.Anastas P, Eghbali N. Green Chemistry: Principles and Practice. ChemSoc Rev. 2010;39(1):301–12.

5.10TH CONGRESS 2D SESSION IN THE SENATE OF THE UNITED STATES. 2008.

6.Ivanković A. Review of 12 Principles of Green Chemistry in Practice. International Journal of Sustainable and Green Energy. 2017;6(3):39.

7.Torosyan G, Hovhannisyan D. Synthesis of allyl phenyl ether and claisen rearrangement. Scientific Study & Research Chemistry & Chemical Engineering, Biotechnology, Food Industry. 2011 Dec 1;12:425–8.

8.Singh A. Polycarbonate Synthesis. In: Encyclopedia of Polymeric Nanomaterials. Berlin, Heidelberg: Springer Berlin Heidelberg; 2015. p. 1793–6.

9. Fukuoka S, Kawamura M, Komiya K, Tojo M, Hachiya H, Hasegawa K, et al. A novel non-phosgene polycarbonate production process using by-product CO2 as starting materialPresented at The First International Conference on Green & Sustainable Chemistry, Tokyo, Japan, March 13?15, 2003. Green Chemistry - GREEN CHEM. 2003 Oct 2;5.

10.Biswal T, BadJena SK, Pradhan D. Sustainable biomaterials and their applications: A short review. Mater Today Proc. 2020;30:274–82.

11.Sheldon RA. Green and sustainable manufacture of chemicals from biomass: state of the art. Green Chem. 2014;16(3):950–63.

12.Kocakaya Z. Green synthetic biomaterials: Synthesis, characterization and antimicrobial properties of lichen-derived nanomaterials. Ceram Int. 2024 May;

13.Jing H, Bardakci F, Akgöl S, Kusat K, Adnan M, Alam M, et al. Green Carbon Dots: Synthesis, Characterization, Properties and Biomedical Applications. J FunctBiomater. 2023 Jan 2;14(1):27.

14.Chafran L, Matias AE, Silva LP. Green Catalysts in the Synthesis of Biopolymers and Biomaterials. ChemistrySelect. 2022 Jul 27;7(28).

15.Puskas JE, Sen MY, Seo KS. Green polymer chemistry using nature's catalysts, enzymes. J PolymSciAPolym Chem. 2009 Jun 15;47(12):2959–76.

16.Bornscheuer UT, Huisman GW, Kazlauskas RJ, Lutz S, Moore JC, Robins K. Engineering the third wave of biocatalysis. Nature. 2012 May 9;485(7397):185–94.

17.Sen S, Puskas J. Green Polymer Chemistry: Enzyme Catalysis for Polymer Functionalization. Molecules. 2015 May 21;20(5):9358–79.

18.Gross RA, Kumar A, Kalra B. Polymer Synthesis by In Vitro Enzyme Catalysis. Chem Rev. 2001 Jul 1;101(7):2097–124.

19.Cipolatti EP, Cerqueira Pinto MC, Henriques RO, da Silva Pinto JCC, de Castro AM, Freire DMG, et al. Enzymes in Green Chemistry: The State of the Art in Chemical Transformations. In: Advances in Enzyme Technology. Elsevier; 2019. p. 137–51.

20.Mendoza-Muñoz N, Leyva-Gómez G, Piñón-Segundo E, Zambrano-Zaragoza ML, Quintanar-Guerrero D, Del Prado Audelo ML, et al. Trends in biopolymer science applied to cosmetics. Int J Cosmet Sci. 2023 Dec 6;45(6):699–724.

21.Sakthivel B, Dhakshinamoorthy A. Chitosan as a reusable solid base catalyst for Knoevenagel condensation reaction. J Colloid Interface Sci. 2017 Jan;485:75–80.

22.Bell EL, Finnigan W, France SP, Green AP, Hayes MA, Hepworth LJ, et al. Biocatalysis. Nature Reviews Methods Primers. 2021 Jun 24;1(1):46.

23.Oke MA, Ojo SA, Fasiku SA, Adebayo EA. Nanotechnology and enzyme immobilization: a review. Nanotechnology. 2023 Sep 17;34(38):385101.

24.Clarke CJ, Tu WC, Levers O, Bröhl A, Hallett JP. Green and Sustainable Solvents in Chemical Processes. Chem Rev. 2018 Jan 24;118(2):747–800.

25.Ragauskas AJ, Williams CK, Davison BH, Britovsek G, Cairney J, Eckert CA, et al. The Path Forward for Biofuels and Biomaterials. Science (1979). 2006 Jan 27;311(5760):484–9.

26.Bozell JJ, Petersen GR. Technology development for the production of biobased products from biorefinery carbohydrates—the US Department of Energy's "Top 10" revisited. Green Chemistry. 2010;12(4):539.

27.Kar S, Sanderson H, Roy K, Benfenati E, Leszczynski J. Green Chemistry in the Synthesis of Pharmaceuticals. Chem Rev. 2022 Feb 9;122(3):3637–710.

28.Allen TM, Cullis PR. Liposomal drug delivery systems: From concept to clinical applications. Adv Drug Deliv Rev. 2013 Jan;65(1):36–48.

29.Place ES, George JH, Williams CK, Stevens MM. Synthetic polymer scaffolds for tissue engineering. ChemSoc Rev. 2009;38(4):1139.

30.Kargozar S, Ramakrishna S, Mozafari M. Chemistry of biomaterials: future prospects. CurrOpin Biomed Eng. 2019 Jun;10:181–90.

31.Ranjbarvan P, Mahmoudifard M, Kehtari M, Babaie A, Hamedi S, Mirzaei S, et al. Natural Compounds for Skin Tissue Engineering by Electrospinning of Nylon-Beta Vulgaris. ASAIO Journal. 2018 Mar;64(2):261–9.

32.Gallezot P. Conversion of biomass to selected chemical products. ChemSoc Rev. 2012;41(4):1538–58.

33.Clomburg JM, Crumbley AM, Gonzalez R. Industrial biomanufacturing: The future of chemical production. Science (1979). 2017 Jan 6;355(6320).

34.Avramescu AM. The Importance and Necessity of New Bio-Based Materials in Industrial Design. MaterialePlastice. 2023 Apr 5;60(1):121–7.

35.Verma N, Jujjavarapu SE, Mahapatra C. Green sustainable biocomposites: Substitute to plastics with innovative fungal mycelium based biomaterial. J Environ Chem Eng. 2023 Oct;11(5):110396.

36.Bhandi S. Biocompatibility of Restorative Materials- A Review. TEXILA INTERNATIONAL JOURNAL OF PUBLIC HEALTH. 2023 Jun 30;11(2):139–43.

37. Paliwal R, Paliwal SR, Kenwat R, Kurmi B Das, Sahu MK. Solid lipid nanoparticles: a review on recent perspectives and patents. Expert OpinTher Pat. 2020 Mar 3;30(3):179–94.

38.Langer R, Peppas NA. Advances in biomaterials, drug delivery, and bionanotechnology. AIChE Journal. 2003 Dec 16;49(12):2990–3006.

39. Murphy S V, Atala A. 3D bioprinting of tissues and organs. Nat Biotechnol. 2014 Aug 5;32(8):773–85.

40.Nerem RM. Regenerative medicine: the emergence of an industry. J R Soc Interface. 2010 Dec 6;7(suppl_6).

41.Ngo TD. Biomaterials Applied to Medical Devices and Pharmacy. In: Synthesis of Nanomaterials. BENTHAM SCIENCE PUBLISHERS; 2023. p. 1–13.

42.Fenton OS, Olafson KN, Pillai PS, Mitchell MJ, Langer R. Advances in Biomaterials for Drug Delivery. Advanced Materials. 2018 Jul 7;30(29).

CHAPTER THREE

# NUCLEIC ACID BIOMATERIALS IN CANCER DRUG DELIVERY

**Mani Sharma[a], Mohini Rawat[b]**

[a] CSIR-Indian Institute of Chemical Technology, Tarnaka, Hyderabad, Secunderabad-500007, Telangana , India

## Introduction

Gene therapy can be defined as a rational therapeutic approach to treat diseases by delivering genes packed in carriers or delivery vectors for site-specific disease intervention. In other words, if a patient is suffering from a known genetic defect, then the delivery of a correct version of the malfunctioning gene (through the use of specially designed carriers) to the diseased site or organ would be expected to correct the genetic defect and hence cure the disease. The goal of gene therapy is to cure the disease at its root- the abnormal or malfunctioning gene. This is in stark contrast to modern-day medical treatments which hardly cure diseases (with a few exceptions) rather modifying the symptoms. In short, gene therapy as a concept is fundamentally sound and attractive.

The idea of using genes for the therapeutic purpose was initially conceived in the late 1960s and early 1970swhen rapid advances were being made in the fields of molecular biology and DNA recombinant technology. Unfortunately, this radical concept was mired up in controversies on the moral, ethical & public-policy issues associated with it and uncertainty on the future promise of gene therapy prevailed for quite a long time. It was not until 1990that the first approved human gene therapy clinical trial was carried out on a four-year-old girl suffering from adenosine deaminase deficiency (ADA, a genetic disease causing a severe immunodeficiency) at the NIH, Maryland, U.S.A. with partial success. Ever since this landmark achievement was reported, a large number of gene therapy clinical trials involving human patients have been completed and an increasing number of gene therapy-based clinical investigations are under progress in different parts of the world.

Gene therapy can be relegated into (i) germ line and (ii) somatic line gene therapy types. In the former, genomes of germ cells (sperms or eggs) are integrated by exogenous functional genes, which can be carried onto the patient's progenies. In the latter, therapeutic genes are introduced into somatic cells and the effects will only be constrained to the individual patient.

Direct modulation of the disease-causing gene, which can be applied to monogenic hereditary diseases; Indirect treatment through gene modulation, which can be applied to multifactorial diseases; and Immunotherapy by gene modulation (DNA vaccines), which leads to the synthesis of the pertinent antigen or an adjuvant are the three major categories of gene therapy according to mode of action.

## Strategies for gene therapy

Gene therapy approaches can be classified into three major categories. The first approach, called *ex vivo* gene therapy, involves, removal of target cells from the patient, transfecting the removed cells outside the body (hence the name *ex vivo*) with the normal gene, and finally, transplanting the ex vivo transfected cells to the patient in a way that allows the new function to be expressed and to ameliorate the disease. The second approach, called *in situ*, introduces the gene of interest directly into the site of disease in the patient (e.g. into a cancer mass). The third approach, called *in vivo*, involves the direct injection of the gene (with a suitable carrier) into the bloodstream which will carry the therapeutic gene in a safe way to target.

In recent years, RNA interference (RNAi) has gained a lot of interest as a tool for functional genomics and probably equally important as a promising therapeutic approach for the treatment of various diseases (Bumcrot et al.; Castanotto and Rossi ; de Fougerolles et al.). RNA interference (RNAi) was first discovered in plants, but it was not widely noted in animals until Fire and Mello demonstrated that double-stranded RNA (dsRNA) can cause greater suppression of gene expression than single-stranded RNA (ssRNA) in Caenorhabditis elegans.

RNA interference (RNAi), an evolutionarily conserved ubiquitous gene silencing mechanism, has potential for clinical development of nucleic acid therapeutics. The delivery vector is crucial for clinical success of therapeutic RNAi. To fully exploit the therapeutic potential of RNAi in cancer therapy, various small interfering RNA (siRNA) delivery strategies have been developed, including stable nucleic acid-lipid particles(SNALP) formulations that encapsulate siRNA designed to silence polo-like kinase 1(PLK1) , siRNA lipoplexes made up of cationic lipid and siRNA

However, despite these bright prospects, a major impediment to the development of siRNA-based strategies for treatment and prevention of diseases is the relatively inefficient means to effectively deliver these macromolecules into the desired target cells or tissues. In recent years ,RNAi (RNA interference) has become more and more important in gene silencing and drug development because of its high specificity, significant effect, minor side effects and ease of synthesis. Naturally, RNAi is an important defense mechanism by which eukaryote cell can degrade exogenous genes. When dsRNA (Double Stranded RNA) enters the cell, it is first cleaved into short double stranded fragments of~20 nucleotide siRNA by enzyme dicer .Then each double stranded siRNA is split into the passenger strand and the guide strand of siRNA pairs with a complementary sequence in a messenger RNA molecule and induces cleavage by Argonaut, which causes gene silencing.

Most siRNAs were administered by local delivery, typically via intravitreal or intranasal routes. Though,local delivery systems may not be appropriate for all diseases. Under some circumstances, systemic drug administration by intravenous (i.v.) injection is needed, and delivery systems will be necessary to administer the siRNA pay load. For example, PRO-040201 (ApoB-SNALP) administrated by i.v. injection was developed by Tekmira with a stable nucleic acid lipid particle (SNALP) system. It was developed for the treatment of hypercholesterolemia by targeting ApoB, which is produced by hepatocytes.. The results revealed that ApoB siRNA was delivered into hepatocytes efficiently and resulted in a significant reduction of LDL and triglycerides in blood. However, Tekmira terminated the clinical trial in January 2010 because one of the two subjects treated with the highest dose experienced flu-like symptoms consistent with stimulation of the immune system caused by the ApoB siRNA payload.Calando Pharmaceuticals (Pasadena, California, USA) has developed an siRNA therapeutic (CALAA-01), which is a cyclodextrin-based polymeric nanoparticle containing the M2 subunit of ribo nucleotide reductase (RRM2) targeted

siRNA.CALAA-01 was modified with the human transferrin (TF) protein and polyethylene glycol (PEG) to improve its stability. Unfortunately, its phase I clinical trial has been terminated in 2013 according to U.S. Food and Drug Administration (FDA). In addition to the above mentioned siRNA drugs, many more are in the developmental pipeline.

In 2001, Tuschl et al. first transferred dsRNA into mammalian cells and solved the interferon effect of dsRNA transfection in these cells, which broadened the therapeutic use of RNAi. In 2010, Davis et al. reported the first targeted siRNA delivery nanoparticle in humans via systemic injection, which provided a reference and a solid foundation for siRNA clinical use.

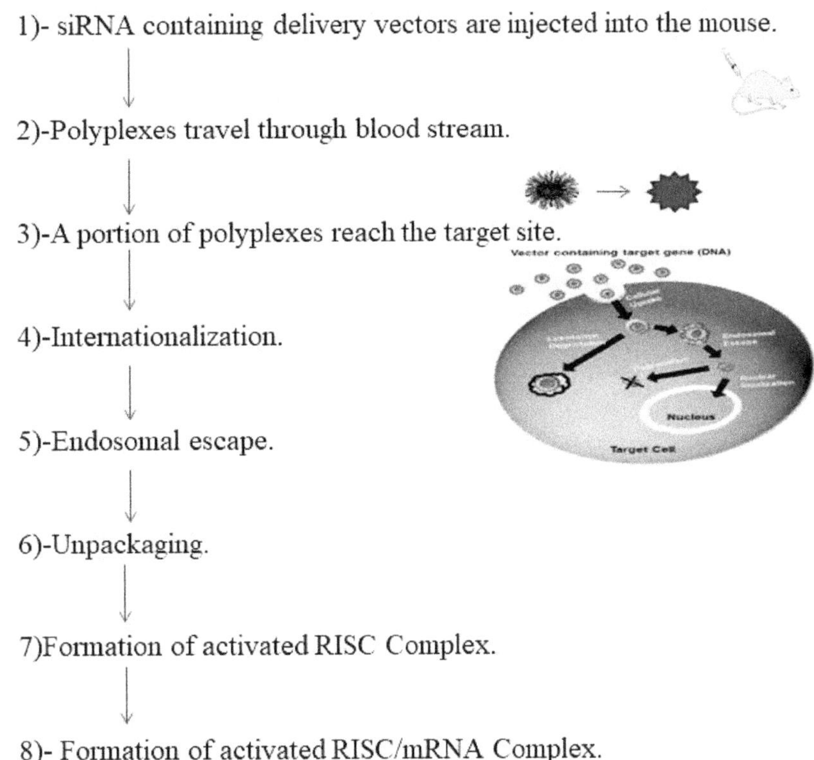


Figure : Schematic Steps involved in direct delivery of siRNA into the tumor cell.

Small interfering RNA(siRNA) has been emerging as one of the most prominent agents for treatment of various diseases, due to its specific silencing of targeted gene. However due to its large molecular weight, negative charge, RNAase degradation and rapid elimination from systemic circulation, naked siRNA is almost impossible to enter the target cells and silence the specific genes.Thus, Cationic lipids (e.g.,1,2 dioleyol-3-trimethylammonium-propane (DOTAP)) or cationic polymers (e.g; polyetherimide (PEI), Poly-L-Lysine (PLL), Polyamidoamine (PAA) and chitosan have been commonly used for siRNA delivery. Mechanism involved is Gene Silencing "Interruption or suppression of the expression of a gene at transcriptional or translational level" gene silencing is a general term used to describe the regulation of expression of genes. Gene Silencing can occur during either transcription or translation, gene silencing is offer considered as gene knockout. Mechanisms include DNA methylation, histone modification and RNAi.The expression of gene is reduced if it is silenced and & when, genes are knocked they are completely erased from the organisms genome, and, thus, have no expression.For efficient siRNA delivery to the cancer cells by cationic liposomes, the cationic liposome/siRNA complex (cationic lipoplex) must be stabilized in the blood by avoiding its agglutination with blood components, and the pharmacokinetics of lipoplex after intravenous injection must be controlled because electrostatic interactions between positively charged lipoplexes and negatively charged erythrocytes cause agglutination, and the agglutinates contribute to high entrapment of lipoplex in the highly extended lung capillaries.

Methods used to silence genes reduce the expression of a gene by at least 70% but do not completely eliminate it. Nanoparticulate systems for carrying nucleic acids may be panoptically classified as lipid- or polymer-based nanoparticles, and each is called a 'lipoplex' or 'polyplex' after it interacts with nucleic acids. The cellular delivery of these complexes is believed to occur via endocytosis followed by endosomal. As a delivery system of nucleic acid, cationic liposomes shave advantages. First, the cationic liposomes are biodegradable after administration in vivo. Lipid components of the liposomes are breakdown by the presence of endogenous enzymes.The unparalleled biocompatibility of liposomes among various nanocarriers resulted in the use of cationic liposomes for delivery of various siRNAs for in vivo studies. The lipid composition-dependent modulation of surface charge density can control the interaction forces with negatively charged nucleic acids. The inclusion of pegylated lipids or functional lipids can make possible the diverse surface modification of liposomes. Moreover, the inclusion of lipophilic chemical drugs in the lipid bilayers of cationic liposomes can provide co-delivery of anticancer drug and therapeutic nucleic acids escape into the cytoplasm.

Over chemotherapeutic anticancer drugs, siRNA has much more advantage:-The first is its high degree of safety, siRNA acts on the post-translational stage of gene expression, so it does not interact with DNA and thereby avoids the mutation and teratogenicity risks of gene therapy. High efficacy of siRNA is its second advantage. In a single cancer cell, siRNA can cause dramatic suppression of gene expression with just several copies. After injection into the blood, siRNA is easily enzymatically degraded by endogenous nucleases, aggregated with serum proteins.

**Nucleic acid drug delivery to combat cancer**

Cancer is a global epidemic and a leading cause of death worldwide, accounting for 7.6 million deaths or around 13% of all deaths. The ratio of mortality and morbidity associated with cancer are increasing day by day and it is an urgent problem faced by developing countries with a large population (e.g. India). Unfortunately, even after so many years of research, the current chemotherapy is not able to deliver the drug to tumors cells or normal organs and tissues, resulting in dose-limiting side-effects and toxicity that underpins the failure of the therapy. Many cancers are caused by over expression of cellular receptors or protein products. RNAi may be a way to regulate the expression of these genes to normal levels and stop the proliferation of tumors. Diseases such as ovarian cancer, prostate cancer, and thyroid cancer have had progress made in developing a cure and hopefully can become a widespread treatment for many cancers. RNAi's ability to fine tune the expression of cancer causing protein products shows promise to become a widespread method of treatment that may be less burdensome than radiation or chemotherapy. The main limitation of chemotherapy is the poor accessibility of anti-neoplastic agents to the tumor and the nonselective nature of these agents. Thus, an effective and safe tumor-targeting delivery system for chemotherapy agents is urgently needed. Currently, a wide range of RNAi based drugs has been developed for various diseases. FDA has approved one of the RNAi based drug Patisiran against transthyretin (TTR) gene for treating hereditary transthyretin-mediated amyloidosis and many RNAi based drugs are in clinical trials. RNAi holds great therapeutic potential for clinical application.

**siRNA on lung cancer**

Lung cancer is the leading cause of cancer-related death in both men and women worldwide with a staggering 28% of total cancer death in United States alone (Jemal et al.) The survival rate of this type of cancer is much less than the other prevalent cancers such as breast and prostate cancers (15%). Although chemotherapy is being the first line of treatment for over 30 years, yet it achieved only limited success with serious dose-limiting side effects (Trussardi et al.; Berger et al.) Science has always burst out from an impossible way to a new approach of accomplishing totally different and novel system in favor of mankind, similarly a potential of microRNAs(miRNAs) and siRNA is enormous in cancer therapeutics, but it is equally tedious to deliver it effectively at the site of solid tumors. Hence an approach is engineered to confirm the adequate reach of siRNA in carcinoma cells for lung cancer. Delivery of siRNA reduce gene expression along with MAPK signaling, increased apoptosis and inhibits the growth of tumor. Regression studies expounds the activity of RNA interference mechanism thus illustrating the effect of siRNA based cancer therapy using cationic lipid as a carrier system.Finally demonstrating that RNA combination therapy is possible in an endemic model, elevating the use of small RNA therapies in patients with lung cancer.(Wen Xue et al.).With immense anticancer effect, siRNA beholds such physio-chemical properties which makes it unstable when delivered naked in bloodstream.Hence, a diligent delivery system is required to fully utilize the potential of this therapeutic solution.This review presents a comprehensive amend for the challenges of the siRNA delivery and ongoing approach to establish unblemished nanoparticle delivery system to attain a promising therapeutic modality.(Katyayani Tatiparti et al.). Large-scale library screening of current chemotherapy siRNA pairs conjugate with positive moiety would help to establish the chemotherapy siRNA-cationic lipid pair selection principle, which could pave the way for delivery of siRNA for cancer treatment in clinic. Following the inherent principle of chemotherapy of lipoplexes, more effective co-delivery vectors can also be designed in the future.(Mingfang Wang et al.).

**siRNA on liver**

Hepatocellular carcinoma (HCC) is still one of the major causes of cancer-related death. Here we encapsulated KNTC2 siRNAs into a lipid nanoparticle (LNP) and investigated their knockdown activity, target engagement marker, antitumoractivity.(Yukimasa Makita et al.) Resistance of hepatocellular carcinoma (HCC) to systemic chemotherapy is partially due to presence of drug-resistant cancer stem cells. Most (85% to 90%) primary liver cancers occurring worldwide are hepatocellular carcinomas (HCC), and treatment options for unresectable HCC are very limited and generally ineffective(Tan Yanget al.) RNA interference is a highly specific as well as efficient technology for gene therapy application in molecular oncology. The present study was planned to develop an efficient and stable tumor selective delivery mechanism for siRNA gene therapy for the purpose of both diagnosis as well as therapy. RNA interference therapy has ability to silence the expression of any disease-related gene in a selective and sequence-dependent manner. However, there is a major hurdle that prevents its use as the goldstandard therapy for cancer. The major barrier is the specific delivery ofsiRNAs to the desired site. To overcome the major problem of siRNA delivery, multiple researchers have worked on variable approaches of efficient in-vivo delivery of siRNA. These approaches included both synthetic as well as natural delivery systems. Synthetic delivery systems included physical methods, conjugation methods, etc. and natural carriers involved viruses and bacteria.We have utilized albumin as a delivery molecule for siRNA in this study. The serum albumin is an endogenous nano-particle and is known for its binding properties to various endogenous metabolites, drugs and metal ions. The biological application of nanoparticles is a rapidly developing area of nanotechnology that raises new possibilities in the diagnosis as well as treatment of human cancers.(Na Liu)

RNA interference (RNAi) therapy, harnessed to produce a new class of drugs for treatment, has drawn attention and seen steady progress over the years. Molecular therapy using biological macromolecules small interfering RNA (siRNA) for gene silencing has received significant attention to target cancer-related genes. Basically, siRNA molecules bind to messenger RNAs (mRNA) by complementary base pairing, to induce degradation of the mRNA and/or block protein synthesis. Numerous genes and gene related proteins have been reported till date to target in siRNA based cancer therapy. Furthermore, a combination of siRNA with traditional anticancer drugs produces synergistic anticancer effect, or overcomes drug resistance, enhances targeting abilities and minimizes side-effects. Current review highlights various functional properties of genes that can be selectively knocked down by siRNAs. In addition, we have also discussed the interaction of siRNA-mediated gene-silencing with chemotherapeutic agents in nanoformulation which constitutes a valuable and safe approach for cancer treatment.(Shweta Jain et al.)

**siRNA on breast cancer**

Breast cancer is the most commonly diagnosed malignancy in American women with an estimated 39,510 fatalities per year, accounting for 14% of all cancer deaths. Most of these fatalities can be attributed to metastatic spread of aggressive forms of breast cancer. Frequent sites of distant breast cancer relapse include the liver, pleural membranes, lungs, lymph nodes and brain with a median survival time of 2.2 to 0.5 years, depending on the subtype significant progress has been made in the development of modern diagnostic tools and surgical treatments, only marginal improvements have been achieved with relapsed metastatic breast cancer. Small interfering RNAs (siRNAs) mediate gene silencing of a target protein by disrupting messenger RNAs in an efficient and sequence-specific manner. One application of this technology is the knockdown of genes responsible for tumorigenesis, including those driving oncogenesis, survival, proliferation and death of cells, angiogenesis, invasion and metastasis, and resistance to treatment.(Jing Zhang et al.)

Since, siRNA offers advantages over traditional pharmaceutical drugs, breast cancer therapy will continue to benefit from the discovery of novel molecular targets. However, siRNA delivery remains a challenge, partly due to the instability of siRNA and its inability to cross cellular membranes. To realize the possible delivery siRNA based therapies, further research must focus on (1)specific target genes involved in tumorigenesis and progression of breast cancer plus rules governing siRNA effectiveness and selectivity;(2)various non-viral nanocarriers have been reported to provide promising application in siRNA delivery in vitro and in vivo, such as liposomes, nanoparticles and inorganic materials. Although significant advancement has been made in the field of siRNA delivery, there is still a need to explore alternative effective strategies. The delivery system should be nontoxic, non-immunogenic, and sufficient for siRNA protection, to reach the target cell and facilitate cell uptake, to release siRNA into the cytoplasm to achieve gene silencing; (3)after injection of siRNA, pharmacokinetic profile and siRNA distribution in organs and tumors are not well investigated in many studies.

Overexpression of RhoA in cancer indicates a poor prognosis, because of increased tumor cell proliferation and invasion and tumor angiogenesis. We showed previously that anti-RhoA small interfering RNA (siRNA)inhibited aggressive breast cancer more effectively than conventional blockers of Rho-mediated signaling pathways. This study reports the efficacy and lack of toxicity of intravenously administered encapsulated anti-RhoA siRNA in chitosan-coated polyisohexylcyanoacrylate (PIHCA) nanoparticles in xenografted aggressive breast cancers (MDA-MB-231). The siRNA was administered every 3 days at a dose of 150 or 1500g/kg body weight in nude mice. This treatment inhibited the growth of tumors by 90% in the 150g group and by even more in the 1500g group. Necrotic areas were observed in tumors from animals treated with anti-RhoA siRNA at 1500 g/kg, resulting from angiogenesis inhibition. In addition, this therapy was found to be devoid of toxic effects, as evidenced by similarities between control and treated animals for the following parameters: body weight gain; biochemical markers of hepatic, renal, and pancreatic function; and macroscopic appearance of organs after 30 days of treatment. Because of its efficacy and the absence of toxicity, it is suggested that this strategy of anti-RhoA siRNA holds significant promise for the treatment of aggressive cancers(J.Y. Pille).

RNAi treatments have additionally visually perceived prosperity in treating spinal mascular atrophy and obviating vision deterioration due to blood vessel magnification. One example is Spinraza, which was approved in tardy 2016 to treat spinal sinewy atrophy by rectifying an mRNA processing error. Macugen treats ocular perceiver degeneration by inhibiting the engenderment of vascular endothelial magnification factor which causes magnification and spread of blood vessels.

Heart disease-currently exists the leading cause of death in the United States in addition to currently exists often tied to high cholesterol. Traditionally, statins were the default treatments for those that object over there suffer from high cholesterol. Statins work to lower blood cholesterol levels by inhibiting the proteins that object over there produce cholesterol. However, their side-effects currently are wide-ranging in addition to may include an increased risk of developing diabetes. For this object over here reason, developing new treatments with fewer serious side effects currently exists an important issue just as the prevalence of diabetes continually increases.

Recently, RNAi treatments have received FDA approval of Inclisiran drug which aims to lower cholesterol levels and is currently undergoing clinical trials.

Blood diseasesrefer to the disorders in the hematopoietic system or plasma components. The development of blood disorders currently exists always thought to exists related with inheritance, the environment, drugs, in addition to biological factors at whatever place the changes in the chromosome in addition to/or genes play a critical role in some specific homeopathies. Therapeutic approaches for blood diseases currently am able to exist divided into different categories, including chemotherapy, radiotherapy, RNAi-based gene therapy, in addition to hematopoietic stem cell transplantation. RNAi-based gene therapy is currently becoming a therapeutic alternative which offers the possibility of a permanent cure for some blood diseases.

Hemophilia-Hemophilia A and B are bleeding disorders resulting from deficiencies of factor VIII and IX, respectively. Gene therapy, utilizing both viral and non-viral delivery vectors *in vivo* and *ex vivo*, has been endeavored for the treatment of both hemophilia A and B.

Given its recent clinical prosperity, adeno-associated vector (AAV)-mediated hepatic gene transfer could be primarily utilized for the treatment of hemophilia B. However, a number of quandaries, such as current immunosuppressive regimen and pre-subsisting neutralizing antibodies, limit the broad applicability of this approach. For hemophilia A, while AAV-mediated gene therapy has potential, a number of circumscriptions reduce its desirabilities, such as packaging capacity and inefficient expression while a number of transgene modifications have incremented the expression levels. These expression constraints lead to further concerns about immune replications to both the capsid and if expression levels are not ample the transgene.

As such, ex vivo gene transfer may be more efficacious for hemophilia A due to its facility to enhance expression through cellular division. While a number of promising gene therapies for hemophilia have been elucidated, there are pellucidly numerous quandaries that still need to be addressed to develop approved gene therapies, especially RNAi, for both hemophilia A and B in humans. RNAi-predicated gene therapy for hemophilia is still in its early stages of development.

β-Thalassemia-β-Thalassemia is an ecumenical-distributed inherited hemoglobin disorder resulting in astringent, chronic anemia.Here, a single β-globin gene is affected and results in the absence or reduced β-globin chain synthesis. The defects of β-globin synthesis lead to an excess of peerless α-globin, which release free iron, non-heme iron, or hemichrome. These iron species promote a rigorous red cell membrane oxidative stress and lead to aberrant β-thalassemic red cell features. The anomalous red cells are determinately abstracted by the macrophage system and result in anemia.

Blood transfusion is a primary way to treat the most rigorous forms of β-thalassemia. Felicitous goals and optimal safety of transfused blood are compulsory for routine administration of red blood cells to patients. The quandary is that the high frequency of blood transfusion can lead to iron overload. In its less rigorous form, chronic transfusions are not required, but iron overload may still develop due to the chronic suppression of the synthesis of the iron regulatory hormone hepcidin by ineffective erythropoiesis.Cardiac complications can be overloaded by untreated iron as it has no fate.

Ergo, handling iron overload is a key factor for the prosperous treatment of this disease. TMPRSS6, a serine protease expressed predominantly in the liver, can inhibit an iron-responsive bone morphogenetic protein-mother against the decapentaplegic (BMP-SMAD) signaling pathway, resulting in the down regulation of hepcidin transcription. Researchers found that therapeutics with the lipid nanoparticle (LNP)-formulated RNAi targeting of TMPRSS6, in conjunction with oral deferiprone therapy, is superior to monotherapy.

**Disease targets for gene therapy**

Majority of human diseases are potential targets of gene therapy as the root cause of almost all the diseases are either single gene or multiple gene defects. Simple, monogenic disorders like ADA deficiency, cystic fibrosis, hemophilia, familial hypercholesterolemia, Gaucher's disease, alpha-1-antitrypsin deficiency etc. are the most suitable and attractive candidates for treatment by gene therapy. A large number of diseases like diabetes, coronary vascular disease, AIDS, arteriosclerosis and many forms of cancer including breast, colon, ovarian, prostate, renal, leukemia, myeloma etc. are known to be caused by multiple gene or polygenic defects (coupled with other environmental factors). These diseases can also be subjected to gene therapy treatments and cured efficiently. With the recent completion of working draft of the human genome and the tentative identification of nearly 40,000-50,000 genes, identifying disease targets for gene therapy are likely to dominate the field of medicine in the coming future. RNA interference (RNAi) can be utilized for gene therapy.

Nucleic acids have garnered significant attention as promising biomaterials for drug delivery due to their unique properties and versatile functionalities. With the advent of molecular biology and advancements in synthetic chemistry, researchers have been able to engineer nucleic acids with precise control over their structure and function, paving the way for innovative applications in medicine. This introduction delves into the rationale behind utilizing nucleic acids as biomaterials in drug delivery systems, highlighting their molecular properties, modes of action, and potential therapeutic implications.Nucleic acid biomaterials have emerged as a promising class of materials for drug delivery, leveraging their unique properties to enhance therapeutic efficacy and minimize side effects. The integration of nucleic acids, such as DNA and RNA, into biomaterials has opened up new avenues for targeted and controlled delivery of therapeutic agents. This introduction provides a comprehensive overview of the role of nucleic acid biomaterials in drug delivery, highlighting their applications, advantages, and challenges.

The development of biomaterials for drug delivery has been driven by the need to overcome the limitations of conventional drug delivery methods. Traditional methods often result in inadequate therapeutic levels, poor bioavailability, and significant side effects due to the lack of control over the release of the therapeutic agent. Nucleic acid biomaterials offer a solution to these challenges by providing a platform for targeted and controlled delivery of therapeutic agents.Nucleic acid biomaterials are designed to incorporate nucleic acids into a matrix that can be tailored to specific therapeutic applications. These biomaterials can be engineered to possess unique properties such as biocompatibility, biodegradability, and specific targeting capabilities. The integration of nucleic acids into biomaterials enhances their therapeutic potential by providing a means to deliver therapeutic agents directly to the site of action, reducing systemic toxicity, and improving efficacy.Nucleic acid biomaterials have been explored for various therapeutic applications, including gene therapy, vaccine development, and targeted drug delivery. These biomaterials have been used to deliver therapeutic agents such as nucleic acids, peptides, and proteins, which can be designed to target specific diseases or conditions.The use of nucleic acid biomaterials in drug delivery offers several advantages, including targeted delivery, controlled release, improved bioavailability, and biocompatibility. Targeted delivery can reduce systemic toxicity and improve efficacy, while controlled release ensures sustained and localized delivery.

Nucleic acid biomaterials can enhance the bioavailability of therapeutic agents, improving their efficacy and reducing side effects, and are biocompatible, reducing the risk of adverse reactions and improving patient safety.Despite the promising applications of nucleic acid biomaterials in drug delivery, several challenges need to be addressed. These include stability and degradation, as nucleic acid biomaterials are susceptible to degradation, which can affect their therapeutic efficacy; targeting and localization, ensuring targeted delivery and localization of therapeutic agents remains a significant challenge; and scalability and manufacturing, as large-scale manufacturing and scalability of nucleic acid biomaterials are essential for widespread adoption.

**Molecular Properties of Nucleic Acids**

Nucleic acids, namely deoxyribonucleic acid (DNA) and ribonucleic acid (RNA), serve as the fundamental building blocks of life, encoding genetic information and orchestrating cellular processes. Their unique chemical structure, consisting of nucleotide monomers linked by phosphodiester bonds, imparts remarkable stability and specificity to these biomolecules. Furthermore, the sequence-specific base pairing between adenine-thymine (A-T) and guanine-cytosine (G-C) enables the formation of double-stranded helical structures with predictable secondary and tertiary conformations. Exploiting these molecular properties, researchers have harnessed nucleic acids for the design and development of sophisticated drug delivery platforms with precise targeting and controlled release capabilities.

**Modes of Action in Drug Delivery**

Nucleic acids exert their therapeutic effects in drug delivery through various mechanisms, including gene silencing, gene editing, and immunomodulation. Small interfering RNA (siRNA) and microRNA (miRNA) molecules can selectively suppress the expression of target genes by harnessing the endogenous RNA interference (RNAi) pathway. By leveraging sequence complementarity, these nucleic acid-based therapeutics can specifically bind to messenger RNA (mRNA) molecules, leading to their degradation or translational inhibition. Additionally, clustered regularly interspaced short palindromic repeats (CRISPR) technology enables precise gene editing by directing the Cas9 nuclease to specific genomic loci, offering unprecedented opportunities for treating genetic disorders and manipulating cellular functions. Moreover, nucleic acids can modulate immune responses through the activation or suppression of innate immune pathways, thereby enhancing the efficacy and safety of drug delivery systems.

**Therapeutic Implications in Medicine**

The application of nucleic acids in drug delivery holds immense promise for addressing unmet medical needs across a wide range of diseases, including cancer, infectious diseases, and genetic disorders. In oncology, targeted delivery of siRNA or miRNA molecules can selectively silence oncogenes or inhibit key signaling pathways involved in tumor progression, offering a personalized approach to cancer therapy with minimal off-target effects. Furthermore, the advent of mRNA-based vaccines has revolutionized the field of vaccinology, enabling rapid development and scalable production of vaccines against emerging infectious diseases, such as COVID-19. Additionally, gene editing technologies, such as CRISPR-Cas9, hold great potential for correcting disease-causing mutations and restoring normal cellular function in monogenic disorders, such as cystic fibrosis and sickle cell anemia.

**RNA interference (RNAi)**

Before understanding how RNAi works, it is first necessary to understand what DNA actually works. DNA is made of small molecules called nucleotides that contain one out of four nitrogen compounds to write a code for protein production. Although DNA holds all of the information necessary to create proteins, it needs to be rewritten as mRNA before it can be translated to a protein that can be useful to the cell. If the protein product of a gene is not made, the gene is not expressed. In the simplest model of gene expression, DNA in cells is transcribed as mRNA which is translated by ribosomes to build proteins. RNAi is a phenomenon that was discovered recently. Using RNAi, short RNA strands that do not encode for proteins can either destroy mRNA or prevent it from being transcribed in the first place. In both cases, the end result is the same; the gene is deactivated and no protein is created.

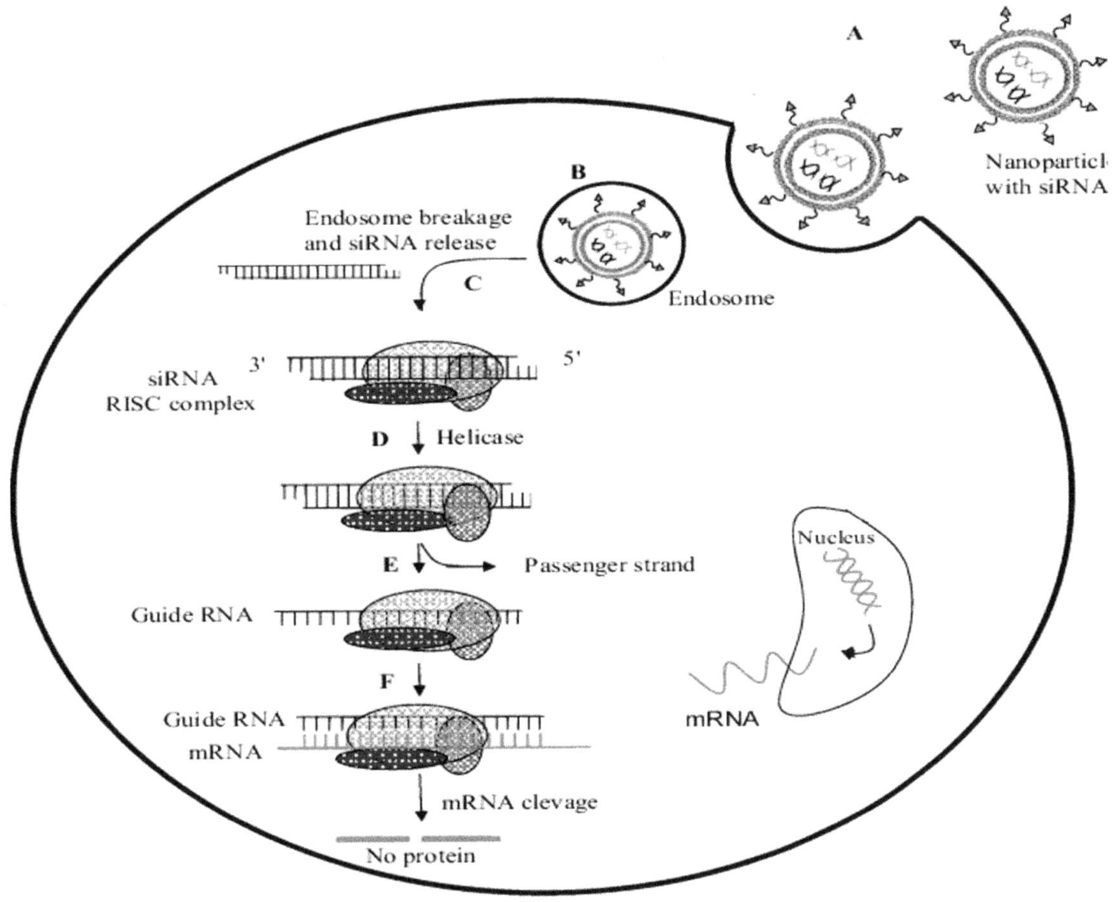


Figure : RNA interference (RNAi) mechanism

There are three strategies for RNAi: 1)Short hairpin RNA (shRNA), 2) endogenous microRNA (miRNA) and 3) small interfering RNA(siRNA) .siRNA is more suitable for drug use because it does not require genome integration and can be easily synthesized. Since rational design of siRNA can specifically inhibit endogenous and heterogenous gene expression, it can modulate any disease related gene expressionThe major advantage of RNAi in cancer therapy is, RNAi can target particular genes of particular pathways and multiple genes of multiple cellular pathways which are involved in diseases. Continuous taking drugs during chemotherapy or overdosing of drugs may cause drug resistance so these approaches also reduce the chance of drug resistance. In recent years, RNA interference (RNAi) has gained a lot of interest as a tool for functional genomics and probably equally important as a promising therapeutic approach for the treatment of various diseases (Bumcrot et al.; Castanotto and Rossi ; de Fougerolles et al.). RNA interference (RNAi) was first discovered in plants, but it was not widely noted in animals until Fire and Mello demonstrated that double-stranded RNA (dsRNA) can cause greater suppression of gene expression than single-stranded RNA (ssRNA) in Caenorhabditis elegans .RNA interference (RNAi), an evolutionarily conserved ubiquitous gene silencing mechanism, has potential for clinical development of nucleic acid therapeutics. The delivery vector is crucial for clinical success of therapeutic RNAi. To fully exploit the therapeutic potential of RNAi in cancer therapy, various small interfering RNA (siRNA) delivery strategies have been developed, including stable nucleic acid-lipid particles(SNALP) formulations that encapsulate siRNA designed to silence polo-like kinase 1(PLK1) , siRNA lipoplexes made up of cationic lipid and siRNA .However, despite these bright prospects, a major impediment to the development of siRNA-based strategies for treatment and prevention of diseases is the relatively inefficient means to effectively deliver these macromolecules into the desired target cells or tissues. In recent years ,RNAi (RNA interference) has become more and more important in gene silencing and drug development because of its high specificity, significant effect, minor side effects and ease of synthesis. Naturally, RNAi is an important defense mechanism by which eukaryote cell can degrade exogenous genes.

Double-stranded RNA (dsRNA) broke into single strand small molecule with a length of 20-25 nucleotide termed as siRNA by an RNaseIII-like enzyme termed Dicer, an endoribonuclease enzyme. When the siRNA is entered into the cell, the endogenous RNAi machinery of the cell initiates gene silencing. Duplex siRNA is loaded into a protein complex called the RNA-induced silencing complex (RISC), and this intermediate proceeds for recognition of complementary mRNAs. After the target sequence is recognized, the mRNA is cleaved by Argonaute-2 of the RISC or inhibition of the translation process, resulting in reduced protein expression from the silenced gene .

| S.No | Name | Indication | Delivery Route | Target | Delivery System | Development Phase |
|---|---|---|---|---|---|---|
| 1. | siRNA-EphA2-DOPC | Advanced solid tumors | Intravenous (I.V) | EphA2 | Lipid-basednanoparticles | Preclinical |
| 2. | APN401 | Metastatic tumors | Intravenous (I.V) injection | E3 ubiquitin ligase Cbl-b | Exvivo transfection | Preclinical |
| 3. | iPsiRNA | Metastatic melanoma, absence of CNS Metastases | Intradermal injection | LMP2, LMP7, MECL1 | Ex vivo transfection | Phase I, completed |
| 4. | Atu027 | Advanced solid tumors | I.V infusion | PKN3 | Lipid-basednanoparticles | Phase-I, completed |
| 5. | siG12D LODER | Pancreatic ductal adenocarcinoma;Pancreatic cancer | Intratumoralimplantation | KRASG1D | LODER polymer | Phase-I, completed |
| 6. | TKM-080,301 | Primary or secondary liver cancer | Hepatic intra-arterial injection | PLK1 | Lipid-basednanoparticles | Phase-I, completed |
| 7. | ND-L02-s0201 | METAVIR F3–4 | Intravenous (I.V)injection | HSP47 | Lipid-basednanoparticles | Phase-I, recruiting |
| 8. | DCR-MYC | Solid tumors; multiple myeloma;non-Hodgkin's lymphoma | I.V infusion | MYC | Lipid-basednanoparticles | Phase-I, recruiting |

Table: Current clinical status of RNAi therapeutics for cancer treatment

|  |  |
|---|---|
| 1998 | • Fire and Mello discovered RNAi mechanism in C. elegans |
| 2001 | • Elbashir proves first in-cell RNAi-Mediated gene silencing |
| 2003 | • Song proves first in-mouse RNAi- Mediated gene silencing |
| 2004 | • First clinical trial on local delivery of siRNA-027 by Allergan and siRNA Therapeutics |
| 2005 | • Song proves first in-mouse carrier- mediated RNAi-Mediated gene silencing |
| 2006 | • Fire and Mello won the Nobel Prize in medicine for discovery of RNAi |
| 2006 | • Alnylam proves first in-primate RNAi-Mediated gene silencing |
| 2008 | • Calando pharmaceutics initiated the first clinical trial of targeted delivery of siRNA; CALAA-01 |
| 2010 | • Alnylam proves first in-human RNAi therapeutics |
| 2013 | • First demonstration of highly potent siRNA-Mediated gene knockdown by Coelho |
| 2018 | • FDA approve the first siRNA therapeutics ONPATTRO |

Table :Timeline of RNAi discovery and the progress of siRNA in clinical application:

**Nucleic acid in drug delivery**

The currently developed siRNA delivey systems for cancer therapy can be divided into four major categories:- chemical modifiction, lipid based nonovectors, polymer-mediated delivery sysatems, conjugate delivery systems, and other (exosomes, RNAi-microphages, oligonucleotide particles).

**Chemical modifications of anti-cancer siRNA**

A great potential can be achieved by chemical modifications and are necessary in cancer therapeutic though they do not provide a carrier for siRNA. siRNA delivery systems. With rational chemical modifications, siRNA can acquire advantages such as serum stability, immune escape ability, and RNAi machinery access .Chemical modifications can be introduced at the 5′ or 3′-terminus, backbone, sugar or nucleobase of siRNA. The most common modification site of siRNA is the 2′ position of the ribose ring, which has been proven to enhance siRNA stability by preventing degradation by endonucleases. The two modification strategies, i.e. 2′-O-methyl and 2′-deoxy-2′-fluoro, are quite well-understood and commercialized, and have been shown to enhance the serum stability of siRNA and increase its in vivo potential. Some other approaches also exist, such as replacement of the phosphor diester (PO4) group with phosphothioate (PS) at the 3′-end of RNA backbone, or the combination of 4′-thiolation with 2′-O-alkyl modification.

Lipid-based vectors for anti-cancer siRNA delivery

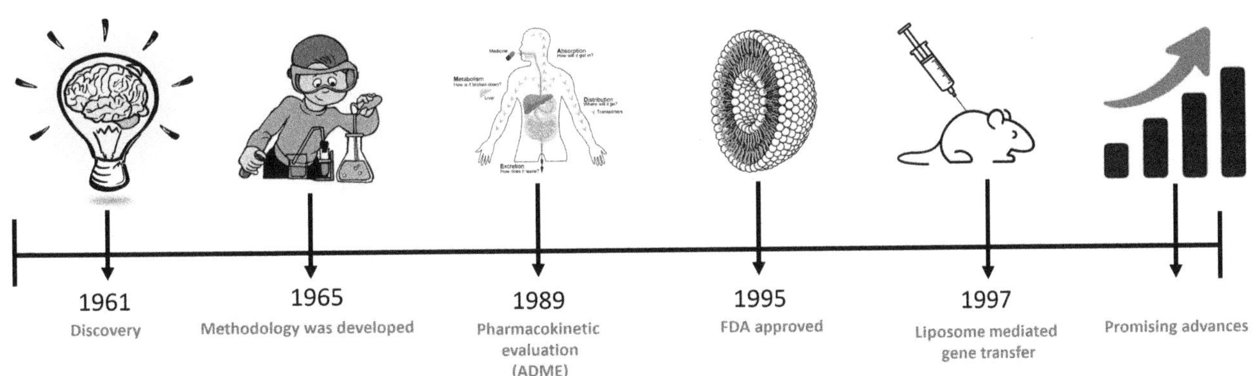


Figure : Journey of Doxil

The most famous lipid based vectors that used for clinical trials are the SNALPs (stable nucleic acid-lipid particles). SNALPs are a kind of lipid nanoparticles which encapsulate siRNA and deliver it to the target cells. SNALPs are microscopic particles approximately 120 nm in diameter.In SNALPs, the siRNA is surrounded by a lipid bilayer containing a mixture of cationic and fusogenic lipids, coated with diffusible polyethylene glycol .With enhanced permeability and retention due to prolonged circulation time in the blood, SNALPs are highly bioavailable, which leads to the accumulation of SNALPs at the sites of vascular leakage, especially at cancer growth sites. After accumulation, SNALPs are easily endocytosed by cancer cells and deliver siRNA into cells successfully.

**Polymer-mediated anti-cancer siRNA delivery**

Polymer-mediated delivery systems, commonly known as polymeric nanoparticles, are solid, biodegradable, colloidal systems which have been widely studied as drug vesicles .According to the material used, polymer-mediated delivery systems can be divided into two categories: water-soluble cationic polymers and polymer nanoparticles.For anticancer siRNA delivery, water-soluble cationic polymers mainly include cyclodextrin or polyethyleneimine (PEI), while polymer nanoparticles are usually based on polycaprolactone(PCL), poly(D,L-lactide) (PLA) and poly(D,L-lactide-co-glycolide) (PLGA).Cyclodextrin is the most promising natural polymer for siRNA delivery.It was first introduced for the delivery of plasmid DNA in 1999 and later reoptimized for siRNA delivery. Within ten years, cyclodextrin polymer (CDP)-based nanoparticles were moved into clinical trials for siRNA delivery. Cyclodextrin polymer nanoparticle was the first targeted siRNA delivery system which entered clinical trials for cancer treatment.

**Conjugate siRNA delivery systems for cancer therapy**

The most common conjugate materials are small drug molecules, aptamers, lipids, peptides, proteins and polymers .This system has a quite obvious advantage for cancer therapeutic clinical use, since the system is simple and well-defined.CPPs (cell-penetrating peptides) are another conjugate material used for siRNA transfection efficacy improvement. A well-known CPP is the TAT trans-activator protein from human immunodeficiency virus type-1 (HIV-1). TAT has been conjugated to the 3′-terminus of the antisense strand of an siRNA using a hetero bi functional cross-linker (HBFC), i.e. sulfosuccinimidyl-4-(p-maleimidophenyl) butyrate. The TAT-siRNA conjugate demonstrated a dramatic improvement in the intracellular delivery of siRNA.

**Approaches**

Viral Vectors: This method is further based on insertion of the modified functional gene into viral vectors to penetrate in the host genome. Once the encapsulated viral vectors enters the cell, the degradation of encapsulated membrane starts and this will release the viral vector that further release the modified gene into the nucleus and switch on the instructions that are necessary for the cell to synthesize the protein that was previously missed or altered. However, unfortunately, due to some adverse effects such as immunogenicity, difficulties in handling large-scale production, and limited length of the genes, this system was not successful. Moreover, potential and real risks of some adenoviruses were also observed during the clinical trials.

Non-viral Vectors: Important non-viral transfer approaches for siRNA delivery include use of: (a) naked siRNA; (b) siRNA complexed to cationic liposomes (so called lipoplexes) and (c) siRNA complexed to cationic polymers. Although naked siRNA gives virtually no transfection under normal conditions, surprisingly efficient transfer of naked siRNA is possible following local injection, notably in muscle and skin. Cationic polymers like poly-L-lysine and polyethyleneimine have been used as gene transfer agents with moderate success.

Physical method: Physical method for gene transfer includes biolistics, jet injection, hydrodynamic injections, ultrasound, and electroporation method. In this method, genes are directly inserted into cytosol of both small and large NA molecule, as well as any other non-permeable molecule with the help of electric impulse, fine needle, or high-pressure gas which may overcome the side effects linked to other gene transfer methods, such as limitation of gene length that can be solved by physical method. Moreover, this system is effective for single or multiple target cells at an intended location and reduce the risk of dispersion of transfection-+ reagents. On other hand, physical method also shows some drawbacks such as: it is difficult for the genes to be transferred to the nucleus because of less permeability through the membrane, naked DNA or RNA digested by enzyme during transfer, damage of cells, difficulty in large-scale manipulation, labor-intensive protocols, and the necessity of costly instruments. These all factors result in decreased transfection efficiency and also curtail its clinical application.

**Systemic Elimination of siRNA**

From the drug delivery standpoint, siRNA molecules have unfavorable physicochemical properties including negative charges, large molecule weight and size, and instability. Naked siRNA is readily degraded by serum endonucleases and is efficiently removed by glomerular filtration, resulting in short plasma half-life of <10 min. These problems are partially overcome by chemical modifications of the RNA backbone and the use of nano-sized carriers.

**Entrapment in the Reticuloendothelial System**

Because naked siRNA is infrequently applied in systemic delivery, this section focuses on siRNA-loaded carriers. Such carriers include nanospheres, nanocapsules, liposomes, micelles, microemulsions, conjugates, and other nanoparticulates. These systems offer a suitable means to deliver small molecular-weight compounds as well as macromolecules such as proteins, peptides, or siRNA. These carrier systems protect siRNA from undesirable interactions with biological milieu components and from metabolism or degradation and, in the case of cancer therapeutics, favorably improve the passive targeting of solid tumors due to the unique tumor features (i.e., leaky vasculature with capillary pore size of 100–800nm and the absence of lymphatic drainage). Upon systemic administration, nano-sized carriers are rapidly distributed to organs in the reticuloendothelial system (RES) and phagocytosed by the mononuclear phagocyte system (e.g., macrophages and liver Kupffer cells). These clearance processes, mediated by the interaction of particles with blood components (e.g., immunoglobulins of the complement system), result in higher particle accumulations in RES organs, such as liver and spleen, relative to non-RES organs. This property has been used to target the siRNA delivery to the RES organs.

Several factors, including surface characteristics, surface charge, and size of the nanoparticles, may affect RES uptake and biodistribution. The general view is that a negative surface charge increases the clearance of particulates from systemic circulation relative to neutral or positively charged particles. Surface modifications using hydrophilic and flexible polyethylene glycol (e.g., pegylation) and other surfactant copolymers, e.g., polyethylene oxide, result in stealth particles that remain in the systemic circulation for a prolonged period of time. These modifications can limit the protein absorption on the particle surface and thereby protect the vectors against opsonization, reduce the complement activation, and promote the cargo stability. These stealth properties are effective for particles within the size range of 70–200 nm.

**Extravasation: Vascular Endothelial Barrier**

One of the unique features of tumor microvessels is their leakiness due to endothelial discontinuity. The pore size of tumor microvessels ranges from 100 to 780 nm in diameter. In comparison, micro vessels in most normal tissues are less leaky; the tight junctions between endothelial cells are usually <2 nm and the pore size in post-capillary venules is <6 nm, whereas fenestrated endothelium of the renal glomeruli and the sinusoidal endothelium of the liver and spleen show larger pore sizes of 40–60 and 150 nm, respectively. Due to vessel leakiness, the major pathway of drug transport across tumor microvascular wall is by extravasation via diffusion and/or convection through the discontinuous endothelial junctions, whereas transcytosis plays a relatively minor role. Leakiness in tumor vessels promotes siRNA/carrier extravasation, but also elevates interstitial fluid pressure and reduces transvascular fluid transport.

**Transport in Tissue Interstitium**

Transport of small molecules in the interstitial space is mainly by diffusion, whereas transport of large molecules is mainly by convection. Diffusion depends on the diffusivity and concentration gradient, and convection depends on the hydraulic conductivity and pressure difference. For tumors, due to the higher interstitial fluid pressure compared to normal tissues, the pressure-driven convective flow in tumor interstitium is outward from the core of a tumor into the surrounding normal tissues. The lack of a lymphatic system in solid tumors increases interstitial fluid pressure, thereby inhibiting the convective transport in tumor interstitial space.

**Internalization of siRNA in Cells**

Naked siRNA does not readily cross the anionic cell membrane through passive diffusion due to the high molecular weight, large size, and negative charges of the phosphate. The major mode of internalization is endocytosis, whereby the drug molecules are internalized together with a component of the cell membrane. Coating of carriers with ligands and antibodies can promote the carrier-specific binding to cell membrane. The positively charged siRNA–Carrier complex interacts with anionic proteoglycans on the cell surface, forms an endocytic vesicle, and enters the cells by endocytosis.

**Intracellular Transport of siRNA**

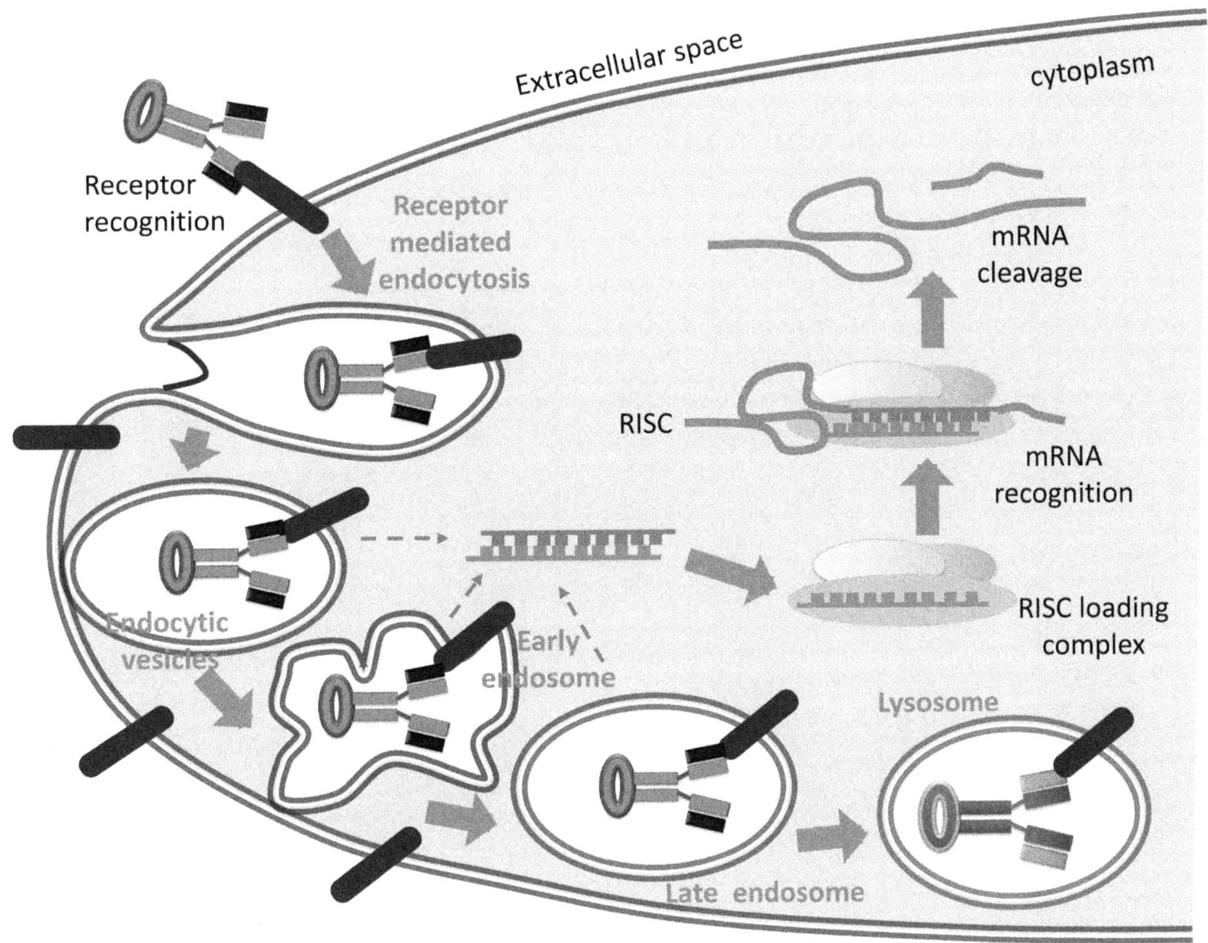

Figure : Endosomal escape mechanism

Following cellular internalization, the siRNA–Carrier complex (in endocytic vesicles) is transported along microtubules to lysosomes that are co-localized with the microtubule organizing center. The endocytotic vesicles sequentially fuse with early endosomes which mature into late endosomes before fusing with lysosomes. The fate of the internalized molecules inside the vesicle depends on the specific type of receptors and includes the following: recycle to the cell surface, degraded inside lysosomes, or released to other intracellular compartments including the cytosol. The endosomal entrapment and lysosomal degradation of siRNA–carrier contributes to the low transfection efficiency and is a major impediment for non-viral carriers. Endosomal escape should happen for successful siRNA delivery. For achieving this, use cationic lipid or polymer because of this increase endosomolysis by destabilization of the cell membrane by their positive charge.

Now a day's siRNA is widely useful techniques for gene silencing because of its ease of synthesis, fewer side effects and successfully reach to target.

**Clinical trial success of nucleic acid drugs**

The advent of nucleic acid drugs has ushered in a new era of therapeutic innovation, offering unprecedented opportunities for the treatment of a wide array of diseases. From cancer to genetic disorders, these therapeutics hold immense promise for revolutionizing medicine by targeting the underlying molecular mechanisms of disease with remarkable precision. This introduction provides an in-depth exploration of the clinical trial successes of nucleic acid drugs, highlighting key milestones, therapeutic breakthroughs, and future prospects in this rapidly evolving field.

**Emergence of Nucleic Acid Drugs**

Nucleic acid drugs encompass a diverse array of therapeutic modalities, including antisense oligonucleotides, small interfering RNA (siRNA), messenger RNA (mRNA) vaccines, and gene editing technologies such as CRISPR-Cas9. The development of these drugs has been fueled by advances in molecular biology, genomics, and bioinformatics, enabling researchers to harness the power of nucleic acids for targeted intervention at the genetic and molecular levels. Unlike traditional small molecule drugs, which often target proteins or enzymes, nucleic acid drugs exert their effects by modulating gene expression, either by inhibiting the production of disease-causing proteins or by correcting genetic mutations.

**Therapeutic Breakthroughs**

One of the most compelling aspects of nucleic acid drugs is their ability to target previously "undruggable" disease targets with unprecedented precision. For example, antisense oligonucleotides have shown remarkable efficacy in treating neurodegenerative disorders such as SMA, where they modulate splicing of the survival motor neuron 2 (SMN2) gene to increase production of functional SMN protein. Similarly, mRNA vaccines have demonstrated exceptional efficacy in preventing infectious diseases, as evidenced by the rapid development and deployment of COVID-19 vaccines based on mRNA technology. Moreover, gene editing technologies like CRISPR-Cas9 hold promise for treating genetic disorders by enabling precise correction of disease-causing mutations at the DNA level.

| Sr.No. | Drug | Company name | Target gene | siRNA carrier | Dissease | Current status |
|---|---|---|---|---|---|---|
| **Ocular diseases** | | | | | | |
| **1.** | Bevasiranib | Opko Health | VEGF | NC | DME | Phase II completed |
| **2.** | AGN-745 | Allergan | VEGFR | NC | AMD | Phase II completed |
| **3.** | PF-655 | Quark | RTP801 | NC | AMD | Phase I completed |
| **4.** | QPI-1007 | Quark | Caspase-2 | NC | NAION | Phase III completed |
| **5.** | SYL1001 (Sylentis) | Sylentis | TRPV1 | NC | Ocular pain | Phase II completed |
| **6.** | SYL040012 Bamosiran | Sylentis | b2-AR | NC | Ocular hypertension | Phase II completed |
| **Lung infections/disorders** | | | | | | |
| **7.** | ALN-RSV01 | Alnylam | RSV-N | NC | RSV infections | Phase II completed |
| **8.** | Excellair | Zabecor | Syk | NC | Astma | Phase II discontinued |
| **Skin diseases** | | | | | | |
| **9.** | TD101 | Transderm | K6a | NC | PC | Phase I completed |

Table : siRNA Drug Candidates in Various Phases of Clinical Trials Using Local Delivery

**Clinical Trial Landscape**

Over the past two decades, nucleic acid drugs have made significant strides in clinical development, with numerous candidates progressing from preclinical studies to late-stage clinical trials. These trials have spanned a wide range of therapeutic areas, including oncology, neurology, rare diseases, and infectious diseases. Notable successes include the approval of antisense oligonucleotide therapies for spinal muscular atrophy (SMA) and hereditary transthyretin amyloidosis (hATTR amyloidosis), as well as the emergency use authorization of mRNA vaccines for COVID-19. These landmark achievements underscore the therapeutic potential and clinical viability of nucleic acid drugs as a new class of medicines.

| Sr.No. | Drug | Company name | Target gene | siRNA carrier | Dissease | Current status |
|---|---|---|---|---|---|---|
| 1. | QPI-1002 | Quark | p53 | Naked siRNA | DGF | Phase III ongoing |
| **Lipid and polymer-based siRNA drugs** | | | | | | |
| 2. | CALAA01 | Calando | RRM2 | CD-NP | Solid tumor | Phase I terminated |
| 3. | TKM-ApoB | Tekmira | ApoB | SNALP | Hypercholesterolemia | Phase I terminated |
| 4. | Atu-027 | Silence | PKN3 | Cationic lipoplex | Advanced solid tumor | Phase II ongoing |
| 5. | ALN-VSP02 | Alnylam | KSP | LNP | Advanced solid tumor | Phase I completed |
| 6. | ALN-TTR02 Patisiran | Alnylam | TTR | LNP | hATTR-PN | Phase III completed |
| 7. | TKM-PLK1 | Tekmira | PLK-1 | LNP | GI-NET/ACC | Phase II ongoing |
| 8. | DCR-MYC | Dicerna | MYC | LNP | HCC | Phase I ongoing |
| 9 | siRNA-EphA2 DOPC | MD Anderson | EphA2 | DOPC liposome | Advanced solid tumor | Phase I ongoing |
| 10. | ALN-PCS02 | Alnylam | PCSK9 | LNP | Hypercholesterolemia | Phase I completed |
| 11. | TKM-100201 | Tekmira | VP24 | LNP | Ebola virus infection | Phase I terminated |
| 12. | ARB-1467 | Arbutus | HBsAg | LNP | Hepatitis B | Phase II ongoing |

Table : siRNA Drug Candidates in Various Phases of Clinical Trials Using Systemic Delivery

In addition to the the clinically applied siRNA delivery options described above, many biotechnology companies-developed delivery platforms were also investigated clinically and preclinically; for example, cyclodextrin-based RONDEL™ technology (Calando Pharmaceuticals), 13,67 polymer-based LODER technology (Silenseed Ltd),68liposome technology (Nitto Denko Corporation,69 Mirna Therapeutics, 70 Sirna Therapeutics,71 Suzhou Ribo Life Science)72 and EDV™ nanocell (EnGeneIC),73 amongst others. Various indications were used for RNAi treatment, among which, topically, siRNA delivery to the eye was evaluated by Quark Pharmaceuticals and Sylentis. However, the two companies did not disclose much information regarding their RNAi delivery technologies. Inspired by the GalNAC conjugate technology, cholesterol, bile acid, aptamer, α-tocopherol, peptide and pRNA-3WJ conjugated siRNAs were developed in laboratories and showed promisingresults.74-77 Some cationic molecules, such as chitosan, peptides, antibodiesand polymers, etc., represent another large class of siRNA delivery carriers and have shown a good performance.78,79 In addition, our laboratory has focused on developing innovative, efficientsiRNA delivery systems for several years. We have developed and thoroughly investigated the siRNA delivery efficiency of ionizable liposome,80 GalNAc conjugate,80 PDMAEMA-based polymers.

siRNA therapeutics undergoing phase III study

Eight siRNAs are undergoing phase III study, which include Fitusiran, Inclisiran, Givosiran, Lumasiran, Vutrisiran, QPI-1002, QPI-1007 and SYL1001. Fitusiran, Inclisiran, Givosiran, Lumasiran and Vutrisiran were originally developed by Alnylam. They employed trivalent GalNAc conjugate as the liver-targeted delivery platform62 andESC91 as the modification strategy. These five modalities were developedfor the treatment of hemophilia and rare bleeding disorders,hypercholesterolemia, acute hepatic porphyria, primary hyperoxaluriatype 1 and ATTR amyloidosis, as a result of targeting antithrombin (AT),92-94 proprotein convertase subtilisin kexin type 9 (PCSK9),95-98 aminolevulinic acid synthase 1 (ALAS1),99-101 glycolate oxidase (GO)102,103 and transthyretin (TTR), respectively.60,61,104 Phase I results for Fitusiran, Inclisiran and Givosiran have been reported.94,98,101 Once-monthly s.c. dosing of Fitusiran induced a dose-dependent mean maximum antithrombin reduction of 70–89% from baseline and also increased thrombin generation in participants with hemophilia A or B.94 Single or multiple doses of Inclisiran resulted in potent and durable reductions in the circulating PCSK9 and lowdensity lipoprotein cholesterol levels, which could be maintained well at day 180 for doses of 300 mg or more.98 Recently disclosed data for Givosiran showed that once-monthly injections of Givosiran triggered sustained reductions in ALAS1 mRNA, delta aminolevulinic acid and porphobilinogen levels to near normal, which was associated with a 79% lower mean annualized attack rate compared to that observed with placebo.101 The most common adverse events of the three therapeutics were injection-site reactions, nasopharyngitis, musculoskeletal or abdominal pain, and diarrhea, etc. Moreover, as long as 1 year of sustained reduction of TTR was achieved with a single dosing of Vutrisiran (ALN-TTRsc02), as shown in the phase I data collected from healthy volunteers, which supports a quarterly dosing of siRNA for the treatment of ATTR amyloidosis.63 QPI-1002105,106 and QPI-10079,107 were developed by Quark Pharmaceuticals, for the treatment of delayed graft function (phase 3) and acute kidney injury (phase 2), as well as nonarteritic anterior ischemic optic neuropathy (phase 3) and acute primary angle closure glaucoma (phase 2), by targeting p53 and caspase 2, respectively. SYL1001 was developed by Sylentis for the treatment of ocular pain and dry eye syndrome, by targeting transient receptor potential cation channel subfamily V member 1 (TRPV1)

**Commercialized siRNA**

ONPATTRO (patisiran) is the first approved RNAi-based therapeutic. DLin-MC3-DMA was employed to form lipid nanoparticle that could entrap siRNA in the complex. siRNA was slightly modified with 11 2'-OMe sugar residues and four 2′-deoxy thymidine (dT) residues.88 Phase III clinical results showed that patisiran not only elevated the modified Neuropathy Impairment Score + 7 (mNIS+7), which assesses motor strength, reflexes, sensation, nerve conduction and posturalblood pressure, but also improved the Norfolk Quality of Life Diabetic Neuropathy (QoL-DN) score. mNIS+7 and QoL-DN assessments constitute the primary and secondary endpoints of the clinical trial.88 The incidence and the severity of adverse events were similar in patients receiving patisiran and placebo. The most common adverse events that occurred more frequently with patisiran compared to placebo were peripheral edema and infusion-related reactions. To reduce the risk of infusion-related reactions, patients will receive pretreatment with antihistamines, nonsteroidal antihistamines and glucocorticoidprior to infusion. Moreover, the results collected in phase I and II studies demonstrated that patisiran significantly reduced the target protein, TTR, in a dose-dependent manner.5,89 Over 80% downregulation of serum TTR protein was achieved when patisiran was dosed 0.3 mg/kg every 3 weeks.89 Accompanied by the reduction of targeted gene and protein, the progression rate of the disease was also remarkably slowed down compared to natural history studies.90 In summary, patisiran can improve measures of polyneuropathy, quality of life, activities of daily living, ambulation, nutritional status and autonomic symptoms relative to placebo in adult patients with hATTR amyloidosis with polyneuropathy.

**Shortcomings of conventional siRNA delivery approaches and strategies to surmount them**

The physicochemical characteristics of siRNA—high molecular weight, anionic charge and hydrophilicity prevent passive diffusion across the plasma membrane of most cell types. Thus, there is a requirement of such delivery mechanisms that allow siRNA to enter cells, avoid endolysosomal compartmentalization and localize in the cytoplasm where it can be loaded into the RNA-induced silencing complex.

Innate immunity, introduction of too much siRNA can result in nonspecific events due to activation of innate immunity responses.

Two significant obstacles to the use of therapeutic siRNA are their macromolecular and polyanionic composition, which restrict their passive diffusion across the cell membrane into the cytosol. Therefore, to function siRNA therapeutics must be actively transported into the cell, but the fate of actively internalized macromolecules is usually catabolism. The job of an effective siRNA delivery vehicle is to direct and deposit functionally active siRNA to the cytosol of a target cell population. The development of effective siRNA vehicles has been an intensely active area of research for the past decade. (del. Vehicle)

**Challenges with siRNA-based therapeutics:**

Off-target effects—siRNAs are designed to knock down specific targets. However, recent studies have shown that they may also silence an unknown number of unintended genes. There are two mechanisms suggested to explain this off-target effect. First, siRNAs can tolerate several mismatches at the mRNA target and retain their ability to silence those targets with imperfect complementarity. The second mechanism involves promiscuous entry of siRNAs into endogenous miRNA machinery. miRNAs recognize targets with perfect complementarity to their 'seed regions' composed of nucleotides 2–8. Complementarity of remaining nucleotides has less importance for recognition. Because siRNAs are very nearly identical to the related class of miRNAs, they can recognize mRNAs with their seed region and lead to degradation of an unpredictable number of mRNAs

Efficacy—During the past few years, a number of siRNAs and other ncRNAs, such as miRNAs, have been successfully used in experimental models. Data from preclinical models are now giving rise to translation of new siRNA and miRNA-based therapies into clinical trials. In the case of siRNAs, the target selection process is extensional, requiring a thorough mining of databases and pathways.Differen t siRNAs targeting different parts of the same mRNA sequence have varying RNAi efficacies, and only a limited fraction of siRNAs has been shown to be functional in mammalian cells. Together with rapid excretion Delivery of siRNAs to target tissues is impeded by many barriers at different levels. siRNAs are easily filtered from the glomerulus and rapidly excreted from the kidney kinetics, the susceptibility to degradation by nucleases is a major problem leading to short half-life (15 min to 1 hour) in plasma, potentially limiting the use of siRNAs. However, some chemical modifications have been shown to protect siRNAs from nuclease degradation without interfering with siRNA silencing efficiency, and some others, such as phosphorothioate (PS) modification or hydrophobic ligands (e.g., cholesterol), were shown to increase protein binding and extend serum lifetime. Besides these, nanocarriers are important tools providing protection.

Unfavorable physicochemical properties such as negative charge, large molecule weight and size complicate passive diffusion of siRNAs through the cell membrane, which makes endocytosis the major way for internalization. This process adds new limitations at different stages of delivery to molecular targets, including endocytosis by tissue cells and release from endosomes into the cytoplasm.

Immune response and toxicity—RNAi is a mechanism involved in the innate immune response to protect cells from invasion by nucleic acids of pathogens such as viruses and bacteria.Several studies demonstrated that siRNAs itself can activate innate immunity by inducing interferon expression, even at low concentrations.Protein kinase

R (PKR) and toll-like receptor (TLR) 3 signaling pathways may be involved in sequence-independent immune activation by siRNAs. However, these mechanisms may play minor roles. Certain siRNAs stimulate production of proinflammatory cytokines via TLR 7 on dendritic cells and TLR 8 on monocytes in a sequence-dependent manner. These two pathways are being discussed as major mechanisms of immune activation by siRNAs. Some sequence motifs such as 5′-UGUGU-3′ or 5′-GUCCUUCAA-3′, some secondary structures and uridine content of the sequence were identified as important for immune activation by these pathways. Chemical modifications such as 2′-O-methylation were shown to prevent immune activation by siRNAs. However, the exact rules of sequence-dependent immune activation are not known yet; hence potential therapeutic siRNAs must be tested for immune stimulatory effects prior to clinical applications.

Small interfering RNA (siRNA) therapeutics face multiple barriers along the pathway from administration to delivery to the intracellular target site. The major barriers for both nanoparticle-formulated and targeting ligand-conjugated siRNAs are indicated with a number (see the figure). The table below provides a brief description of each barrier and suggests possible strategies to overcome them.

**Conclusion and future perspectives**

The future of cancer therapy lies at the intersection of precision medicine and advanced drug delivery technologies. Nucleic acid biomaterials are poised to play a pivotal role in this landscape, offering unprecedented opportunities for targeted and personalized cancer treatment. As researchers continue to unravel the complexities of cancer biology and refine drug delivery strategies, several advanced perspectives emerge, promising to reshape the way we diagnose, treat, and manage cancer.

**Targeted Nanoparticle Delivery Systems**

One of the most promising advancements in cancer drug delivery is the development of targeted nanoparticle delivery systems. By encapsulating nucleic acid drugs within nanoparticles, researchers can enhance their stability, prolong circulation time, and improve their accumulation at the tumor site through passive or active targeting mechanisms. Advanced nanoparticle formulations, such as liposomes, polymeric micelles, and lipid nanoparticles, offer precise control over drug release kinetics and intracellular trafficking, enabling efficient delivery of nucleic acid therapeutics to cancer cells while minimizing systemic toxicity.

**Multifunctional Nanocarriers for Combination Therapy**

Another key future perspective is the design of multifunctional nanocarriers capable of delivering multiple therapeutic payloads simultaneously. By incorporating nucleic acid drugs alongside conventional chemotherapeutic agents, targeted inhibitors, or immunomodulatory agents, researchers can exploit synergistic interactions and overcome drug resistance mechanisms in cancer cells. Moreover, the integration of diagnostic imaging agents or stimuli-responsive elements into these nanocarriers enables real-time monitoring of therapeutic response and controlled release of drugs in response to specific microenvironmental cues within the tumor.

**Intracellular Delivery and Subcellular Targeting**

Advancing our understanding of intracellular delivery mechanisms and subcellular targeting strategies represents another frontier in nucleic acid drug delivery for cancer therapy. By engineering nanocarriers with precise surface modifications or functional moieties, researchers can enhance cellular uptake, escape from endosomal compartments, and achieve targeted delivery of nucleic acid drugs to specific subcellular organelles or compartments within cancer cells. This level of precision enables tailored interventions, such as targeting oncogenic signaling pathways, modulating gene expression, or inducing apoptosis, with minimal off-target effects on healthy tissues.

**Immune Modulation and Immunotherapy**

The convergence of nucleic acid drug delivery and immunotherapy holds immense potential for transforming cancer treatment paradigms. By harnessing the immunomodulatory properties of nucleic acids, such as Toll-like receptor agonists or cytokine-encoding mRNA, researchers can stimulate antitumor immune responses, enhance dendritic cell maturation, and overcome immunosuppressive barriers within the tumor microenvironment. Furthermore, the development of personalized cancer vaccines based on tumor-specific antigens or neoantigens holds promise for priming the immune system to recognize and eliminate cancer cells, offering a novel approach for cancer prevention and immunotherapy.

**Theranostic Approaches for Precision Medicine**

Theranostics, which integrate therapeutic and diagnostic functionalities into a single platform, represent a cutting-edge approach for precision cancer medicine. By combining nucleic acid-based drug delivery with molecular imaging techniques, such as positron emission tomography (PET), magnetic resonance imaging (MRI), or fluorescence imaging, researchers can non-invasively monitor drug distribution, pharmacokinetics, and therapeutic response in real-time. This enables clinicians to tailor treatment regimens to individual patients based on their unique tumor biology and therapeutic response profile, optimizing therapeutic outcomes and minimizing adverse effects.

In conclusion, the future perspectives in nucleic acid biomaterials for cancer drug delivery are characterized by a convergence of advanced technologies, interdisciplinary collaborations, and a patient-centric approach to precision medicine. By harnessing the power of targeted nanoparticle delivery systems, multifunctional nanocarriers, intracellular delivery mechanisms, immune modulation, and theranostic approaches, researchers are poised to overcome existing challenges and revolutionize the way we diagnose, treat, and manage cancer. These advancements promise to usher in a new era of precision oncology, where tailored interventions based on the molecular characteristics of individual tumors offer new hope for patients with cancer.

Compared with small molecular drugs and monoclonal antibody drugs, RNAi-based therapeutics has its innate advantages .siRNA- based therapeutics hold great potential for cancer therapy and treatment of other diseases. However, many challenges, including rapid degradation, poor cellular uptake and off-target effects, need to be addressed in order to carry these molecules into clinical trials. These new class of therapeutics holds great promise for the treatment of various cancers by targeting signaling pathways and oncogenes that promote cell proliferation, cell cycle progression, invasion/metastasis and resistance mechanisms in tumors. Improvements in rational design strategies, selection algorithms, chemical modifications and nanocarriers have the potential to make the translational process faster and more effective in the near future and to open the door to development of highly effective and safe therapeutics for clinical applications.The success of LNP in hepatic applications is due, at least in part, to the liver's ideal physiology, notably being highly perfused with fenestrated endothelium. A number of challenges remain to be overcome for LNP siRNA to be used as therapeutics in a broad range of diseases. The existing LNP siRNA systems for liver applications have to be modified to extend their utility for non-hepatic tissues such as distal tumors. Novel small molecule targeting ligands will be required to facilitate LNP uptake into these non-hepatic tissues, especially when the siRNA is not tissue-specific. In order to reach tumor cores or tumors with poor vascularization, small LNP may be useful [60,61]. LNP siRNA systems as small as 25 nm can be made using microfluidic micromixing technology [22]; however, the relatively small siRNA payload may compromise activity and alternative methods to increase potency will have to be explored. Furthermore, LNP composition will likely require modifications for other routes of administration such as intraperitoneal, subcutaneous, intranasal or topical.

Since the first publication of RNAi in 1998, this technology has already advanced rapidly from the laboratory bench to the early or mid stage clinical trials. Although several RNAi-based drugs indicate strong promise in clinical applications, occasional recent frustrations in clinical trials have tempered the excitement and have triggered extensive efforts to surmount these key hurdles. Cytoplasmic delivery of siRNAs is one of the most important limitations. As described in Section 2, systemic RNAi delivery involves multi-step processes and endosomal escape is the most challenging bottleneck of translation of RNAi therapeutics. Therefore, it is not surprising that even slight inefficiencies at any particular stage would ultimately lead to a marginal or no gene silencing activity. Nanotechnology offers an assortment of versatile targeted delivery platforms for RNAi therapeutics. A precisely engineered, multifunctional nanocarrier with combined passive and active targeting capabilities may address the delivery challenge to the widespread use of RNAi as a therapy. Different nanotechnology platforms have their inherent niche and function differently by various routes of delivery (e.g. local vs. systemic) that subsequently affect the disease type (Table 1). For example, naked siRNAs, which are rapidly degraded in biological serum, are confined to easily accessible organs; the biodistribution of lipid particles (SNALPs) and dendrimers are more suitable for liver disease by systemic delivery; and aptamer-siRNA chimera and pRNA nanoparticles are multivalent that are suitable for viral diseases. Although SNALPs appear to be the most promising approach in the clinical development pipeline, it is expected that other nanotechnology platforms will display advantages in other disease areas.To effectively translate preclinical proof-of-concept to clinical efficacy, the following developments must be achieved to advance the field of RNAi therapeutics, 1) optimization of gene silencing activity of RNAi agents with increased nuclease resistance and reduced immune activation; 2)discovery of proper delivery formulation with prolonged circulation time and enhanced biodistribution; 3) specific tissue and cellular uptake; 4) efficient endosomal release of siRNA and incorporation of siRNA into the multi-protein RNA-induced silencing complex (RISC); and 5) elucidation of RISC loading and Ago2 function. A better understanding of intracellular fate of siRNA-nanocarriers will provide more rational rules for designing and optimizing an ideal siRNA-nanocarrier delivery system.

## REFERENCES


1. Saito Y., Liang G., Egger G., Friedman J.M., Chuang J. C., Coetzee G. A. and Jones P. A. 2006 Specific activation of microRNA-127 with down regulation of the proto-oncogene BCL6 by chromatin modifying drugs in human cancer cells. Cancer Cell 9, 435–443.
2. Scherr M., Battmer K., Winkler T., Heidenreich O., Ganser A. and Eder M. 2003 Specific inhibition of bcr-abl gene expression by small interfering RNA. Blood 101, 1566–1569.
3. Michael M. Z., O'Connor S. M., van Holst Pellekaan N. G., Young G. P. and James R. J. 2003 Reduced accumulation of specific microRNAs in colorectal neoplasia. Mol. Cancer Res. 1, 882–891.
4. Brummelkamp T. R., Bernards R. and Agami R. 2002 Stable suppression of tumorigenicity by virus-mediated RNA interference. Cancer Cell 2, 243–247.
5. Reddy K. S. 2007 India wakes up to the threat of cardiovascular diseases. J. Am. Coll. Cardiol. 50, 1370–1372.
6. Colussi P. A., Quinn L. M., Huang D. C., Coombe M., Read S. H., Richardson H. and Kumar S. 2000 Debcl, a proapoptotic Bcl-2 homologue, is a component of the Drosophila melanogaster cell death machinery. J. Cell Biol. 148, 703–714.
7. Jacque J. M., Triques K. and Stevenson M. 2002 Modulation of HIV-1 replication by RNA interference. Nature 418, 435–438.
8. Song E., Lee S. K., Wang J., Ince N., Ouyang N., Min J. et al. 2003 RNA interference targeting Fas protects mice from fulminant hepatitis. Nature Med. 9, 347–351.
9. Schiffelers, R.M.; Xu, J.; Storm, G.; Woodle, M.C.; Scaria, P.V. Effects of treatment with small interfering RNA on joint inflammation in mice with collagen-induced arthritis. Arthritis Rheum. 2005, 52, 1314–1318.
10. Nakasa, T.; Shibuya, H.; Nagata, Y.; Niimoto, T.; Ochi, M. The inhibitory effect of microRNA-146a expression on bone destruction in collagen-induced arthritis. Arthritis Rheum. 2011, 63, 1582–1590.
11. Khoury, M.; Louis-Plence, P.; Escriou, V.; Noel, D.; Largeau, C.; Cantos, C.; Scherman, D.; Jorgensen, C.; Apparailly, F. Efficient new cationic liposome formulation for systemic delivery of small interfering RNA silencing tumor necrosis factor alpha in experimental arthritis. Arthritis Rheum. 2006, 54, 1867–1877.
12. Lam, J. K., Chow, M. Y., Zhang, Y., & Leung, S. W. (2015). SiRNA Versus miRNA as Therapeutics for Gene Silencing. Molecular Therapy—Nucleic Acids, 4.
13. Sattar, Naveed et al. Statins and risk of incident diabetes: a collaborative meta-analysis of randomised statin trials. The Lancet, Volume 375, Issue 9716, 735–742.
14. Ray, K. K., Landmesser, U., Leiter, L. A., Kallend, D., Dufour, R., Karakas, M., Kastelein, J. J. (2017). Inclisiran in Patients at High Cardiovascular Risk with Elevated LDL Cholesterol. New England Journal of Medicine, 376(15), 1430–1440.
15. Porada CD, Stem C, Almeida-Porada G. Gene therapy: the promise of a permanent cure. N C Med J. 2013; 74: 526–9.
16. Linden R, Matte U. A snapshot of gene therapy in Latin America. Genet Mol Biol. 2014; 37: 294–98.
17. Chodisetty S, Nelson EJ. Gene therapy in India: A focus. J Biosci. 2014; 39: 537–41.
18. Razi Soofiyani S, Baradaran B, Lotfipour F, Kazemi T, Mohammadnejad L. Gene therapy, early promises, subsequent problems, and recent breakthroughs. Adv Pharm Bull. 2013; 3:249–55.

19. Rogers GL, Herzog RW. Gene therapy for hemophilia. Front Biosci (Landmark Ed).2015; 20: 556–603.
20. Kalpravidh RW, Tangjaidee T, Hatairaktham S, Charoensakdi R, Panichkul N, Siritanaratkul N, Fucharoen S. Glutathione redox system in beta-thalassemia/Hb E patients.Sci World J. 2013; 7: 543973.
21. Ghosh YK, Visweswariah SS, Bhattacharya S. Nature of linkage between the cationic headgroup and cholesteryl skeleton controls gene transfection efficiency. FEBS Lett. 2000; 473:341–344.
22. Rajesh M, Sen J, Srujan M, et al. Dramatic influence of the orientation of linker between hydrophilic and hydrophobic lipid moiety in liposomal gene delivery. J Am Chem Soc. 2007; 129:11408–11420.
23. Ishiwata H, Suzuki N, Ando S, et al. Characteristics and biodistribution of cationic liposomes and their DNA complexes. J Control Release. 2000; 69:139–148.
24. J.-y. Pillé, h. Li, e. Blot, j.-r. Bertrand, l.-l. Pritchard, p. Opolon, a. Maksimenko, h. Lu, j.-p. Vannier, j. Soria, c. Malvy, and c. Soria Intravenous Delivery of Anti-RhoA Small Interfering RNA Loaded in Nanoparticles of Chitosan in Mice: Safety and Efficacy in Xenografted Aggressive Breast Cancer human gene therapy 17:1019–1026 (October 2006).
25. Jemal, A., Thun, M.J., Ries, L.A., Howe, H.L., Weir, H.K., Center, M.M., 2008. Annual report to the nation on the status of cancer, 1975–2005, featuring trends in lung cancer, tobacco use, and tobacco control. J. Natl. Cancer Inst. 100, 1672–1694.
26. Trussardi, A., Poitevin, G., Gorisse, M.C., Faroux, M.J., Bobichon, H., Delvincourt, C., Jardillier, J.C., 1998. Sequential overexpression of LRP and MRP but not P-gp 170 in VP16-selected A549 adenocarcinoma cells. Int. J. Oncol. 13, 543–548.
27. Berger, W., Setinek, U., Hollaus, P., Zidek, T., Steiner, E., Elbling, L., Cantonati, H., Attems, J., Gsur, A., Micksche, M., 2005. Multidrug resistance markers Pglycoprotein, multidrug resistance protein 1, and lung resistance protein in nonsmall cell lung cancer: prognostic implications. J. Cancer Res. Clin. Oncol. 131, 355–363.
28. Review Toxicity of cationic lipids and cationic polymers in gene delivery Hongtao Lv, Shubiao Zhang b, Bing Wang, Shaohui Cui b, Jie Yan, Journal of Controlled Release 114 (2006) 100–109.
29. R. Bottega, R.M. Epand, Inhibition of protein kinase C by cationic amphiphiles, Biochemistry 31 (1992) 9025–9030.
30. I. van der Woude, A. Wagenaar, A.A. Meekel, M.B. ter Beest, M.H. Ruiters, J.B. Engberts, D. Hoekstra, Novel pyridinium surfactants for efficient, nontoxic in vitro gene delivery, Proc. Natl. Acad. Sci. U. S. A. 94 (1997) 1160–1165.
31. N.S. Tempelton, D.D. Lasic, P.M. Frederik, H.H. Strey, D.D. Roberts, G. N. Palvakis, Improved DNA: liposomes complexes for increased systemic delivery and gene expression, Nat. Biotechnol. 15 (1997) 647–652.
32. P. Pinnaduwage, L. Schmitt, L. Huang, Use of a quaternary ammonium detergent in liposome mediated DNA transfection of mouse L-cells, Biochim. Biophys. Acta 985 (1989) 33–37.
33. F.X. Tang, J.A. Hughes, Synthesis of a single-tailed cationic lipid and investigation of its transfection, J. Control. Release 62 (1999) 345–358.
34. V. Floch, S. Loisel, E. Guenin, A.C. Herve, J.C. Clement, J.J. Yaouanc, H. des Abbayes, C. Ferec, Cation substitution in cationic phosphonolipids: a new concept to improve transfection activity and decrease cellular toxicity, J. Med. Chem. 30 (2000) 4617–4628.
35. A.M. Aberle, F. Tablin, N.J.Walker, D.C. Gruenert, M.H. Nantz, A novel tetraester construct that reduces cationic lipid-associated cytotoxicity. Implications for the onset of cytotoxicity, Biochemistry 37 (1998) 6533–6540.
36. J. Stekar, G. Nössner, B. Kutscher, J. Engel and P. Hilgard, Angew. Chem. Int. Ed., 1995, 34, 238-240.
37. C. Ornelas-Megiatto, P. R. Wich and J. M. J. Fréchet, J. Am.Chem. Soc., 2012, 134, 1902-1905.
38. Delivery of siRNA Therapeutics: Barriers and Carriers Jie Wang, Ze Lu, M. Guillaume Wientjes, and Jessie L.-S. Au1, The AAPS Journal, Vol. 12, No. 4, December 2010.
39. Chen, Y., Gao, D. Y., & Huang, L. (2015). In vivo delivery of miRNAs for cancer therapy: challenges and strategies. Advanced drug delivery reviews, 81, 128-141.
40. Guo, P., Huang, J., Wang, L., Jia, Y., Zhang, H., & Li, J. (2019). Advances in the development and application of nucleic acid drugs. Journal of controlled release, 305, 130-150.

41. Li, J., & Huang, L. (2016). Targeted delivery of RNA-based cancer therapy: the role of siRNA and miRNA. Expert opinion on drug delivery, 13(5), 7-25.
42. Meng, Z., & Lu, M. (2017). RNA interference-induced innate immunity, off-target effect, or immune adjuvant?. Frontiers in Immunology, 8, 331.
43. Pecot, C. V., Calin, G. A., Coleman, R. L., Lopez-Berestein, G., & Sood, A. K. (2011). RNA interference in the clinic: challenges and future directions. Nature Reviews Cancer, 11(1), 59-67.
44. Li, J., & Huang, L. (2016). Targeted delivery of RNA-based cancer therapy: the role of siRNA and miRNA. Expert opinion on drug delivery, 13(5), 7-25.
45. Wang, J., & Lu, Z. (2014). Wientjes and J. L. Au. Delivery of siRNA therapeutics: barriers and carriers. The AAPS journal, 16(4), 1-11.
46. Yin, H., & Kanasty, R. L. (2014). Eltoukhy, A. Vegas, J. R. Dorkin, R. Anderson. Non-viral vectors for gene-based therapy. Nature Reviews Genetics, 15(8), 541-555.
47. Langer, R., & Folkman, J. (1976). Polymers for the sustained release of proteins and other macromolecules. Nature, 263(5580), 797-800.
48. Lee, S. K., & Han, M. S. (2016). Asokan and D. G. Choi. Delivery and therapeutic potential of gene editing technologies: A review. Journal of Controlled Release, 240, 256-270.
49. Yu, A. M., & Tu, M. J. (2018). RNA drugs and RNA targets for small molecules: principles, progress, and challenges. Pharmacological reviews, 70(2), 214-346.
50. Han, H., & Lee, H. (2017). Recent advances in the development of gene delivery systems. Biomaterials research, 21(1), 1-12.
51. Yin, H., & Kanasty, R. L. (2014). Eltoukhy, A. Vegas, J. R. Dorkin, R. Anderson. Non-viral vectors for gene-based therapy. Nature Reviews Genetics, 15(8), 541-555.
52. Ma, X., & Yu, H. (2016). Drug delivery systems mediated by mesoporous silica nanoparticles: an updated review. Frontiers of Medicine, 10(2), 1-9.
53. Li, J., & Huang, L. (2016). Targeted delivery of RNA-based cancer therapy: the role of siRNA and miRNA. Expert opinion on drug delivery, 13(5), 7-25

CHAPTER FOUR

# LIPIDS AS BIOMATERIALS IN DRUG DELIVERY AGAINST CANCER

**Mani Sharma**[a]

[a] CSIR-Indian Institute of Chemical Technology, Tarnaka, Hyderabad, Secunderabad-500007, Telangana , India

**Introduction**

In the realm of pharmaceutical sciences, the exploration of lipids as biomaterials for drug delivery against cancer stands as an intriguing frontier. This burgeoning field amalgamates the intricate disciplines of chemistry, biology, and materials science to harness the unique properties of lipids in combatting one of the most formidable diseases afflicting mankind. As the search for more efficacious and targeted cancer therapies intensifies, lipids emerge as promising candidates owing to their biocompatibility, versatility, and ability to encapsulate a diverse array of therapeutic agents. This discourse endeavors to delineate the multifaceted roles of lipids in drug delivery systems tailored for combating cancer, elucidating their molecular intricacies, design principles, and therapeutic implications.

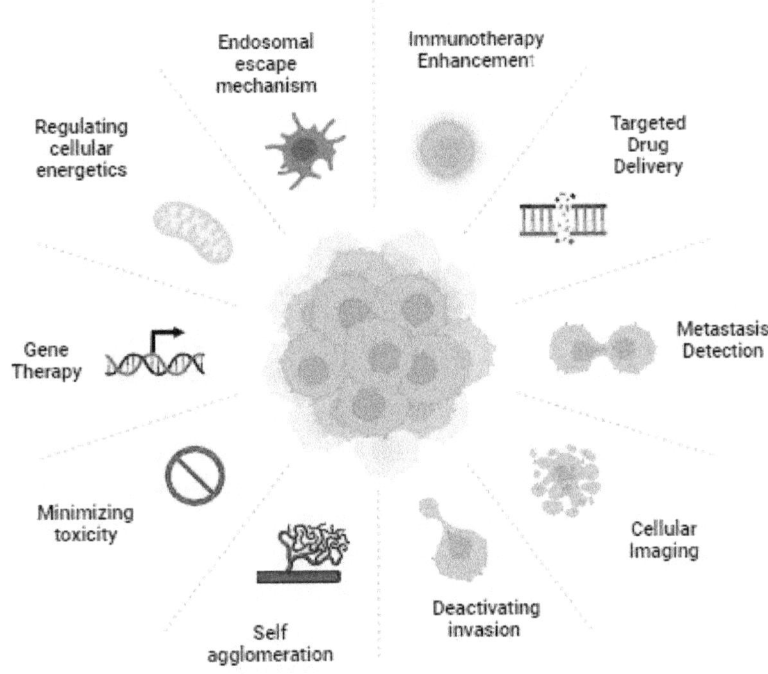


Figure : Role of lipids in the treatment of cancer

Central to comprehending the application of lipids in cancer therapeutics is a nuanced understanding of their structural diversity and physicochemical properties. Lipids, encompassing a spectrum of molecules from simple fatty acids to complex phospholipids and sterols, exhibit a remarkable array of structures and functionalities. Such structural diversity imparts distinct attributes to lipid-based drug delivery systems, influencing their solubility, stability, and interaction with biological entities. Moreover, the amphiphilic nature of lipids, characterized by hydrophilic headgroups and hydrophobic tails, facilitates the formation of various nanostructures such as liposomes, micelles, and lipid nanoparticles, thereby enabling the encapsulation and targeted delivery of anticancer agents.

In the design and fabrication of lipid-based drug delivery systems, meticulous attention is directed towards tailoring their physicochemical properties to optimize therapeutic efficacy and minimize adverse effects. Fundamental to this endeavor is the rational selection of lipids based on their biocompatibility, biodegradability, and potential for controlled release. Additionally, the integration of targeting ligands onto lipid nanoparticles augments their specificity towards cancer cells, thereby mitigating off-target effects and enhancing therapeutic selectivity. Furthermore, the incorporation of stimuli-responsive elements enables the spatiotemporal control of drug release, capitalizing on the unique microenvironment of the tumor milieu for site-specific drug delivery.

The advent of lipid-based nanocarriers has revolutionized the landscape of cancer therapeutics, offering a myriad of advantages over conventional drug delivery modalities. Chief among these is the ability to encapsulate hydrophobic as well as hydrophilic drugs within lipid bilayers or cores, thereby circumventing issues pertaining to poor aqueous solubility and bioavailability. Moreover, the nanoscale dimensions of lipid-based carriers endow them with favorable pharmacokinetic properties, including prolonged circulation times and enhanced accumulation within tumor tissues via the enhanced permeability and retention (EPR) effect. Additionally, the amenability of lipid nanoparticles to surface modification facilitates the co-delivery of multiple therapeutic agents or imaging probes, thereby enabling multimodal cancer therapy and diagnostics.

The therapeutic potential of lipid-based drug delivery systems extends beyond conventional chemotherapy to encompass a spectrum of emerging modalities, including nucleic acid-based therapies and immunomodulatory agents. By virtue of their ability to encapsulate nucleic acids such as siRNA, miRNA, and mRNA, lipid nanoparticles serve as efficacious carriers for gene silencing and modulation, thereby offering a promising avenue for targeted cancer gene therapy. Furthermore, the immunomodulatory properties of certain lipids, exemplified by lipid-based adjuvants and immune-stimulating complexes, hold immense potential for potentiating anticancer immune responses and overcoming immune evasion mechanisms employed by malignant cells.

Lipids, a diverse class of biomolecules, have gained significant attention in the field of drug delivery due to their unique properties and potential applications in the treatment of various diseases, including cancer. The use of lipids as biomaterials in drug delivery systems offers several advantages, such as improved bioavailability, targeted drug delivery, and reduced side effects. In the context of cancer therapy, the development of lipid-based drug delivery systems has shown promising results in enhancing the efficacy of anti-cancer drugs while minimizing their adverse effects on healthy tissues.One of the key advantages of using lipids as biomaterials in drug delivery is their ability to encapsulate and protect therapeutic agents from degradation in the body. Lipids can form various structures, such as liposomes, micelles, and solid lipid nanoparticles, which serve as carriers for drugs, proteins, and genetic materials. These lipid-based carriers can protect the encapsulated drugs from premature degradation and clearance, thereby increasing their circulation time in the body.Another important aspect of lipid-based drug delivery systems is their potential for targeted drug delivery. Lipids can be modified with specific ligands or antibodies that recognize and bind to receptors overexpressed on cancer cells. This targeted approach helps to increase the accumulation of drugs in tumor tissues while minimizing their exposure to healthy cells, leading to improved therapeutic efficacy and reduced side effects.The versatility of lipids as biomaterials in drug delivery is further enhanced by their ability to be tailored for specific applications. The composition and structure of lipid-based carriers can be adjusted to control drug release kinetics, improve stability, and enhance cellular uptake. For instance, the incorporation of PEGylated lipids can prolong the circulation time of liposomes, while the use of cationic lipids can facilitate the delivery of nucleic acids for gene therapy.In the context of cancer therapy, lipid-based drug delivery systems have been extensively studied for the delivery of various anti-cancer agents, including chemotherapeutic drugs, small interfering RNAs (siRNAs), and immunotherapeutic agents. These systems have shown promising results in preclinical and clinical studies, demonstrating improved therapeutic outcomes and reduced toxicity compared to conventional drug formulations.One notable example of a lipid-based drug delivery system in cancer therapy is Doxil®, a liposomal formulation of the chemotherapeutic drug doxorubicin. Doxil® has been approved for the treatment of various types of cancer, including ovarian cancer, multiple myeloma, and AIDS-related Kaposi's sarcoma. By encapsulating doxorubicin in PEGylated liposomes, Doxil® has shown reduced cardiotoxicity and improved therapeutic efficacy compared to free doxorubicin.Despite the promising results, the development of lipid-based drug delivery systems for cancer therapy also faces challenges. These challenges include the optimization of drug loading efficiency, the development of scalable manufacturing processes, and the need for further research to understand the long-term safety and efficacy of these systems in clinical settings.

**Cationic lipids as biomaterials in drug delivery**

Cationic lipids were introduced as carriers for DNA and RNA over 20 years ago. Cationic lipids interact with negatively charged nucleic acids through electrostatic interactions composing complexes called lipoplexes. The proposed mechanism of formation of lipoplexes is that negatively charged nucleic acids bind to positively charged lipid vesicles. Supplemental positively charged vesicles adsorb to the solvent-exposed nucleic acids. This process causes the formation of a multilamellar structure of positively charged lipid bilayers 3.7 nm thick, spaced 2 nm apart from each other by negatively charged nucleic acids. One of the first cationic lipids to be utilized for DNA distribution is DOTMA. Upon hydration, DOTMA will compose liposomes either alone, or in presence of other lipids. These liposomes can be downsized into minute unilamellar vesicles (SUVs) <100 nm in diameter. Liposomes differ from micelles; liposomes are spherical vesicles in which a single or several perpetual lipid bilayers disunite the external aqueous medium from the intra liposomal aqueous core, whereas micelles have an inner oil core. Predicated on the efficacy of DOTMA and other cationic lipids some structural features common to those lipids most efficacious for DNA distribution in vivo.

These features include: (i) a cationic head group and its neighbouring aliphatic chain being in a 1, 2-relationship on the backbone; (ii) an ether bond for bridging the aliphatic chains to the backbone; and (iii) paired oleyl chains as the hydrophobic anchor into the lipid assembly. More recently, a combinatorial library of lipidlike molecules, termed lipidoids, was developed for siRNA distribution. The performance of the lipidoids was compared with different structural motifs including alkyl chain length and the degradability of the linker between amine and alkyl groups. Highest calibers of knockdown were achieved utilizing lipidoids with the following properties: (i) more than two amines per head unit; (ii) amide bonds between the amine 'core' and acyl tails; (iii) more preponderant than two acyl chains; (iv) acyl chains between 8 and 12 carbon atoms; and (v) at least one secondary amine. An example of a lipidoid, called 98N12, together with other commonly used cationic lipids.

Cholesterol plays a role in many cellular membrane cognate events such as membrane fusion, macropinocytosis and caveolin and lipid-raft-mediated endocytosis Conjugating cholesterol to siRNA amends cellular uptake and transfection, and decreases siRNA degradation in serum. Cholesterol may play a dual role in the distribution of siRNA. When incorporated in the carrier, cholesterol may avail facilitate cell fusion or endosomal internalization of the carrier. When conjugated to siRNA, cholesterol seems to act as a targeting entity.

PEG coated polymeric nanoparticles are the most promising non-viral vectors for systemic delivery of siRNA. PEGylation not only reduces the toxicity of cationic lipids (CL) and cationic polymers such as Polyethyleneimine (PEI) but also inhibits particle aggregation Self-assembled; LPD (liposome-polycation-DNA complex) is a potent nanocarrier for systemic delivery of siRNA.

For efficient liposomal siRNA distribution, sundry types of cationic lipids have been synthesized and efficaciously distributed siRNA both in vitro and in vivo. Concretely, cholesterol- and glycerol-predicated cationic lipids have been used extensively for a cationic liposome mediated siRNA distribution. The general structure of a cationic lipid has three components: (1) a hydrophobic lipid anchor group (e.g. cholesterol, dialkyl, or trialkyl lipid), which avails to compose the liposomal structure; (2) a linker arm, such as an ester, amido, or carbamate; and (3) a positively charged head group, mainly composed of cationic amine (e.g. secondary, tertiary, or quaternary amine).

The linker arm controls the conformational flexibility, degree of stability, biodegradability, and transfection efficacy. Concerning the head group, it has been reported that inclusion of a cationic cholesterol derivative having a hydroxyethyl group at the amine head group into the formulation of the lipid predicated nanoparticles achieved high transfection facility for gene distribution. Consequently, in cationic cholesterol derivative predicated liposomes, we used cationic cholesterol derivatives such as OH-Chol, OH-C-Chol, HAPC-Chol, MHAPC-Chol, and DMHAPC-Chol, which had a hydroxyethyl group at the amine head group.

Most cationic lipids are coupled with helper lipids for incrementing transfection efficiency. For example, Cholesterol and DOPE are utilized for incrementing stability and safety, as well as siRNA complexation. DOPE that was utilized in this study is one of the most commonly used helper lipids. DOPE has fusogenic properties and has been found to promote membrane perforation, amend particle stability and lower toxicity. Particles made from DOPE and DOTAP in ratios of 1:1 and 3:1 were found to facilitate endosomal fusion and cargo release. Our study employs the same DOPE to DOTAP ratios and we withal found that DOPE integration incremented transfection efficiency. It has anteriorly been proposed that DOPE pushes the structure of lipid complexes towards a more efficacious inverted hexagonal phase and this could be responsible for the higher transfection rate. An alternative or complementary explication may be that the neutral helper lipid DOPE promotes a more impotent binding of the siRNA in the particle sanctioning a more expeditious relinquishment of the siRNA to the RISC within the cytoplasm.

Lipid-predicated carriers are promising candidates for therapeutic siRNA distribution. When designing carriers, consideration of both the molecular and meta-molecular scales must be taken into consideration. On the molecular scale, the building blocks, i.e. the lipids, must be able to assemble into stable distribution systems, which may or may not be affected by the nucleic acid payload. Complexation with siRNA often occurs via electrostatic interactions; ergo, the polar head of the lipid should contain a positive charge during siRNA complexation, carried in most cases by the amine groups. Electrostatic interactions must be stable enough to sustain the nucleic payload in the carrier en route but must sanction dissociation, to execute the therapeutic activity, at the distribution site. Molecules containing several amines per head group, in which marginal spacing subsists between one amine to the other, are able to adhere to the negatively charged backbone of siRNA in a better manner than several lipids containing a single positive charge per headgroup. When assembling carriers from positively charged lipids, stability may be enhanced by the additament of neutral lipids (sometimes referred to as helper lipids) to reduce repulsion between homogeneous charges in the bilayer. Integrating cholesterol, which resides in the hydrophobic region of the bilayer, amends carrier stability, and seems to play a consequential role in facilitating cellular uptake of siRNA. PEG lipids, which elongate out of the lipid bilayer, presenting a highly hydrated corona circumventing the carrier, enhance circulation time and reduce carrier uptake by RES components. To enable carrier uptake and permeation across fenestrae, a size limit of less than 100 nm should be maintained.

Phosphonium cationic lipid

Phosphonium salt-containing polymers have very recently started to emerge as attractive materials for the engineering non-viral gene delivery systems. Compared to more frequently utilised ammonium-based polymers, some of these materials can enhance binding of nucleic acid at lower polymer concentration, and mediate good transfections efficiency, with low cytotoxicity.

P vs. N: Toxicity profiles in vitro and in vivo

A potential benefit of some phosphonium-containing materials is a lower cytotoxicity compared to their ammonium analogues. This was first described in a study by Stekar et al. which focussed at identifying analogues of anti-neoplastic synthetic phospholipids edelfosine and miltefosine, with better tolerability and higher cytostatic activity. Novel analogues were synthesised by replacing the nitrogen atom (N) of 2-O-methyl-1-O-octadecyl-rac-glyceryl-3-phosphocholine and octadecyl phosphosphocholine with either arsenic (As) or phosphorus (P), and the resulting phosphonium and arsonium phospholipids were found to have comparatively lower acute toxicity in a mouse model, when compared to their parent choline phospholipids. However, the new analogues retained a similar antineoplastic activity of their parent phospholipids, as assessed in vitro in various cell lines (lymphocytic leukemia cells (L1210), KB cells (a subline of HeLa cells) and DS cells (B lymphocyte)) and in vivo using rat bearing 7,12-dimethylbenz(a)anthracene induced carcinomas. Although the exact mechanism(s) behind the observed differences was not investigated at this stage, the reduced acute toxicity resulting in weaker parasympathomimetic activity could be potentially related to the reater covalent radii of phosphonium and arsonium ions, which resulted in larger complexes. A study by Clément and co-coworkers on cationic phosphonolipids demonstrated that changing the nature of the cationic polar head from ammonium to phosphonium or arsonium, resulted in more efficient DNA transfection of β-galactosidase in airway epithelial cells (CFT1 cells) and HeLa cells. Furthermore, reduced cytotoxicity was observed in myelogenous leukemia cells (K562) transfected with a phosphonolipids containing phosphorus or arsenic-based quaternary groups compared to the corresponding ammonium lipids.

In a subsequent work the same authors investigated a large library of cationic phosphonolipids with variable structural parameters, including the nature of cationic quaternary moieties - ammonium, phosphonium or arsonium, as part of gene delivery vectors, both in vitro and in vivo. Using a luciferase assay, it was found that the replacement of ammonium groups with analogue phosphonium or arsenium moieties improved cell transfection and reduced cytotoxicity in a range of cell lines (HeLa, CFT1, K562). In terms of phosphonium-containing polymers, a seminal work by Frechet and co-workers showed that structurally analogous polyacrylates bearing triethyl-phosphonium repeating units had lower cytotoxicity compared to the corresponding triethylammonium analogues. Cell viability was assessed using a metabolic WST-1 proliferation assay employing a range of polymer concentrations (50-500 µg mL-1), and was measured 48 hours after polymer exposure. Furthermore, better cell viability was observed for the triethyl-phosphonium based polymer after transfection with siRNA polyplexes in comparison to its ammonium analogues. In a subsequent work using similar polymers in 3T3 mouse cell line, we found no significant difference in cytotoxicity between phosponium and ammonium-containing polymers. Using tributyl- and triethyl-ammonium and phosphonium polystyrenes, no differences in cytotoxicity profiles were found for both polymers and corresponding polynucleotide polyplexes in HeLa cells, as estimated by a MTT cell viability assay. Overall, current evidence suggests that phosphonium polymers generally possess a cytotoxicity profile equivalent or more favourable than their ammonium-based analogues, which could open the way for a more widespread application of these materials in gene delivery.

**Why Cationic liposomes in gene delivery?**

Cationic liposomes are prepared from cationic lipids containing two hydrophobic aliphatic long chains and positively charged functionalities in their head-group region. Cationic lipids are generally formulated in combination with neutral lipids like DOPE or cholesterol for use as gene transfer vectors. Because of their opposite surface charge, cationic liposomes can form a charged complex with negatively charged siRNA molecule. The resulting charged lipid-siRNA complexes (popularly known as "lipoplexes") do not experience the electrostatic barrier faced by the naked siRNA in entering biological cells and get endocytosed by the cell plasma membrane. In addition, cationic liposomes also protect siRNA from attack by the en-route RNases. Broadly speaking, cationic transfection lipids are designed to protect siRNA so that favorable interactions with plasma membrane occur leading to efficient endocytosis and subsequent destabilization of endosomes. In 1987, Felgner et al. for the first time, used chemically designed and synthesized cationic lipid in transfecting cultured cells with plasmid DNA. Since then, a large number of efficient cationic lipids having different molecular architectures have been reported till date.The main advantages associated with the use of cationic transfection lipids include their: (a) robust manufacture; (b) ease in handling & preparation techniques; (c) ability to inject large lipid:DNA complexes and (d) low immunogenic response etc.

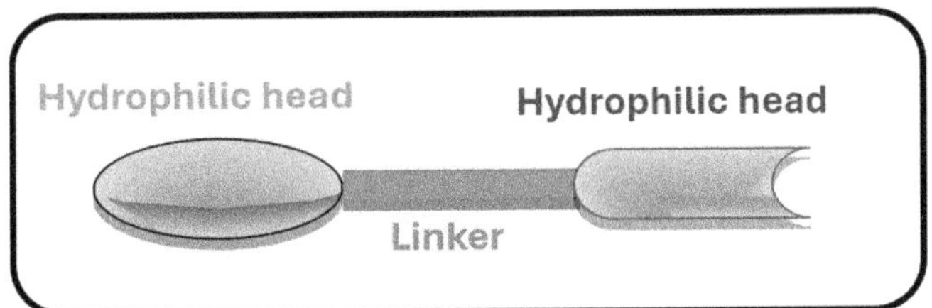


Figure : General structure of Cationic lipid

Cationic lipids are amphiphilic molecules and generally consist of three parts: a hydrophobic domain (for example, aliphatic chains), a hydrophilic head group (for example, quaternary ammonium), and a spacer including a linker bond (for example, ester bond) and backbone domain (for example, glycerol)) between these two parts. One of the critical factors that influence siRNA delivery is the composition of the cationic head group. A solution of cationic lipids, often formed with neutral helper lipids, can be mixed with siRNA to form a lipoplex Well-characterized and widely used commercial reagents for cationic lipid transfection include N-[1-(2,3-dioleyloxy) propyl]-N,N,N-tri methyl ammonium chloride (DOTMA), [1,2-bis(oleoyloxy)-3-(trimethyl ammonio) propane] (DOTAP), and 3β[N-(N', N'-dimethyl aminoethane)-carbamoyl] cholesterol (DCChol). Dioleoyl phosphatidyl-ethanol amine (DOPE), a neutral lipid, is often used in conjunction with cationic lipids because of its membrane destabilizing effects at low pH, which aid in endolysosomal escape.

**Hydrophobic Tail group**

There are two major types of hydrophobic moieties, namely aliphatic chains and lipid-based derivatives. Traditionally, for aliphatic chains, single-tailed cationic lipids are more toxic and less efficient than their double-tailed counterparts. Pinnaduwage et al. reported that cetyl trimethyl ammonium bromide (CTAB) was more toxic and less efficient than DOTMA. However, Tang and Hughes demonstrated that 6-lauroxyhexyl ornithinate (LHON) with one tail was more efficient and of lower cytotoxicity compared with DOTAP. This result shows that we cannot completely abolish the possibility of one tail cationic lipids for gene therapy application.

The effect of hydrophobic chain on toxicity has not been adequately addressed. Many scientists have been trying to give a proper explanation; however, there is still a long way to go. In any case, the influence of hydrophobic chain length on the parameter may well depend on the physicochemical features of the other two domains.

**Hydrophilic Head group**

The cytotoxic effect is associated with the cationic nature of the vectors, which is mainly determined by the structure of its hydrophilic group. The head group often consists of primary, secondary, tertiary amines or quaternary ammonium salts, but guanidino and imidazole groups have also been trialed. In addition, Floch et al. developed a class of cationic lipids characterized by a cationic charge carried by a phosphorus or arsenic atom instead of a nitrogen atom. The cationic lipids can become cytotoxic by interacting with critical enzymes such as PKC. The research shows that many derivatives of cholesterol which contain tertiary or quaternary nitrogen headgroups can inhibit PKC activity. Quaternary ammonium amphiphiles are more toxic than their tertiary amine counterparts. A recent solution to circumvent these problems was to spread the positive charge of the cationic head by delocalizing it into a heterocyclic ring. Heterocyclic cationic lipids containing imidazolium or pyridinium polar heads have been reported to display higher transfection efficiency and reduced cytotoxicity when compared with classical transfection systems. Ilies et al. reported that 1-(2, 3-dioleoyloxy propyl)-2, 4, 6-trimethyl pyridinium lipid, a kind of pyridinium lipid, was able to transfect several cancer cell lines with similar or better efficiency than DOTAP, while producing lower cytotoxicity. The import of a heterocyclic ring as the substitution of the liner amine headgroup, such as pyridinium and guanidine, can spread the positive charge of the cationic head, and then toxicity is decreased significantly.

**Linker bonds**

Most of the linker bonds in the above mentioned synthesized lipids are ether, ester carbamate and amide bond. Although compounds with ether linker render better transfection efficiency, they are too stable to be biodegraded thus cause toxicity. Cationic lipids with ester bonds such as DOTAP in the linker zone are more biodegradable and associated with less cytotoxicity in cultured cells, but those with ester or amide linkers are liable to decompose in the circulation system. In recent years, carbamate-linked lipids which with lower toxicity as novel cationic lipids have been developed. It is familiar to chemists that compounds comprising carbamate bond is stable in the neutral circumstance and is liable to acid-catalyzed hydrolysis. As well known, the pH value in endosomes is 1–2 lower than that of the circulation system, and it is expected that these carbamate-linked lipids can keep stable in the circulation system while decompose to release siRNA after entering endosomes in cell because of the pH decreasing. The lipids may be rapidly degraded into nontoxic low molecules in cell. Aberle et al. proposed that cytotoxicity due to cationic lipids may occur at a stage before the lipoplexes were encapsulated into endosomes. An increase in the length of the linker segment led to decreased toxicity in cell culture. These results show that the cytotoxicity is lowered while the linkage is degradable.

**Cationic lipids as Delivery Vectors**

Lipofectamine 2000

Dalby et al.used Lipofectamine 2000 to examine the effect of transfection efficiency and they proved that Lipofectamine 2000 provides high transfection efficiency and high levels of transgene expression in a range of mammalian cell types in vitro using a simple protocol. The most commercially existing cationic liposome/lipid-based systems are Lipofectamine 2000 and CDAN based liposome composed of CDAN: DOPE at different molar ratios.

1, 2-bis (oleoyloxy)-3-(trimethylammonio) propane (DOTAP):

Leventis and Silvius were first synthesized the DOTAP in 1990. Its structure made up of glycerol in which two oleoyl chains bound by an ester bond as a spacer and one with a quaternary amine. By using cationic DOTAP liposome's Sorensen *et al.* injected anti- TNF- α siRNA in a mice and they were successfully inhibited lipopolysaccharide-induced TNF- α gene expression. Ma *et al.* also reported that this cationic lipid, used with cholesterol in 55:45 ratios is able to deliver siRNA.

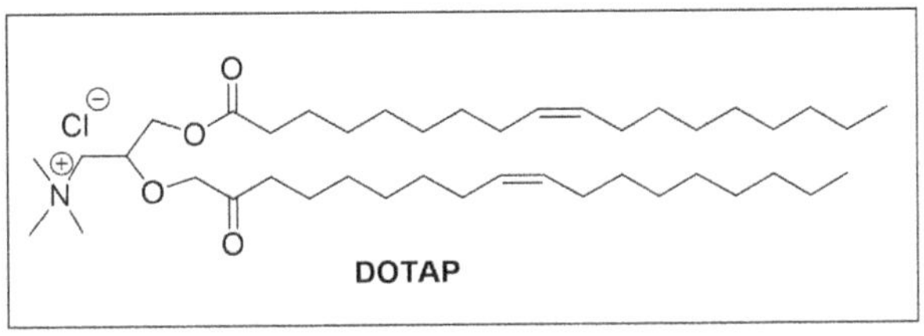

Figure: Structure of DOTAP

**N-[1-(2, 3-dioleyloxy) propyl]-N, N, N-trimethylammonium chloride (DOTMA):**

First synthesized and commercially available cationic lipid to be designed for gene delivery is DOTMA. It is made up of glycerol in which two oleoyl chains bound by an ether bond as a spacer and one with a quaternary amine. When compared to other cationic lipids, DOTMA has better in vivo transfection efficiency. "Lipofectin" which is used as a transfection reagent is the combination of 1:1 ratio of DOTAP and DOPE.

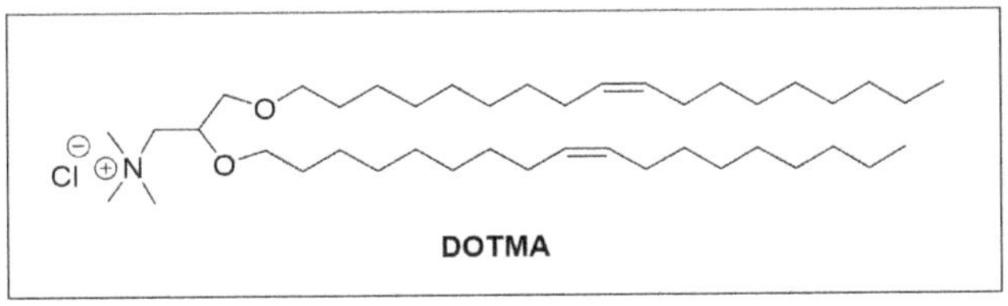

Figure: Structure of DOTMA

**3β [N-(N',N'-dimethylaminoethane)-carbamoyl]cholesterol (DC-Chol):**

Among the existing gene delivery systems, DC-Chol/DOPE liposome is one of the most effective systems in gene delivery. Yajun Guo and Jianming Chen examined the effect on the siRNA and plasmid DNA (pDNA) transfection by using DC-Chol/DOPE liposomes with different molar ratio. These results disclose that the mechanism of siRNA and pDNA transfection efficiency depend on the DC-Chol/DOPE liposomes at a different molar ratio.

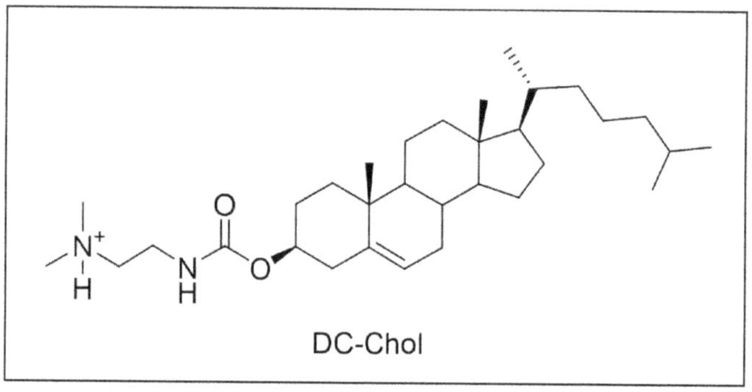

DC-Chol

Figure: Structure of DC-Chol

In conclusion, there are two main types of gene delivery vectors commonly in use- viral and non-viral vectors. Among these, the most efficient delivery vectors are the cationic lipids. So far, the siRNA delivery strategies are based on single agent therapies, but combinational therapy is more effective when compared to a single agent in curing cancer.

**Cationic lipids as anticancer agents**

Estradiol

Estradiol is a steroid and primary female sex hormone. Apart from its physiological functions, it is also involved in many disease-promoting processes notably in certain cancers, originating in estrogen sensitive tissue such as breast cancer. Estradiol, the endogenous ligand for Estrogen receptor (ER) is chemically modified to modulate the ER function, which is of high importance for treating variety of diseases including breast cancer and osteoporosis.

Rajkumar Banerjee et al. reported a new class of highly efficient anti–breast cancer agents that contain a novel combination of estradiol and cationic lipid moieties. Among their reported novel ES-cationic lipid derivatives eight carbon chain derivative of estradiol (ES-C8) exhibited excellent anti-proliferative activity in both estrogen-receptor-positive and estrogen-receptor-negative breast cancer cells but with no toxicity to normal cells. This warrants further *in vivo* efficacy studies in human breast cancer models.

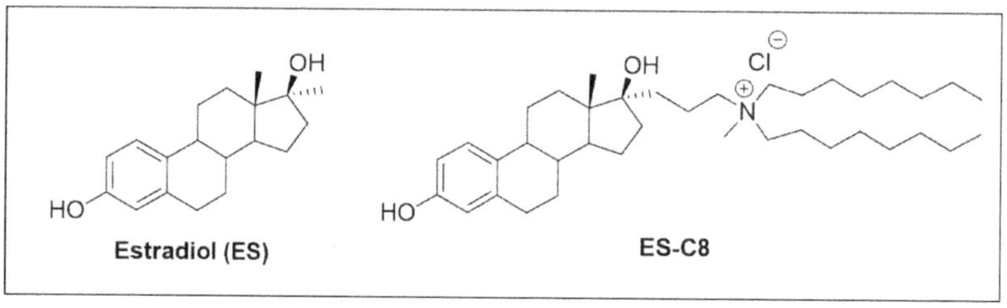

Estradiol (ES)

ES-C8

Figure: Structure of Estradiol

Haloperidol

Haloperidolis a neuroleptic drug that shows high affinity towards σ (sigma) receptors (SR) and it has been shown to induce apoptosis at higher concentrations in SR over-expressing melanoma and carcinoma.Ithas been shown that it exhibits anticancer activity and induces apoptosis in different tumor cell lines at moderate concentrations. Interestingly structural alteration of haloperidol by conjugation with a quaternary ammonium lipid moiety enhanced its anti-proliferative activity without hampering the targeting ability.

In 2011, Pal and co-workers reported that the conjugation of an eight carbon twin chain cationic lipid moiety to haloperidol generated a new σ receptor targeted anti-proliferative therapeutic activity via caspase-3-mediated apoptosis and Akt protein down-regulation.

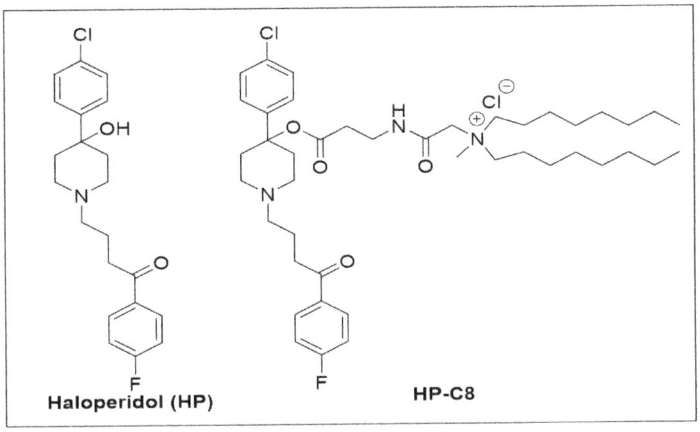

Figure: Structure of Haloperidol

Dexamethasone

Dexamethasone (Dex) is a type of steroidal medicine that acts as a ligand for glucocorticoid receptors. It is used as an anti-inflammatory agent and also shows moderate anticancer activity.However, it exhibits certain side effects associated with it's steroidal nature, while being used for antitumor treatments. For effective anticancer treatment, controlled and structural alteration of Dex is needed.

Rajkumar Banerjee et al. modified Dex with cationic lipid in which the molecule Dex with eight carbon chain-length exhibit better anti-proliferative activity than the Dex, most probably via modulation of JAK3/STAT3 pathway.

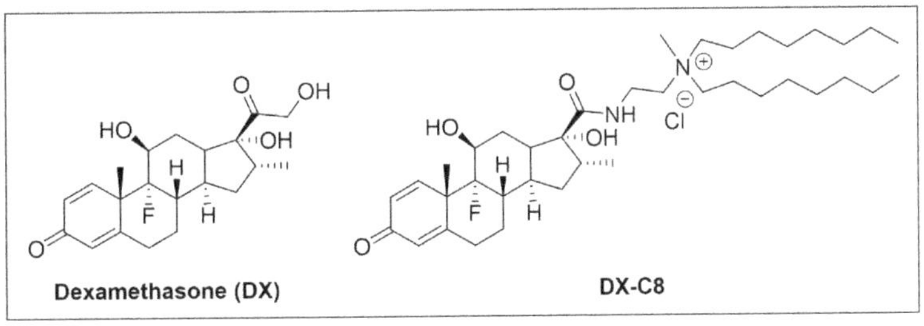

Figure: Structure of Dexamethasone

Emodin

Emodin (1, 3, 8-trihydroxy-6-methyl-9, 10-anthraquinone) is a natural chemical supplement found in Rhubarb. It possesses anti-tumor, anti-viral and anti-bacterial activities. Among them, only anti cancer activity is more widely reported. However, to potentiate the anticancer effects of emodin molecule, certain chemical modifications are necessary. Teich and Gu both affirmed that the cationic side chain containing emodin derivatives showed stronger cytotoxic activity compared to simple emodin molecule.

Wenfeng Wang at al. synthesized a series of cationic lipo-emodins and screened for in vitro antiproliferative activities against a panel of cancer and non-cancer cells. The molecule with eight and ten carbon chain-lengths (EM-C8, EM-C10) significantly inhibited proliferation of cancer cells via arresting the cell cycle predominantly in the G0/G1 phase, and at the same time, exhibited low cytotoxicity to non-cancerous cells. In vivo studies also revealed that the 10 mg/kg of EM-C8 derivative and 25 mg/kg of EM-C10 derivative showed significant anti-proliferative activity compared to emodin molecule.

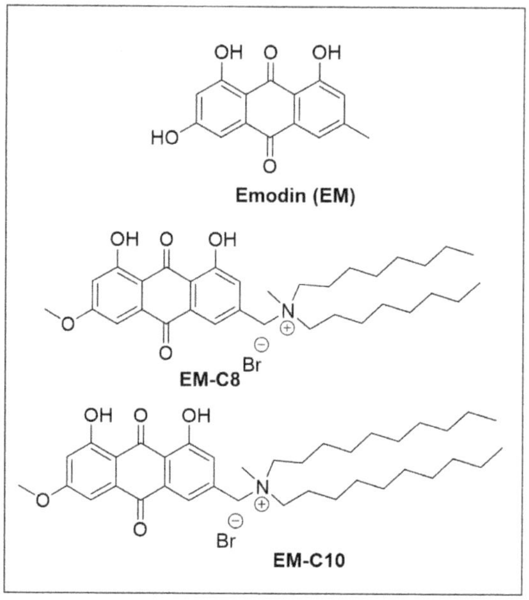

Figure: Structure of Emodin

**Classification of Cationic Lipids**

Cationic lipids play a crucial role in various fields such as drug delivery, gene therapy, and biotechnology due to their unique properties and applications. Understanding the classification of cationic lipids is essential for researchers, scientists, and professionals working in these areas. This comprehensive guide aims to delve into the intricate world of cationic lipids, exploring their diverse structures, functions, and applications.

**Importance of Cationic Lipids**

Cationic lipids are a class of lipids that carry a positive charge, making them particularly useful in interacting with negatively charged molecules such as nucleic acids. This property is exploited in gene delivery systems where cationic lipids form complexes with nucleic acids to facilitate their transport across cell membranes. Additionally, cationic lipids are known for their ability to self-assemble into lipid bilayers, making them valuable in drug delivery systems and as components of liposomes.

Classification Based on Structure

Cationic lipids can be classified based on their structure, which influences their physicochemical properties and biological activities. One common classification is based on the nature of the cationic headgroup. For example, there are quaternary ammonium cationic lipids, which contain a positively charged nitrogen atom, and guanidinium cationic lipids, which have a guanidinium group as the cationic headgroup. These structural differences impact the interactions of cationic lipids with biological membranes and molecules.

Classification Based on Chain Length

Another way to classify cationic lipids is based on the length of their hydrophobic tails. Short-chain cationic lipids have fewer carbon atoms in their hydrophobic tails, leading to differences in their solubility, stability, and transfection efficiency. In contrast, long-chain cationic lipids exhibit different membrane interactions and cellular uptake mechanisms. Understanding the implications of chain length on the behavior of cationic lipids is crucial for designing effective delivery systems.

Classification Based on Linker Groups

Cationic lipids can also be classified based on the linker groups that connect the cationic headgroup to the hydrophobic tail. Linker groups play a significant role in determining the flexibility, stability, and transfection efficiency of cationic lipids. Examples of linker groups include ester linkages, amide linkages, and ether linkages, each influencing the overall properties of the cationic lipid. Researchers often tailor the linker groups to optimize the performance of cationic lipids in specific applications.

**Advantages of cationic lipids**

Cationic lipids play a crucial role in drug delivery systems, offering several advantages that make them valuable tools in pharmaceutical research and development. Here are some key advantages explained in detail:

Efficient Cellular Uptake: One of the primary advantages of cationic lipids is their ability to facilitate efficient cellular uptake of therapeutic agents. Cationic lipids possess a positive charge, which enables them to interact favorably with negatively charged cell membranes. This electrostatic interaction promotes cellular internalization of the drug-loaded lipid nanoparticles, enhancing drug delivery to target tissues or cells. This feature is particularly advantageous for delivering nucleic acid-based therapeutics, such as siRNA or mRNA, which often face challenges related to cellular uptake.

Enhanced Stability of Lipid Nanoparticles: Cationic lipids contribute to the stability of lipid nanoparticles by aiding in the formation of compact, stable complexes with therapeutic agents. The positive charge of cationic lipids facilitates the condensation of negatively charged nucleic acids or other drugs into nanoparticles, shielding them from enzymatic degradation and premature release. This enhanced stability prolongs the circulation time of the nanoparticles in the bloodstream, thereby improving the pharmacokinetics and bioavailability of the encapsulated drug.

Facilitated Endosomal Escape: Another significant advantage of cationic lipids is their ability to promote endosomal escape of encapsulated drugs. Upon cellular uptake, drug-loaded lipid nanoparticles are typically internalized into endosomes. However, the acidic environment of endosomes can lead to drug degradation or entrapment within the endosomal compartment, limiting therapeutic efficacy. Cationic lipids can destabilize endosomal membranes through a process known as the "proton sponge effect," wherein the influx of protons into the endosome causes osmotic swelling and rupture, facilitating the release of encapsulated drugs into the cytoplasm. This mechanism enhances the intracellular delivery of therapeutics, particularly macromolecules like nucleic acids, which require access to the cytoplasm for their biological activity.

Versatility in Formulation Design: Cationic lipids offer versatility in the design of lipid-based drug delivery systems. They can be easily modified or functionalized to fine-tune their physicochemical properties, such as particle size, surface charge, and membrane permeability, to suit specific therapeutic applications. Additionally, cationic lipids can be combined with other lipid components or polymers to form hybrid nanoparticles with complementary properties, such as increased stability or enhanced targeting ability. This flexibility in formulation design allows researchers to tailor lipid-based delivery systems to meet the unique requirements of different drugs and disease targets, thereby maximizing therapeutic efficacy while minimizing off-target effects.

In summary, cationic lipids represent a promising class of materials for drug delivery applications, offering advantages such as efficient cellular uptake, enhanced stability of lipid nanoparticles, facilitated endosomal escape, and versatility in formulation design. These features make them valuable tools for delivering a wide range of therapeutics, including nucleic acids, small molecules, and peptides, with improved efficacy and therapeutic outcomes.

**Anionic lipuds as biomaterials in cancer drug delivery**

Introduction

In the realm of cancer therapy, the quest for effective treatment strategies continues unabated. Anionic lipids, a class of biomaterials, have emerged as promising candidates for revolutionizing cancer therapy due to their unique physicochemical properties and versatile applications. In this chapter, we delve into the diverse roles anionic lipids play in cancer therapy, from drug delivery to imaging and beyond. Understanding their mechanisms of action and potential applications is crucial for advancing the field of oncology.

Structure and Properties

Anionic lipids, characterized by their negatively charged head groups, form a crucial component of cell membranes. The amphiphilic nature of these lipids, comprising hydrophobic tails and hydrophilic head groups, enables them to self-assemble into various nanostructures, including liposomes, micelles, and lipid nanoparticles. This structural versatility facilitates their interactions with therapeutic agents and biological systems, making them ideal candidates for drug delivery and targeting in cancer therapy.

**Applications of Anionic Lipids in Cancer Therapy**

Drug Delivery

Anionic lipids serve as excellent carriers for delivering anticancer drugs to tumor sites. By encapsulating chemotherapeutic agents within liposomal or lipid nanoparticle formulations, anionic lipids can enhance drug stability, improve pharmacokinetics, and minimize off-target effects. Furthermore, the negative charge of these lipids enables electrostatic interactions with positively charged drugs, enhancing encapsulation efficiency and payload capacity. Liposomal formulations containing anionic lipids have shown promising results in preclinical and clinical studies, demonstrating enhanced therapeutic efficacy and reduced systemic toxicity compared to conventional chemotherapy.

Targeted Therapy

The ability to functionalize anionic lipids with targeting ligands further enhances their utility in cancer therapy. Surface modification of liposomal or lipid nanoparticle formulations with tumor-targeting moieties, such as antibodies, peptides, or aptamers, enables precise delivery of therapeutic payloads to cancer cells while sparing healthy tissues. This targeted approach not only improves therapeutic efficacy but also reduces adverse effects associated with systemic drug administration. Anionic lipids play a pivotal role in facilitating ligand conjugation and maintaining the stability and integrity of targeted drug delivery systems.

Imaging Agents

In addition to drug delivery, anionic lipids find applications as imaging agents for cancer diagnosis and monitoring. By incorporating contrast agents or fluorescent dyes into lipid-based nanostructures, anionic lipids can enable non-invasive imaging modalities, such as magnetic resonance imaging (MRI), computed tomography (CT), and fluorescence imaging. These imaging probes can provide valuable insights into tumor morphology, metastatic spread, and treatment response, aiding clinicians in personalized cancer management strategies.

**Challenges and Future Perspectives**

Despite their considerable potential, the translation of anionic lipid-based therapeutics from bench to bedside poses several challenges. Issues such as batch-to-batch variability, scale-up production, and regulatory hurdles need to be addressed to facilitate clinical translation. Moreover, optimizing the pharmacokinetic properties and tumor-targeting specificity of anionic lipid-based formulations remains a priority for future research. Advances in nanotechnology, biomaterials science, and precision medicine are poised to unlock new opportunities for leveraging anionic lipids in cancer therapy.

**Conclusion**

Anionic lipids represent a versatile class of biomaterials with immense potential in cancer therapy. Their unique physicochemical properties, coupled with their ability to self-assemble into various nanostructures, make them attractive candidates for drug delivery, targeted therapy, and imaging applications. By harnessing the inherent properties of anionic lipids and leveraging innovative strategies, researchers can continue to innovate and advance the field of cancer therapeutics, ultimately improving patient outcomes and quality of life.

Ionic lipids as biomaterials in cancer drug delivery

In the ever-evolving landscape of cancer therapeutics, the emergence of ionic lipids as biomaterials has sparked considerable interest and promise. These unique molecules, characterized by their charged head groups, offer a versatile platform for designing innovative strategies in cancer diagnosis, treatment, and imaging. This chapter explores the multifaceted roles of ionic lipids in oncology, highlighting their potential applications and contributions to advancing cancer care.

Ionic Lipids: Structure and Properties

Ionic lipids, also known as charged lipids, possess a polar head group that imparts an electrical charge to the molecule. This distinguishing feature distinguishes them from their neutral counterparts and endows them with distinctive properties crucial for biomedical applications. The amphiphilic nature of ionic lipids enables them to self-assemble into various nanostructures, including liposomes, micelles, and lipid nanoparticles, thereby facilitating drug delivery and targeting in cancer therapy. Additionally, the charge of these lipids enables electrostatic interactions with therapeutic agents and biological entities, enhancing their stability and efficacy in biomedical applications.

**Applications of Ionic Lipids in Cancer Therapy**

Drug Delivery

One of the primary applications of ionic lipids in cancer therapy is as carriers for delivering therapeutic agents to tumor sites. By encapsulating chemotherapeutic drugs within liposomal or lipid nanoparticle formulations, ionic lipids can enhance drug stability, improve pharmacokinetics, and minimize off-target effects. The charged nature of these lipids enables precise control over drug loading and release kinetics, allowing for tailored therapeutic regimens. Furthermore, surface modification of lipid-based nanostructures with targeting ligands facilitates selective accumulation of drugs within tumor tissues, thereby enhancing therapeutic efficacy while minimizing systemic toxicity.

Gene Delivery

In addition to conventional chemotherapy, ionic lipids hold immense potential for nucleic acid delivery in cancer gene therapy. Cationic lipids, a subclass of ionic lipids, interact with negatively charged nucleic acids to form lipid-nucleic acid complexes (lipoplexes), which can efficiently deliver therapeutic genes or RNA molecules to target cells. These lipoplexes protect nucleic acids from degradation and facilitate their intracellular uptake, enabling targeted modulation of gene expression pathways implicated in cancer progression. Moreover, the tunable physicochemical properties of ionic lipids offer opportunities for optimizing transfection efficiency and minimizing immunogenicity, thereby advancing the clinical translation of gene-based cancer therapies.

**Imaging Agents**

Ionic lipids play a crucial role in cancer diagnosis and monitoring through their applications as imaging agents. By incorporating contrast agents or fluorescent dyes into lipid-based nanostructures, ionic lipids enable non-invasive imaging modalities such as magnetic resonance imaging (MRI), computed tomography (CT), and fluorescence imaging. These imaging probes can provide valuable insights into tumor morphology, metastatic spread, and treatment response, aiding clinicians in devising personalized cancer management strategies. Additionally, the biocompatibility and customizable properties of ionic lipids make them ideal candidates for developing multimodal imaging probes for comprehensive cancer imaging and staging.

**Challenges and Future Directions**

Despite their considerable potential, the clinical translation of ionic lipid-based therapeutics faces several challenges. Issues such as systemic toxicity, immunogenicity, and regulatory approval hurdles necessitate rigorous preclinical evaluation and optimization of formulation parameters. Furthermore, advancements in nanotechnology, biomaterials science, and personalized medicine are poised to unlock new avenues for leveraging ionic lipids in cancer therapy. Future research efforts should focus on elucidating the mechanisms underlying the interactions between ionic lipids and biological systems, as well as refining their design and functionalization strategies to enhance therapeutic efficacy and safety profiles.

Conclusion

Ionic lipids represent a versatile class of biomaterials with diverse applications in cancer therapy, ranging from drug delivery and gene therapy to imaging and diagnostics. Their unique physicochemical properties and customizable characteristics make them attractive candidates for addressing the multifaceted challenges of cancer treatment. By harnessing the inherent capabilities of ionic lipids and leveraging innovative strategies, researchers can continue to innovate and advance the field of oncology, ultimately improving patient outcomes and quality of life.

**Future of lipids as biomaterials in cancer**

In the realm of cancer therapy, the quest for innovative and effective treatment modalities continues to drive research and development. Lipids, once considered mere structural components of cell membranes, have emerged as versatile biomaterials with immense potential in cancer diagnosis, treatment, and imaging. This chapter explores the future of lipids as biomaterials in cancer therapy, highlighting recent advancements, challenges, and opportunities in harnessing lipid-based nanostructures for precision medicine and personalized oncology. From drug delivery and targeted therapy to imaging and diagnostics, lipids are poised to revolutionize the landscape of cancer care, offering novel solutions for combating this complex disease.

Cancer remains one of the most pressing global health challenges, with a significant impact on morbidity and mortality worldwide. Despite advancements in conventional therapies, such as chemotherapy, radiation therapy, and surgery, the heterogeneity and adaptability of cancer cells pose formidable obstacles to effective treatment. In recent years, the field of cancer therapy has witnessed a paradigm shift towards precision medicine, emphasizing the development of tailored therapeutic strategies that target specific molecular aberrations driving tumorigenesis. In this context, biomaterials play a pivotal role in facilitating the delivery of therapeutic agents, enabling targeted interventions, and monitoring disease progression. Among biomaterials, lipids have garnered considerable attention due to their inherent biocompatibility, versatility, and tunable properties. This chapter explores the transformative potential of lipids as biomaterials in cancer therapy, elucidating their diverse applications and future directions in personalized oncology.

**Lipids: Versatile Building Blocks in Cancer Therapy**

Lipids encompass a diverse array of molecules, including fatty acids, phospholipids, sterols, and glycerides, which serve as fundamental building blocks of cellular membranes. Beyond their structural roles, lipids exhibit remarkable functional diversity, participating in essential biological processes such as cell signaling, energy storage, and membrane trafficking. In the context of cancer therapy, lipids offer unique advantages as biomaterials, owing to their amphiphilic nature, self-assembly properties, and biocompatibility. By harnessing these inherent characteristics, researchers have developed innovative lipid-based nanostructures for various applications in cancer diagnosis, treatment, and imaging.

**Drug Delivery Strategies Using Lipid-Based Nanostructures**

One of the most promising applications of lipids in cancer therapy is drug delivery, wherein therapeutic agents are encapsulated within lipid-based nanostructures to improve their pharmacokinetics, enhance tumor targeting, and minimize off-target effects. Liposomal formulations, composed of lipid bilayers encapsulating aqueous compartments, represent a widely studied drug delivery platform with numerous clinical applications. Liposomes offer several advantages, including high drug loading capacity, controlled release kinetics, and the ability to encapsulate both hydrophilic and hydrophobic drugs. Moreover, the surface properties of liposomes can be modified to impart stealth characteristics, prolonging circulation time in the bloodstream and enhancing accumulation within tumor tissues through the enhanced permeability and retention (EPR) effect.

In addition to liposomes, lipid nanoparticles, such as solid lipid nanoparticles (SLNs) and nanostructured lipid carriers (NLCs), have emerged as promising drug delivery systems for cancer therapy. These lipid-based nanostructures offer distinct advantages, including enhanced stability, tunable release profiles, and facile surface functionalization. Furthermore, lipid-based nanoparticles can be engineered to overcome biological barriers, such as the blood-brain barrier (BBB), enabling targeted delivery of therapeutics to otherwise inaccessible sites. By leveraging the versatility of lipids as biomaterials, researchers continue to innovate drug delivery strategies that improve the efficacy and safety of cancer therapeutics, ultimately enhancing patient outcomes and quality of life.

**Targeted Therapy and Personalized Medicine**

In addition to conventional chemotherapy, lipids play a crucial role in facilitating targeted therapy approaches that selectively inhibit cancer cell proliferation and survival pathways. By functionalizing lipid-based nanostructures with targeting ligands, such as antibodies, peptides, or aptamers, researchers can achieve precise delivery of therapeutic agents to tumor cells while sparing healthy tissues. This targeted approach not only enhances therapeutic efficacy but also minimizes systemic toxicity, thereby improving the therapeutic index of anticancer drugs. Moreover, by integrating molecular profiling data and patient-specific biomarkers, researchers can tailor lipid-based nanomedicines to individual patients, advancing the paradigm of personalized oncology. Through the convergence of nanotechnology, biomaterials science, and molecular diagnostics, lipid-based targeted therapy holds promise for revolutionizing cancer treatment paradigms and overcoming therapeutic resistance mechanisms.

**Lipid-Based Imaging Agents for Cancer Diagnosis and Monitoring**

Beyond therapeutic applications, lipids serve as valuable components of imaging agents for cancer diagnosis, staging, and monitoring. By incorporating contrast agents or fluorescent dyes into lipid-based nanostructures, researchers can develop multimodal imaging probes that provide real-time insights into tumor morphology, vascularization, and metabolic activity. Magnetic resonance imaging (MRI), positron emission tomography (PET), computed tomography (CT), and fluorescence imaging are among the imaging modalities that leverage lipid-based nanostructures for enhanced sensitivity and specificity in cancer detection. Moreover, by functionalizing lipid nanoparticles with targeting ligands, researchers can achieve molecular imaging of specific biomarkers associated with tumor aggressiveness and treatment response. These advances in lipid-based imaging agents hold promise for improving early detection, prognostication, and therapeutic monitoring in cancer patients, paving the way for more effective and personalized oncologic care.

**Challenges and Opportunities in Lipid-Based Cancer Therapy**

Despite the remarkable progress in lipid-based cancer therapy, several challenges and opportunities lie ahead on the path to clinical translation and widespread adoption. Among the key challenges are issues related to scalability, reproducibility, and regulatory approval of lipid-based nanostructures. Furthermore, optimizing the pharmacokinetic properties, biodistribution, and tumor-targeting specificity of lipid-based therapeutics remains an ongoing endeavor. Additionally, concerns regarding the immunogenicity and long-term safety profiles of lipid-based nanostructures necessitate comprehensive preclinical evaluation and translational research efforts. Nevertheless, the versatility and tunability of lipids as biomaterials offer exciting opportunities for overcoming these challenges and advancing the frontier of cancer therapy.

**Future Directions and Emerging Trends**

Looking ahead, several emerging trends and future directions are poised to shape the landscape of lipid-based cancer therapy in the years to come. Integration of artificial intelligence (AI) and machine learning algorithms holds promise for accelerating the design and optimization of lipid-based nanostructures tailored to individual patient profiles. Moreover, advancements in genome editing technologies, such as CRISPR-Cas9, present opportunities for developing lipid-based gene editing therapies that target oncogenic mutations and restore tumor suppressor functions. Furthermore, the advent of theranostic platforms, combining diagnostic imaging and therapeutic capabilities within a single nanostructure, represents a paradigm shift towards personalized, multifunctional cancer therapeutics. By leveraging these emerging technologies and interdisciplinary collaborations, researchers can unlock new avenues for harnessing lipids as biomaterials and realizing the full potential of precision medicine in oncology.

**Conclusion**

In conclusion, lipids stand at the forefront of biomaterials innovation in cancer therapy, offering unprecedented opportunities for precision medicine and personalized oncology. From drug delivery and targeted therapy to imaging and diagnostics, lipid-based nanostructures have demonstrated remarkable versatility and efficacy in combating this complex disease. Through continued research efforts, interdisciplinary collaborations, and translational initiatives, the future of lipid-based cancer therapy holds promise for transforming the landscape of oncologic care, improving patient outcomes, and ultimately, eradic.

## References


1. Allen, T. M., & Cullis, P. R. (2013). Liposomal drug delivery systems: from concept to clinical applications. Advanced drug delivery reviews, 65(1), 36-48.
2. Torchilin, V. P. (2011). Multifunctional nanocarriers. Advanced drug delivery reviews, 63(9), 853-862.
3. Batist, G., Ramakrishnan, G., Rao, C. S., Chandrasekharan, A., Gutheil, J., Guthrie, T., ... & Hoelzer, K. (2001). Reduced cardiotoxicity and preserved antitumor efficacy of liposome-encapsulated doxorubicin and cyclophosphamide compared with conventional doxorubicin and cyclophosphamide in a randomized, multicenter trial of metastatic breast cancer. Journal of Clinical Oncology, 19(5), 1444-1454.
4. Sercombe, L., Veerati, T., Moheimani, F., Wu, S. Y., Sood, A. K., & Hua, S. (2015). Advances and challenges of liposome assisted drug delivery. Frontiers in pharmacology, 6, 286.
5. Bulbake, U., Doppalapudi, S., Kommineni, N., & Khan, W. (2017). Liposomal formulations in clinical use: an updated review. Pharmaceutics, 9(2), 12.

6. Gabizon, A., & Shmeeda, H. (2006). Barenholz and A. (2012). Doxil®--the first FDA-approved nano-drug: lessons learned. Journal of Controlled Release, 160(2), 117-134.
7. Barenholz, Y. (2012). Doxil®--the first FDA-approved nano-drug: lessons learned. Journal of controlled release, 160(2), 117-134.
8. Danhier, F., Feron, O., & Préat, V. (2010). To exploit the tumor microenvironment: Passive and active tumor targeting of nanocarriers for anti-cancer drug delivery. Journal of Controlled Release, 148(2), 135-146.
9. Li, S. D., & Huang, L. (2010). Pharmacokinetics and biodistribution of nanoparticles. Molecular pharmaceutics, 7(3), 287-289.
10. Ta, T., & Porter, T. M. (2013). Thermosensitive liposomes for localized delivery and triggered release of chemotherapy. Journal of Controlled Release, 169(1-2), 112-125.
11. Wang, J., Mongayt, D., Torchilin, V. P., & Weissig, V. (2005). Factors controlling the biodistribution behavior of lipophilic drug carriers liposomes, micelles, stealth micelles and solid lipid nanoparticles. Advanced Drug Delivery Reviews, 59(7), 491-504.
12. Gabizon, A., & Shmeeda, H. (2006). Barenholz and A. (2012). Doxil®--the first FDA-approved nano-drug: lessons learned. Journal of Controlled Release, 160(2), 117-134.
13. Barenholz, Y. (2012). Doxil®--the first FDA-approved nano-drug: lessons learned. Journal of controlled release, 160(2), 117-134.
14. Parhi, P., Mohanty, C., & Sahoo, S. K. (2012). Nanotechnology-based combinational drug delivery: an emerging approach for cancer therapy. Drug discovery today, 17(17-18), 1044-1052.
15. Gubernator, J. (2011). Active methods of drug loading into liposomes: recent strategies for stable drug entrapment and increased in vivo activity. Expert opinion on drug delivery, 8(5), 565-580.
16. Liu, D., He, C., & Liu, Z. (2013). Xu, and X. Chen. Applications of polymeric micelles with tumor targeted in chemotherapy. Progress in Polymer Science, 38(3-4), 421-446.
17. Koudelka, S., & Turánek, J. (2012). Liposomal paclitaxel formulations. Journal of controlled release, 163(3), 322-334.
18. Chang, H. I., & Yeh, M. K. (2012). Clinical development of liposome-based drugs: formulation, characterization, and therapeutic efficacy. International journal of nanomedicine, 7, 49.
19. Bulbake, U., Doppalapudi, S., Kommineni, N., & Khan, W. (2017). Liposomal formulations in clinical use: an updated review. Pharmaceutics, 9(2), 12.
20. Kieler-Ferguson, H. M., & Fréchet, J. M. (2011). Designing macromolecules for therapeutic applications: polyester dendrimer–drug conjugates. Journal of the American Chemical Society, 133(22), 8424-8427.
21. Allen, T. M., & Cullis, P. R. (2013). Liposomal drug delivery systems: from concept to clinical applications. Advanced drug delivery reviews, 65(1), 36-48.
22. Lee, S. M., & Lee, E. J. (2017). Liposomal drug products and recent advances in the synthesis of supercritical fluid-mediated liposomes. International journal of nanomedicine, 12, 8055.
23. Li, X., Hirsh, D. J., & Cabral-Lilly, D. (2006). Liposome binding and destabilization induced by the cationic amphiphilic drugs quinacrine and chlorpromazine. Biochimica et Biophysica Acta (BBA)-Biomembranes, 1758(11), 1711-1716.
24. Torchilin, V. P. (2005). Recent advances with liposomes as pharmaceutical carriers. Nature reviews drug discovery, 4(2), 145-160.
25. Dagar, S., Sekar, V., Verma, P., Sharma, A., & Kumar, L. (2013). Liposome: classification, preparation, and applications. International Journal of Pharmaceutical Sciences and Research, 4(3), 863.
26. Papahadjopoulos, D., Allen, T. M., & Gabizon, A. (1991). Sterically stabilized liposomes: improvements in pharmacokinetics and antitumor therapeutic efficacy. Proceedings of the National Academy of Sciences, 88(24), 11460-11464.
27. Torchilin, V. P. (2011). Multifunctional nanocarriers. Advanced drug delivery reviews, 63(9), 853-862.
28. Bulbake, U., Doppalapudi, S., Kommineni, N., & Khan, W. (2017). Liposomal formulations in clinical use: an updated review. Pharmaceutics, 9(2), 12.

29. Sercombe, L., Veerati, T., Moheimani, F., Wu, S. Y., Sood, A. K., & Hua, S. (2015). Advances and challenges of liposome assisted drug delivery. Frontiers in pharmacology, 6, 286.
30. Li, S. D., & Huang, L. (2010). Pharmacokinetics and biodistribution of nanoparticles. Molecular pharmaceutics, 7(3), 287-289.
31. Wang, J., Mongayt, D., Torchilin, V. P., & Weissig, V. (2005). Factors controlling the biodistribution behavior of lipophilic drug carriers liposomes, micelles, stealth micelles and solid lipid nanoparticles. Advanced Drug Delivery Reviews, 59(7), 491-504.
32. Barenholz, Y. (2012). Doxil®--the first FDA-approved nano-drug: lessons learned. Journal of controlled release, 160(2), 117-134.
33. Allen, T. M., & Cullis, P. R. (2013). Liposomal drug delivery systems: from concept to clinical applications. Advanced drug delivery reviews, 65(1), 36-48.
34. Kieler-Ferguson, H. M., & Fréchet, J. M. (2011). Designing macromolecules for therapeutic applications: polyester dendrimer–drug conjugates. Journal of the American Chemical Society, 133(22), 8424-8427.
35. Chang, H. I., & Yeh, M. K. (2012). Clinical development of liposome-based drugs: formulation, characterization, and therapeutic efficacy. International journal of nanomedicine, 7, 49.
36. Ta, T., & Porter, T. M. (2013). Thermosensitive liposomes for localized delivery and triggered release of chemotherapy. Journal of Controlled Release, 169(1-2), 112-125.
37. Bulbake, U., Doppalapudi, S., Kommineni, N., & Khan, W. (2017). Liposomal formulations in clinical use: an updated review. Pharmaceutics, 9(2), 12.
38. Torchilin, V. P. (2011). Multifunctional nanocarriers. Advanced drug delivery reviews, 63(9), 853-862.
39. Liu, D., He, C., & Liu, Z. (2013). Xu, and X. Chen. Applications of polymeric micelles with tumor targeted in chemotherapy. Progress in Polymer Science, 38(3-4), 421-446.
40. Sercombe, L., Veerati, T., Moheimani, F., Wu, S. Y., Sood, A. K., & Hua, S. (2015). Advances and challenges of liposome assisted drug delivery. Frontiers in pharmacology, 6, 286.
41. Needham, D., & Dewhirst, M. W. (2001). The development and testing of a new temperature-sensitive drug delivery system for the treatment of solid tumors. Advanced drug delivery reviews, 53(3), 285-305.
42. Lammers, T., Subr, V., Ulbrich, K., Peschke, P., Huber, P. E., Hennink, W. E., & Storm, G. (2009). Simultaneous delivery of doxorubicin and gemcitabine to tumors in vivo using prototypic polymeric drug carriers. Biomaterials, 30(20), 3466-3475.
43. Prabhakar, U., Maeda, H., Jain, R. K., Sevick-Muraca, E. M., Zamboni, W., Farokhzad, O. C., ... & Chauhan, V. P. (2013). Challenges and key considerations of the enhanced permeability and retention effect for nanomedicine drug delivery in oncology. Cancer research, 73(8), 2412-2417.
44. Lammers, T., Kiessling, F., Hennink, W. E., & Storm, G. (2012). Drug targeting to tumors: principles, pitfalls and (pre-) clinical progress. Journal of controlled release, 161(2), 175-187.
45. Peer, D., Karp, J. M., Hong, S., Farokhzad, O. C., Margalit, R., & Langer, R. (2007). Nanocarriers as an emerging platform for cancer therapy. Nature nanotechnology, 2(12), 751-760.
46. Alexis, F., Pridgen, E., Molnar, L. K., & Farokhzad, O. C. (2008). Factors affecting the clearance and biodistribution of polymeric nanoparticles. Molecular pharmaceutics, 5(4), 505-515.
47. Lammers, T., Hennink, W. E., & Storm, G. (2008). Tumour-targeted nanomedicines: principles and practice. British journal of cancer, 99(3), 392-397.
48. Alexis, F., Pridgen, E. M., & Langer, R. (2010). Farokhzad. Nanoparticle technologies for cancer therapy. Handbook of experimental pharmacology, 197, 55-86.
49. Ferrari, M. (2005). Cancer nanotechnology: opportunities and challenges. Nature reviews cancer, 5(3), 161-171.
50. Gradishar, W. J., Tjulandin, S., Davidson, N., Shaw, H., Desai, N., Bhar, P., ... & O'Shaughnessy, J. (2005). Phase III trial of nanoparticle albumin-bound paclitaxel compared with polyethylated castor oil–based paclitaxel in women with breast cancer. Journal of Clinical Oncology, 23(31), 7794-7803.
51. Duncan, R. (2006). Polymer conjugates as anticancer nanomedicines. Nature Reviews Cancer, 6(9), 688-701.

52. Peer, D., & Margalit, R. (2004). Loading mitomycin C inside long circulating hyaluronan targeted nano-liposomes increases its antitumor activity in three mice tumor models. International Journal of Cancer, 108(5), 780-789.
53. Iyer, A. K., Khaled, G., Fang, J., & Maeda, H. (2006). Exploiting the enhanced permeability and retention effect for tumor targeting. Drug discovery today, 11(17-18), 812-818.
54. Maeda, H. (2010). Tumor-selective delivery of macromolecular drugs via the EPR effect: background and future prospects. Bioconjugate chemistry, 21(5), 797-802.
55. Iyer, A. K., Khaled, G., Fang, J., & Maeda, H. (2006). Exploiting the enhanced permeability and retention effect for tumor targeting. Drug discovery today, 11(17-18), 812-818.
56. Koo, A. N., Lee, H. J., Kim, S. E., Chang, J. H., Park, C., Kim, C., ... & Kim, K. (2011). Disulfide-cross-linked PEG-poly (amino acid)s copolymer micelles for glutathione-mediated intracellular drug delivery. Chemical communications, 47(15), 4665-4667.
57. Farokhzad, O. C., & Langer, R. (2009). Impact of nanotechnology on drug delivery. ACS nano, 3(1), 16-20.
58. Wong, C., Stylianopoulos, T., Cui, J., Martin, J., Chauhan, V. P., Jiang, W., ... & Bawendi, M. G. (2011). Multistage nanoparticle delivery system for deep penetration into tumor tissue. Proceedings of the National Academy of Sciences, 108(6), 2426-2431.
59. Torchilin, V. P. (2011). Multifunctional nanocarriers. Advanced drug delivery reviews, 63(9), 853-862.

CHAPTER FIVE

# Current Advancement of Biomaterial for Implant Scaffolds

**Alina Khan[a], Sahil Hussain[b]Arun Kumar[b], Bidhyut Kumar Dubey[c]**

*[a]Department of Toxicology and Medical Elementology, Jamia Hamdard, New Delhi,110062, India*

*[b]Department of pharmacy, Integral University, Lucknow,226026, India.*

*cEra college of Pharmacy, Era University, Sarfarazganj, Lucknow 226003, India*

**Introduction**

The commercialization of biomedical devices and tissue engineering, a technique which aims to unleash the regenerative potential inherent to human organs and tissues in a state of degeneration and repair or reestablish normal biological function, have been greatly aided by the creation of biomaterials. The rapidly expanding area of regenerative medicine may encounter new challenges as a result of advances in our knowledge of biomaterials that regenerate and their functions in the creation of new tissues. The function and multi-component design of native extracellular matrix (ECMs) for cell lodging serve as an inspiration for the role that biologically active elements play in the production of synthetic biological materials that are routinely used today. These components characterize an artificial in vivo milieu with intricate and dynamic interactions that both promote and control stem cells, just like what happens in a natural cellular microenvironment. (1).

Biomaterials have become a highly active and fascinating field of research in recent years because of the constant push to produce new and inventive materials while also minimizing the economic effect on humanity and improving healthcare. Modern scientific fields and modern technology in materials science, healthcare, molecular and cellular biology, the field of biochemistry nanotechnology, multiscale modeling, enhanced design, and biological production are all included in the most current version of biomaterials. This greatly advances our knowledge of materials and broadens the range of potential biological applications.(2) .

Numerous novel substances and compounds have been developed via research, which have enhanced cell survival, multiplication, and printing capabilities. The biomimicry technique is used to arrange various biological elements (such as testosterone and hormones) in a way that mimics genuine tissues in order to make further modifications(3). [a2] That is carried out to improve collagen synthesis or cell signaling. environmentally friendly scaffolds are also used in the administration of pharmaceuticals, growth hormones, amino acids, and other therapeutic items. During an efficient loading operation, the scaffold's connection of these materials is crucial(4).

Figure 1 illustrates how biomaterials, which are used to build components of medical gadgets, surgical procedures, systems for delivering drugs, scaffolds for tissue creation, and diagnostic tools, have enabled advancements in regenerative medicine, tailored healthcare, and disease management.The goal of this book chapter is to examine the most current developments in implantable scaffold materials for various tissues.

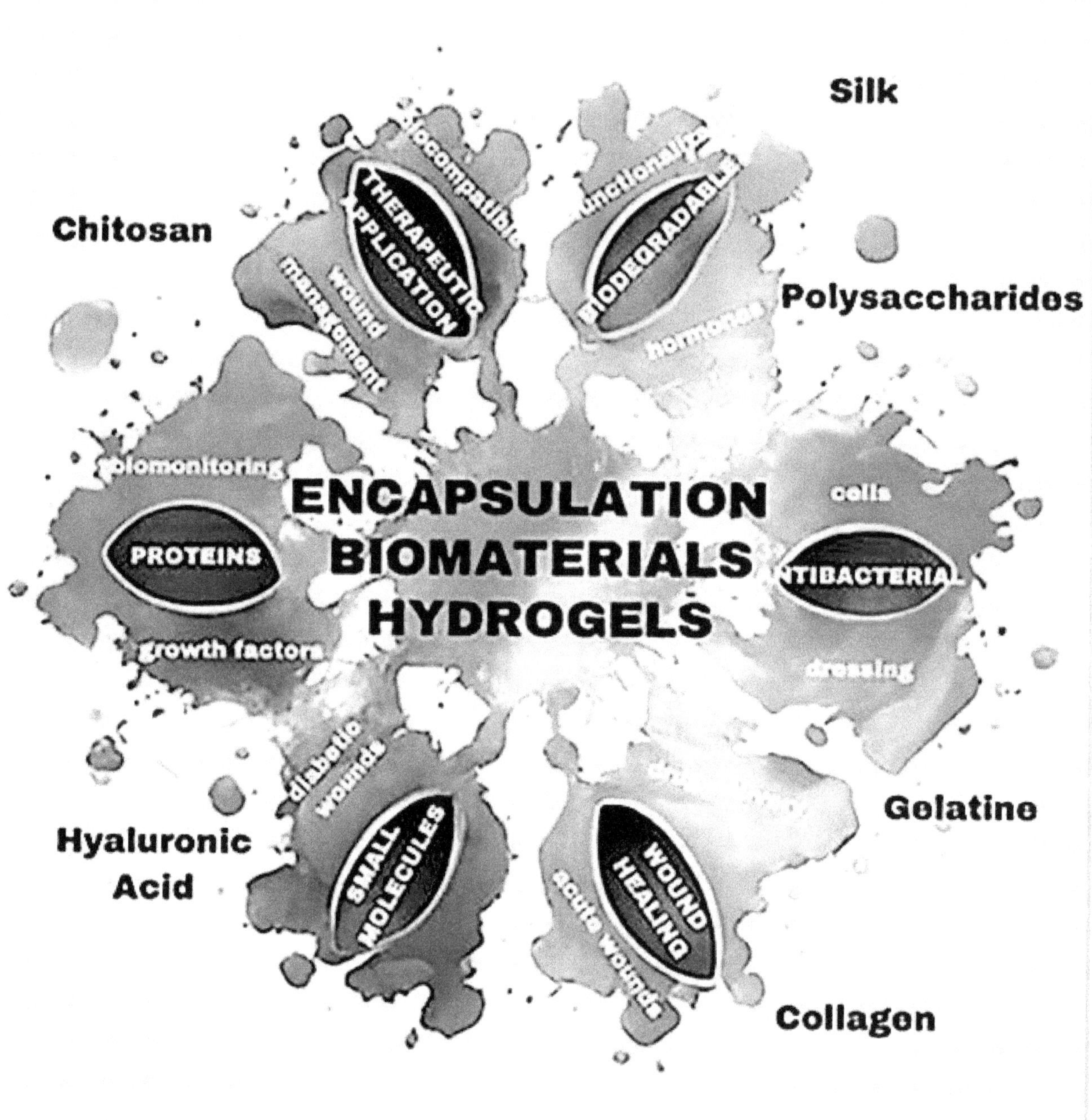


**Fig 1.Biomaterial scaffolds with therapeutics application(4)**

**Classification of Biomaterial Used for Implant Scaffolds**

Polymer degradability and hydrophilicity or hydrophobicity are determined by the structure-property relationship (SPR), arrangement, and functional groups of each unit(5).Figure 2 displays the classification of monomers intended to form distinct scaffolds according to their sources and their decomposition patterns.

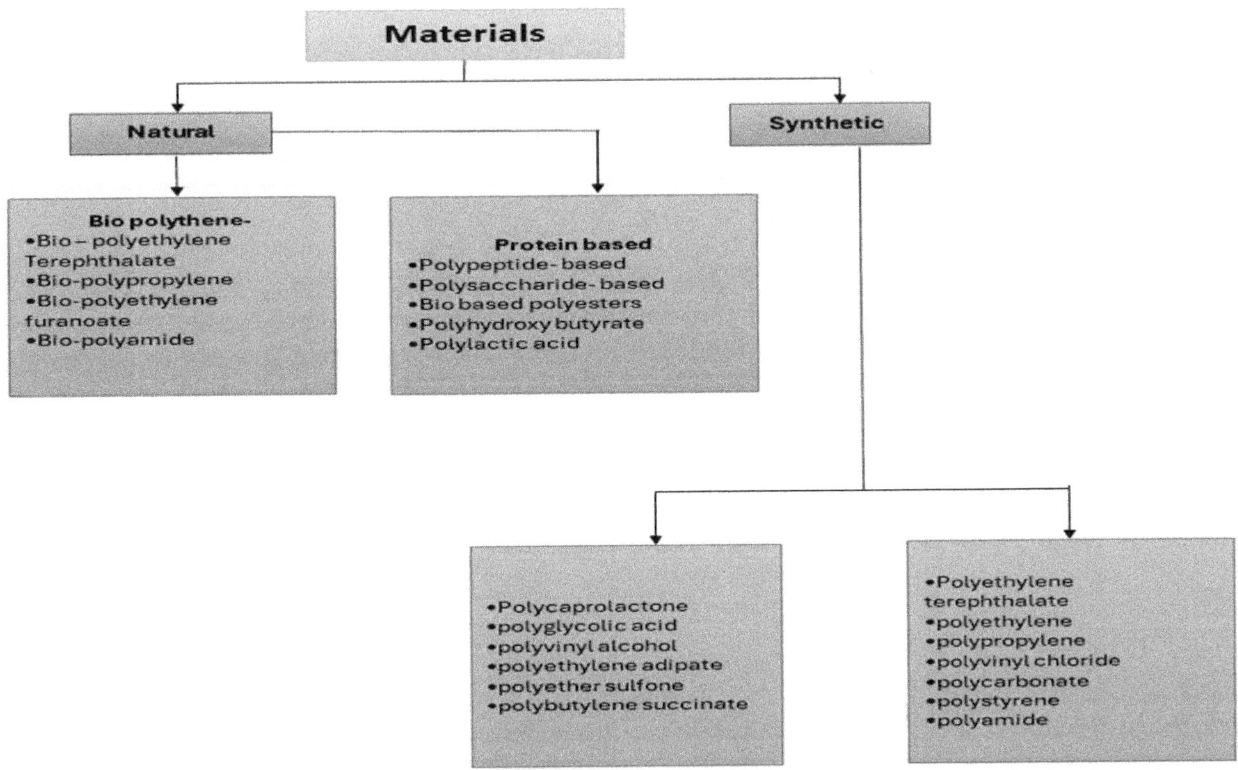


**Fig 2.Classification of biomaterialsused to build various scaffolds.**

**NaturalBio-Composites**

Polymers made from natural resources were exploited for many decades to produce a spectrum of scaffolds as chemotherapy for tumors. Particles are usually divided into distinct groups owing to its content& elements: polypeptide-based, protein-based, polysaccharide-based and bio-functional units reflect their activity, hemocompatibility, three-dimensional form, and underpinning composition within them. Whereas polymers made from natural materials provide an ease in creating anticancer scaffolds, they also have negatives, among them being exposed to microbial or fungal contamination, unwanted antigenicity,poor breakdown characteristic(6).For examplepolysaccharides are inexpensive to produce, easily derivatized, and have strong bio-resorb ability and biological compatibility. They are a good fit for therapeutic usage since they include features that are comparable to the ECM. There are two distinct types of polysaccharides: stored polysaccharides and structured polysaccharides. Crustacean shells contain chitin, which is a structural polysaccharide, while starch and glycogen are instances of storing polysaccharides(7). Dextran is one of the several polysaccharides that has been effectively used in therapeutic applications. This is a hydrophilic biopolymer of carbohydrates that breaks down unsuitable physical surroundings without compromising the survival of cells(8).Therefore, these polymers may be adjusted to have the perfect properties for producing a framework that enables the key beneficial effects against cancer, depending on the kind, phase, and ecology of the disease.

**Synthetic Bio-Composites**

Synthetic biocompatible materials are artificially created mostly from petroleum-based hydrocarbons and polymers that exist naturally . These biomolecules are categorized into three distinct kinds, such as thermoplastic, elastomeric, and synthetic polymers. A synthetic polymer could provide birth to a new synthetic polymer by altering its primary structure,secondary chains . A structural framework of a synthetic material isinitially made up of connections composed of carbon but it also contain hydrogen and/or oxygen linkages . A deviation from this tendency amongst created substances is silicon, it consists of fewer carbon atoms & was consequently considered to be an inorganic substance. For instancePCL, or poly(ε-caprolactone), (7)PCL is a very resilient aliphatic polymer that finds extensive use in several biological contexts (9). It is a polymer with a low melting point of 60 °C with recurring hexanoate units. In addition to its outstanding physical elasticity, thermal resistance, bioresorbability, and rheological and viscous qualities, PCL is also bioresorbable. Rigid tissues (with the bones and dentistry applications) and soft tissues such as (skin, liver, cartilage, tendons, muscle, nerve endings, cornea, and vessels for blood) (10)have all been produced using PCL.

**Role of Advance Biomaterial in Medical Devices**

Introduction: Modern science, notably biomaterials, has altered various areas, including healthcare. Such biologically-interactive materials have permitted novel medical discoveries, better patient outcomes, and extended research and development. This section covers biomaterials' vast and vital relevance to health care and beyond.(12)

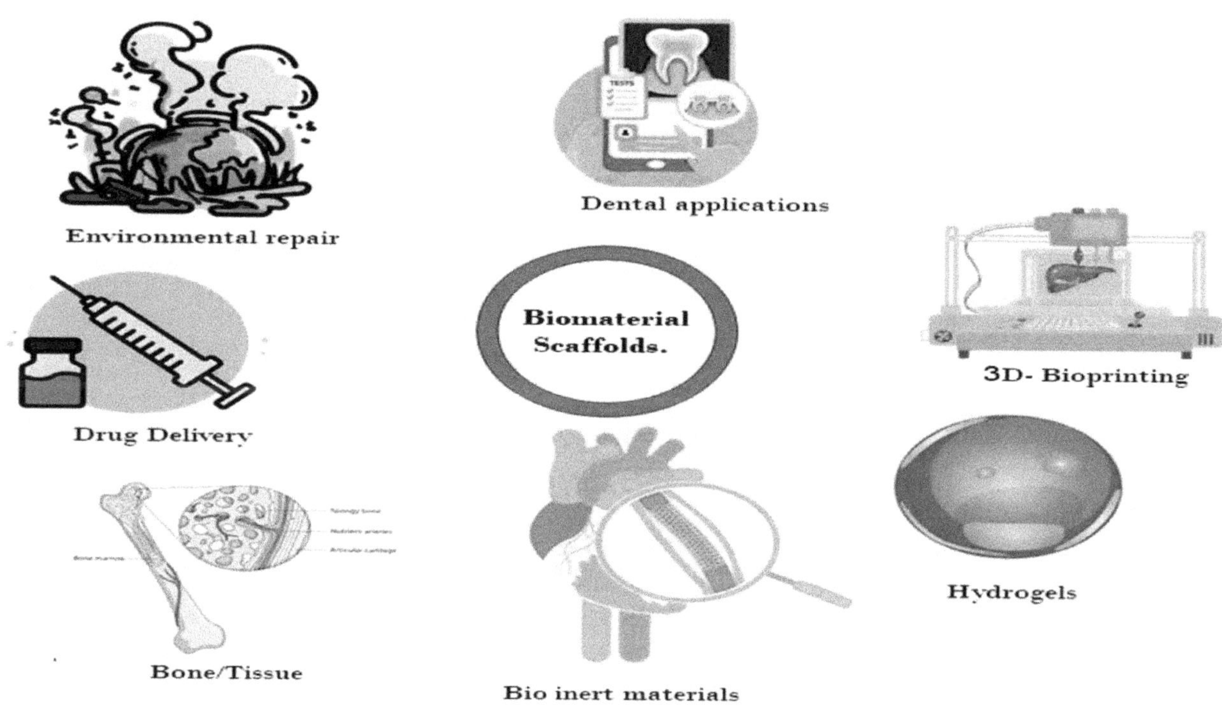


**Fig 3. Role of Bio medical in medical devices.**

**Supporting Healthcare Equipment and Implantable devices:**

Biomaterials play a vital role in medical device and implant development. Biomaterials support life-changing technology like pacemakers and knee replacements. The non-toxic, biocompatible, and body-integrating components are carefully selected. In addition to increasing comfort for patients, biomaterials in medical devices have increased implant lifespan and decreased problems(13).

**Polymers bring new potential in tissue engineering and medical regeneration[a10].**

- Scaffold materials, such as polymers that decompose and decellularized extracellular matrix, give a three-dimensional framework for tissue formation and regeneration. Coupled alongside stem cells and growth factors, these biomaterial-based scaffolds induce tissue repair, making it conceivable to reconstruct damaged organs and tissues(14).

**Improving Drug Delivery Systems.**

- In pharmaceuticals, biomaterials play a crucial role in drug delivery systems. Liposomes, micelles, and nanoparticles created from biomaterials aid encapsulate drugs, letting targeted and regulated release. These technologies provide for proper pharmaceutical dosing, limit unwanted effects, and increase treatment success. Biomaterial-based pharmaceutical delivery has altered medical interventions, particularly in cancer therapy and chronic disease management(15).

**Supporting Dental Applications.**

- Biomaterials are crucial to numerous dental applications. Dental implants manufactured from materials that are biocompatible, such as titanium, combine with jawbones to deliver strong tooth replacements. Furthermore, dental composites manufactured from resin-based materials are applied for tooth restorations, giving better aesthetics and strength(16).

**Improving Biocompatibility in Transplantation.**

- Biomaterials have boosted its biocompatibility in donor and tissue transplants. Surface modifications of implanted biomaterials have lowered immune responses and promoted tissue integration. That has resulted to improved rates of survival in transplant surgery and lessened the necessity for immunosuppressive drugs(17).

**Stimulating Cell Culture and Research.**

- In research laboratories, biomaterials are significant instruments for cell culture and tissue engineering studies. Biomaterial matrices create a setting that simulates the natural tissue microenvironment, promoting cell proliferation and differentiation. These matrices are used frequently in exploring cell conduct, pharmaceutical screening, and disease simulation(18).

**Application**

It is impossible to overestimate the significance of biomaterial for implant scaffolds in medicine as they're essential to the advancement of healthcare in many different ways. The following table lists the essential biomaterials applications that are significant to the medical field:

**Application**

**Hydrogels**

Hydrogels are three-dimensional, hydrophilic networks that can hold significant amounts of biological fluids like water. This property makes them useful for a variety of applications, including medication delivery, cell carriers, biosensors, and scaffolds in biological tissue technology. These show enormous potential for biological applications and can grow greatly in aqueous environments, mimicking the water content of the human body.

**Hydrogels for Autoimmune Repair**

Because self-healing hydrogels can mend themselves, much like organic materials like skin and bones, they have potential biological uses. By using techniques like free radical polymerization to produce hydrogels containing reversible oxime crosslinks, scientists may improve the mechanical characteristics of hydrogels and increase their ability to mend themselves. Hydrogels with self-healing properties also depend heavily on hydrophobic interactions.

**Biomaterial Scaffolds in Tissue Engineering and Regenerative Healthcare**

Damaged tissues and organs may heal and regenerate more easily with the use of biomaterial scaffolds and matrices. They are vital for novel therapies for diseases ranging from transplantation of organs to defects of the bones because they provide structural support and signals for development, differentiation, and tissue creation.

**Implants for Medical Purposes and Devices**

Dental implants, prosthetic limbs, coronary stents, replacements for joints, and other medical devices are all made using biomaterial scaffold implants. For millions of patients worldwide, these implants enhance quality of life, reduce pain, and restore function.

**Pharmaceutical Delivery Systems**

To increase pharmaceutical medications' efficacy, safety, and targeted distribution, drug delivery systems use biomaterials. By encapsulating medications in biodegradable carriers that enable local targeting, prolonged circulation, and controlled release, they improve treatment results and lessen side effects.

**Medical Imaging Contrast Agents and Mapping Probes**

Materials enhance the visibility of physique, pathologic changes, and molecular markers in medical imaging tests including CT, MRI, and ultrasonography. These imaging agents provide prompt diagnosis, accurate problem identification, and efficient therapeutic result monitoring.

**Biosensors and Diagnostic Tests**

Biomaterial composite are used in diagnostic tests and biological sensors for the purpose of identifying biological variables, biomolecules, and pathogens. Their capacity for biorecognition, signal transmission, and amplification enables the rapid, precise, and focused identification of illness biomarkers.

**Devices for Surgery and Wound Care**

To help with hemostasis, closure of wounds, and healing of tissues, biomaterials are utilized in medical sutures, tissue adhesives, and wound dressings. Those techniques improve patient rehabilitation, improve surgery results, hasten recovery, and lower healthcare expenses.

**Biological Compatibility Studies and Screening**

Biomaterials are useful research instruments for both in vitro and in vivo studies of biological compatibility, organ responses, and cell–material interactions. They contribute to the advancement of theragnostic and individualized medical research, which combines diagnosis and treatment into integrated platforms for accurate diagnosis, therapy monitoring, and customized care.

Hydrogels are hydrophilic, 3-D with the capacity to incorporate large volumes of water or biological fluids, they may be used as great options for biosensors, drug delivery vehicles, and cell transporters as well as scaffolds in biological tissue technology(19). In addition to their hydrophilic character, hydrogels—crosslinked three-dimensional networks of hydrophilic polymer chains—having capacity which stores enormous amounts of water(20) .As a result, in an aqueous media, the hydrogel structures may expand greatly.Given that water makes up the majority of the human body(21),hydrogels, which possess a tremendous deal of promise for biological applications .

**Hydrogelsfor Autoimmune Repair**

The capacity of organic materials, such as wood, skin, and bones, to repair themselves, is among their most amazing features. Thus, self-healing hydrogels provide an additional avenue for biological applications. Even though synthetic hydrogels are designed to resemble tissues from living organisms, majority of the moment they are incapable of healing themselves.This restriction will prevent it from being used for many applications that need a lot of stress. Because of this, scientists work very hard to enhance hydrogels‘ mechanical properties, especially their capacity for self-healing. For our ecosystems, an energy dissipation process is often involved in the process of fracture healing. Self-healing may occur in the presence of sacrificial bonds, which have the ability to break and then dynamically reconstruct either before to or during the failure. It has been reported that a variety of covalent and non-covalent interactions result in a regenerative hydrogel(22).

The process of creating novel hydrogels with reversible oxime crosslinks was explained. Because of their dynamic nature, they are capable of mending themselves. Free radical polymerization was used to copolymerize N,N-dimethylacrylamide (DMA) and diacetone acrylamide (DAA), resulting in copolymers with keto functional groups that were used to make these hydrogels(23). The hydrophilic copolymers that were supplied were then covalently crosslinked with difunctional alkoxyamine to produce hydrogels using the oxime manufacturing process. In addition to their ability to repair themselves effectively, oxime linkages' flexibility led to mutable gel-to-sol transitions when more monofunctional alkoxyamine was introduced at ambient temperature.

Hydrophobic interactionsmay play a vital function in addition to their chemical equivalents as a cross-linker for hydrogels that mend themselves. By copolymerizing a hydrophilic monomer, acrylamide, with an enormous hydrophobic monomer, stearyl methacrylate and dococyl acrylate, within a micellar solution of sodium dodecyl sulfate, Okay's group produced a hydrogel (24). Micelles form once the salt is added, and they dissolve hydrophobes. It has been shown that this hydrogel has a high level of toughness because of the short hydrophobic contact lifetime between the dococyl acrylate and stearyl methacrylate blocks.

In a recent work, free-radical polymerization was used to create hydrogels with cationic substituents. Because the cationic replacements in the gel networks intercalated into the Micromica interlayers, the hydrogels stuck strongly when an aqueous dispersion of Micaromica was applied to the surface. As the hydrogels' water to mineral component ratio dropped, the bonding strength increased and achieved a breaking load of 10 kg(25).

**Biomaterials are used in tissue engineering and regenerative healthcare** :Biomaterial scaffolds and matrices areused facilitate the repair and regrowth of injured tissues and organs. The creation of innovative therapeutics for illnesses ranging from organ transplantation to bone abnormalities is made possible by their ability to offer structural support and signals for development, differentiation, and tissue formation (26).

**Implants for medical purposes and devices:**Scaffold implants for teeth, artificial limbs, cardiac stents, replacing joints, and other devices using biomaterials are among the many applications for which they are used. To millions of patients globally, implants like these enhance quality of life, relieve pain, and recover function (27).

**Pharmaceutical delivery systems:** To improve the effectiveness, safety, and targeted distribution of pharmacological drugs, materials are used in systems for drug delivery. Biomaterials improve therapeutic results and reduce adverse effects by enclosing pharmaceuticals inside biocompatible carriers that allow for controlled release, extended circulation, and site-specific targeting (28).

Biomaterials are used for contrast agents and mapping probes for medical imaging tests including computed tomography (CT), ultrasonography, and electromagnetic resonance imaging (MRI). Overall improved visibility of anatomy, pathologic alterations, and molecular markers made possible by these biomaterial-based imaging compounds makes it easier to identify problems early, make precise diagnoses, and track the effectiveness of therapy (29). Composites play a crucial role in biosensors and diagnostic tests that identify infections, biomolecules, and biological variables. They possess distinct qualities including biorecognition, transmission of signals, and multiplication capabilities. Disease biomarkers may be found quickly, accurately, and selectively thanks to biological sensors .

**Devices for surgery and wound care:** To aid in hemostasis, wound closure, and tissue healing, biomaterials are used in medical sutures, tissue adhesives, and dressings for wounds(30),(31). These biomaterial-based solutions speed up the recovery process, improve surgical results, and save healthcare expenses while also increasing patient rehabilitation.

**Screening and studies on biological compatibility:** Materials are useful instruments for investigating biological compatibility, organ responses, and cell–material interactions both in vitro and in vivo (32).

Materials are driving advances in the fields of theragnostic and individualized healthcare, which integrate treatment and diagnosis into unified platforms (33),(34). Theranostic techniques provide accurate evaluation, therapy tracking, and customized therapy by combining biomaterial-based drug delivery systems with targeted medicines and image analysis technologies.

**Challenges**

Current breakthroughs in biomaterials for implanted scaffolds in cancer therapy have showed considerable promise in boosting treatment results. (35).However, some difficulties still need to be solved to further increase their effectiveness.Despite the fact that biomaterial scaffold-based implants have been successfully explored for cancer immunotherapy, a number of issues still need to be resolved before they can be more easily clinically translated.

A few of the main obstacles include batch variability, the composition and function of biomaterials, the pharmacokinetics and release mechanism of bioactive substances or gene therapies, and the difficulty of controlling cell behavior for cell-based products. The usage of numerous nucleic acid combinations or the release of a therapy involving the use of additional materials are examples of how this becomes more difficult as complexity increases(36).

Initially, a variety of imaging-guided injection methods have to be created in order to inject the biomaterials into deep tumors. Secondly, as the majority of the study mentioned above overlooked the complex scenario of tumor-induced immunosuppression, more attention needs to be focused on developing an immunosuppressive tumor model.

Third, it is important to guarantee the reproducibility of biomaterial scaffold-based implants, particularly with regard to the drug release profile. Furthermore, a comprehensive assessment of the possible long-term toxicity of biomaterial scaffold-based implants is necessary, with particular attention to the chronic inflammation and immunological response triggered by the degradation products(37).

It should be mentioned that the biomaterial scaffold itself has the ability to stimulate and/or activate an innate immune response that may already be present and contribute to the anticancer process(38). Given that biomaterial scaffold-based implants often pass through regulatory barriers pertaining to medications, devices, and tissue/cell transplants. As acellular techniques are much simpler to get clinical approval for than cell-based treatments, the present formula choices should be as straightforward as feasible(39).

**Clinical Significance**

Cancer therapy has witnessed tremendous breakthroughs with the introduction of biomaterials for implant scaffolds. These biomaterials serve a key role in increasing the success of cancer treatment by providing a supporting framework for tissue regeneration and targeted medication administration(40).

Clinical Significance in Current Advancements of Biomaterials for Implant Scaffolds Related to cancer are-

**Cancer Scaffolds Immunotherapy**

Along with surgery, chemotherapy, and radiation therapy, immunotherapy is another tactic used in the battle against cancer. It has lately been regarded as an additional anti-cancer therapeutic approach. Immunotherapy aims to produce a strong and long-lasting immune response against cancerous cells. Immunotherapy techniques may work by either supplying extrinsic immune system elements, including certain proteins that the immune system can target, or by boosting the intrinsic immune system. Immune system inhibitors, cancer vaccines, and monoclonal antibodies are the three major categories of traditional immunotherapy for cancer. Current immune oncology has a modest success rate, despite the field's tremendous developments. These treatments currently require laborious and costly laboratory procedures, which have led to poor ex vivo engineered cell homing in lymph nodes thus far. This suggests that current approaches should be combined with other scientific fields in order to successfully treat a larger population of cancer patients and eradicate the disease permanently(41).

**Local Concurrent Chemotherapy Delivery& Agent Anti-Angiogenic**

Anti-angiogenic treatment often has a lower toxicity and incidence to cause resistance in contrast to chemotherapy, which makes it advantageous to employ as an anti-neoplastic agent. Nevertheless, anti-angiogenic therapy by itself has only modestly improved patient survival; as a result, anti-angiogenic therapy must be combined with other cutting-edge therapeutic approaches. Thus far, local administration of anti-angiogenic medications has included the systemic introduction of a chemotherapeutic agent.(42).

**Local Polychemotherapy Delivery**

Combined chemotherapy has been used extensively because it allows for the delivery of lower dosages of each agent to minimize cytotoxicity and resistance development. It is crucial to consider the following factors when creating a combinational chemotherapy regimen that will work well together, have minimal cytotoxicity, and reduce the likelihood of resistance: (i) selecting medications with distinct modes of action; (ii) employing agents with distinct toxicities; and (iii) using medications with demonstrated monotherapy efficacy.The systemic administration of combinational medication has been the focus of current methods.

**Gene Therapy as a Drug Delivery Alternative**

Delivering a gene that replaces a damaged gene was the initial goal of gene therapy. To change or regulate the course of cellular function, gene therapy has expanded to include the insertion of a new gene that encodes a particular therapeutic protein to a faulty spot. Scientists have successfully found proteins for a variety of therapeutic applications, including the treatment of cancer. Nevertheless, the delivery of recombinant proteins has proven to be problematic, prompting the employment of gene therapy as a substitute method for delivering the gene encoding the desired protein. Since DNAs have longer half-lives than proteins, gene therapy enables growth factors to be more bioavailable for longer than protein delivery.

In addition, producing these recombinant proteins is more costly and challenging than producing the genes encoding the growth factors. The proteins are produced in vivo using gene therapy, which enables the delivery of the proteins in a form that is more physiologically active and allows for more precise post-translational modification and tertiary structure creation.(43)

**Advantage and Disadvantage**[a15]

**Advantages**

Biomaterials for implant scaffold serves a number of advantages, including the following:

**Biocompatibility**: Materials ought to be accepted by the human body without triggering harmful reactions or unfavorable immune responses. Biomaterials which are appropriate for medical applications and implants should be compatible as it guarantees that they may interact with human tissues and fluids and not cause damage (44).

**Bioactivity**: Certain biomaterials are naturally bioactive, which means they may interact with biological substances or stimulate certain cell reactions. Bioactive biomaterials promote molecular signaling, cell adhesion, or tissue regeneration, aiding in the body's repair and healing processes (45).

**Mechanical characteristics**: In order to endure physiological stresses and preserve structural integrity in vivo, biomaterials need to have the right mechanical characteristics. These features vary based on the intended use, with materials ranging from flexible polymers for scaffolds used in tissue engineering to stiff metal for bearing load implants (27).

**Degradation kinetics**: Enzyme or hydrolytic polymer chain cleavage is two ways in which some biomaterials are intended to break down over time. Biodegradable materials provide the regulated release or provisional support of medicinal substances, which may then be gradually assimilated or reabsorbed by the body (28).

**Surface alterations**: The biocompatibility, bioactivity, or usefulness of biomaterial surfaces may all be improved. To enable customized interactions with biological systems, surface alterations might include coating with bioactive compounds, anchoring of cell-adhesive peptides, or inclusion of drug-releasing particles(46).

**Disadvantages**

**Immunogenicity and biological compatibility**

Hydrogels must be biocompatible in order for their usage in biomedical applications to be both safe and successful. The therapeutic value of hydrogel breakdown products or persistent crosslinking agents may be limited due to the possibility of inducing inflammatory or immunological responses in vivo(4).

**Durability and mechanical features**

Hydrogels must have sufficient mechanical stability and characteristics in order to maintain their firmness and functional capabilities in vivo. The durability and effectiveness of hydrogel-based treatments may be jeopardized by poor mechanical qualities or quick deterioration(47).

**Regulating the release of drugs kinetics**

In drug delivery uses, precise control of drug release kinetics is crucial for maximizing therapeutic effectiveness and reducing adverse effects, especially in complex biological contexts(15).

**Biomimetic structures for tissue engineering**

It is still very difficult to fabricate scaffolds for synthetic tissue engineering that have the right structural and biochemical signals to encourage regeneration of tissue. In tissue science to be effective, hydrogel-based constructions must mimic the intricate hierarchical organization and milieu of genuine tissues(48).

**Conclusive remark**

The fields of immunotherapy and biomaterials have united to form a growing body of research that has the potential to overcome clinical and scientific obstacles that now limit cancer immunotherapy(49).Both cancer treatment and the creation of biomaterials are expanding at startling speeds, with new findings and clinical trials every year. New developments in biomaterial delivery are constantly being published, demonstrating our growing ability to selectively and proactively control medicines. (50),(51)Findings such as those discussed in this book chapter emphasizes the fascinating potential of biomaterial delivery techniques, whether injected, sprayed, or added into the body, as well as the potential for a potent synergy with the expanding array of diminutive molecule, amino acid, or cell-based immunotherapies.

Further studies must expand our grasp of the layout requirements in order for academics to identify which issues will probably affect the direction for future study on this subject. Which is needed to create the "ideal" immunotherapeutic biomaterial—assuming that for instance material can be produced. The essential release patterns of adjuvants and antigenics among several criteria, such as the acceptable durability of the material vs. degradation rates, is a difficult process to accomplish. An excessively quick absorption of adjuvants to the immune system might lead to immunity tolerance, while an excessively delayed release could not properly align with antigen presentation, resulting in inadequate stimulation of dendritic cells(36).

An inherent defensive reaction to an intrinsically foreign carrier component and its impact (or lack thereof) on immunological therapy, whether overt or covert, are further concerns. Additionally, new research indicates that personalized healthcare is the way of the future, and biomaterial-based medications would recquire to be adjusted to each patient's distinctive immunological response patterns. Therefore, even though the modern designs indicate that the field has a lot to provide in regards to improving therapeutic results and bringing back informative pharmacological courses, which continue to be very important problem and research avenues that need to be thoroughly examined in order to bring such a wide range of biomaterial antigens to the clinic.

**Reference**


1. Chen FM, Liu X. Advancing biomaterials of human origin for tissue engineering. Prog Polym Sci. 2016 Feb 1;53:86–168.

2. Li Q, Mai YW. Biomaterials for Implants and Scaffolds. Vol. 8. 2017.

3. Tripathi S, Mandal SS, Bauri S, Maiti P. 3D bioprinting and its innovative approach for biomedical applications. MedComm. 2022 Dec 24;4(1):e194.

4. Chelu M, Musuc AM, Chelu M, Musuc AM. Biomaterials-Based Hydrogels for Therapeutic Applications [Internet]. IntechOpen; 2024 [cited 2024 Jun 23]. Available from: https://www.intechopen.com/online-first/1183935

5. ResearchGate [Internet]. [cited 2024 Jun 3]. Figure 1. Classification of biomaterials used to prepare 3D scaffolds... Available from: https://www.researchgate.net/figure/Classification-of-biomaterials-used-to-prepare-3D-scaffolds-according-to-their-sources_fig1_366013812

6. Shahriar S, Andrabi SM, Islam F, An J, Schindler S, Matis M, et al. Next-Generation 3D Scaffolds for Nano-Based Chemotherapeutics Delivery and Cancer Treatment. Pharmaceutics. 2022 Dec 3;14:2712.

7. Vach Agocsova S, Culenova M, Birova I, Omanikova L, Moncmanova B, Danisovic L, et al. Resorbable Biomaterials Used for 3D Scaffolds in Tissue Engineering: A Review. Materials. 2023 Jun 8;16(12):4267.

8. Ghaffari R, Salimi-Kenari H, Fahimipour F, Rabiee SM, Adeli H, Dashtimoghadam E. Fabrication and characterization of dextran/nanocrystalline β-tricalcium phosphate nanocomposite hydrogel scaffolds. Int J Biol Macromol. 2020 Apr 1;148:434–48.

9. Kannan R, Wei G, Ma PX. Chapter 2 - Synthetic polymeric biomaterials for tissue engineering. In: Boccaccini AR, Ma PX, Liverani L, editors. Tissue Engineering Using Ceramics and Polymers (Third Edition) [Internet]. Woodhead Publishing; 2022 [cited 2024 Jun 23]. p. 41–74. (Woodhead Publishing Series in Biomaterials). Available from: https://www.sciencedirect.com/science/article/pii/B9780128205082000234

10. Ilha J, Figueiro A, Grando MC, Macuvele DLP, Fiori MA, Padoin N, et al. Nanosilica:Polycaprolactone ratio and heat treatment modify the wettability of nanosilica/polycaprolactone coatings for application in aqueous systems. Surf Interfaces. 2022 Jul 1;31:101997.

11. ResearchGate [Internet]. [cited 2024 Jun 5]. Table 2: List of commercial polymeric scaffolds' products. Available from: https://www.researchgate.net/figure/List-of-commercial-polymeric-scaffolds-products_tbl2_258379053

12. Todros S, Todesco M, Bagno A. Biomaterials and Their Biomedical Applications: From Replacement to Regeneration. Processes. 2021 Nov;9(11):1949.

13. Bhat S, Kumar A. Biomaterials and bioengineering tomorrow's healthcare. Biomatter. 2013 Jul 1;3(3):e24717.

14. Loh QL, Choong C. Three-Dimensional Scaffolds for Tissue Engineering Applications: Role of Porosity and Pore Size. Tissue Eng Part B Rev. 2013 Dec;19(6):485–502.

15. Ezike TC, Okpala US, Onoja UL, Nwike CP, Ezeako EC, Okpara OJ, et al. Advances in drug delivery systems, challenges and future directions. Heliyon. 2023 Jun 24;9(6):e17488.

16. Hakim LK, Yari A, Nikparto N, Mehraban SH, Cheperli S, Asadi A, et al. The current applications of nano and biomaterials in drug delivery of dental implant. BMC Oral Health. 2024 Jan 24;24:126.

17. Lee KY, Mooney DJ. Hydrogels for tissue engineering. Chem Rev. 2001 Jul;101(7):1869–79.

18. Eldeeb AE, Salah S, Elkasabgy NA. Biomaterials for Tissue Engineering Applications and Current Updates in the Field: A Comprehensive Review. AAPS PharmSciTech. 2022 Sep 26;23(7):267.

19. Chai Q, Jiao Y, Yu X. Hydrogels for Biomedical Applications: Their Characteristics and the Mechanisms behind Them. Gels. 2017 Jan 24;3(1):6.

20. Daniele MA, Adams AA, Naciri J, North SH, Ligler FS. Interpenetrating networks based on gelatin methacrylamide and PEG formed using concurrent thiol click chemistries for hydrogel tissue engineering scaffolds. Biomaterials. 2014 Feb;35(6):1845–56.

21. Billiet T, Vandenhaute M, Schelfhout J, Van Vlierberghe S, Dubruel P. A review of trends and limitations in hydrogel-rapid prototyping for tissue engineering. Biomaterials. 2012 Sep;33(26):6020–41.

22. MD DLT. News-Medical. 2022 [cited 2024 Jun 5]. Applications of Biomaterials in Healthcare and Medicine. Available from: https://www.news-medical.net/health/Applications-of-Biomaterials-in-Healthcare-and-Medicine.aspx

23. Ding R, Yu X, Wang P, Zhang J, Zhou Y, Cao X, et al. Hybrid photosensitizer based on amphiphilic block copolymer stabilized silver nanoparticles for highly efficient photodynamic inactivation of bacteria. RSC Adv. 2016;6(24):20392–8.

24. Nathan R. Richbourg, Richbourg NR, Nicholas A. Peppas, Peppas NA, Vassilios I. Sikavitsas, Sikavitsas VI. Tuning the biomimetic behavior of scaffolds for regenerative medicine through surface modifications. J Tissue Eng Regen Med. 2019 Aug 1;13(8):1275–93.

25. Yu X, Chen X, Chai Q, Ayres N. Synthesis of polymer organogelators using hydrogen bonding as physical cross-links. Colloid Polym Sci. 2016 Jan 1;294(1):59–68.

26. Processes | Free Full-Text | Advanced Biomedical Applications of Multifunctional Natural and Synthetic Biomaterials [Internet]. [cited 2024 Jun 23]. Available from: https://www.mdpi.com/2227-9717/11/9/2696

27. Polymers | Free Full-Text | Biomaterials as Implants in the Orthopedic Field for Regenerative Medicine: Metal versus Synthetic Polymers [Internet]. [cited 2024 Jun 23]. Available from: https://www.mdpi.com/2073-4360/15/12/2601

28. Gels | Free Full-Text | Polymer-Based Hydrogels Applied in Drug Delivery: An Overview [Internet]. [cited 2024 Jun 23]. Available from: https://www.mdpi.com/2310-2861/9/7/523

29. Zhang YS, Yao J. Imaging Biomaterial–Tissue Interactions. Trends Biotechnol. 2018 Apr 1;36(4):403–14.

30. Pharmaceutics | Free Full-Text | Polymeric Materials for Hemostatic Wound Healing [Internet]. [cited 2024 Jun 23]. Available from: https://www.mdpi.com/1999-4923/13/12/2127

31. IJMS | Free Full-Text | Chitosan-Based Biomaterials for Hemostatic Applications: A Review of Recent Advances [Internet]. [cited 2024 Jun 23]. Available from: https://www.mdpi.com/1422-0067/24/13/10540

32. Processes | Free Full-Text | Advanced Biomedical Applications of Multifunctional Natural and Synthetic Biomaterials [Internet]. [cited 2024 Jun 23]. Available from: https://www.mdpi.com/2227-9717/11/9/2696

33. Kim H, Kwak G, Kim K, Yoon HY, Kwon IC. Theranostic designs of biomaterials for precision medicine in cancer therapy. Biomaterials. 2019 Aug 1;213:119207.

34. JPM | Free Full-Text | The Promise of Nanotechnology in Personalized Medicine [Internet]. [cited 2024 Jun 23]. Available from: https://www.mdpi.com/2075-4426/12/5/673

35. Li J, Luo Y, Li B, Xia Y, Wang H, Fu C. Implantable and Injectable Biomaterial Scaffolds for Cancer Immunotherapy. Front Bioeng Biotechnol [Internet]. 2020 Nov 30 [cited 2024 Jun 7];8. Available from: https://www.frontiersin.org/articles/10.3389/fbioe.2020.612950

36. Biomaterial-assisted targeted modulation of immune cells in cancer treatment | Nature Materials [Internet]. [cited 2024 Jun 7]. Available from: https://www.nature.com/articles/s41563-018-0147-9

37. Bersani F, Lee J, Yu M, Morris R, Desai R, Ramaswamy S, et al. Bioengineered implantable scaffolds as a tool to study stromal-derived factors in metastatic cancer models. Cancer Res. 2014 Dec 15;74(24):7229–38.

38. Yang C, Blum NT, Lin J, Qu J, Huang P. Biomaterial scaffold-based local drug delivery systems for cancer immunotherapy. Sci Bull. 2020 Sep 15;65(17):1489–504.

39. Beatty GL, Gladney WL. Immune escape mechanisms as a guide for cancer immunotherapy. Clin Cancer Res Off J Am Assoc Cancer Res. 2015 Feb 15;21(4):687–92.

40. Peer D, Karp JM, Hong S, Farokhzad OC, Margalit R, Langer R. Nanocarriers as an emerging platform for cancer therapy. Nat Nanotechnol. 2007 Dec;2(12):751–60.

41. Langer R, Phd D. Langer, R. & Tirrell, D. A. Designing materials for biology and medicine. Nature 428, 487-492. Nature. 2004 May 1;428:487–92.

42. Tissue engineering--current challenges and expanding opportunities - PubMed [Internet]. [cited 2024 Jun 7]. Available from: https://pubmed.ncbi.nlm.nih.gov/11834815/

43. Chew SA, Danti S. Biomaterial-Based Implantable Devices for Cancer Therapy. Adv Healthc Mater. 2017 Jan;6(2):1600766.

44. Processes | Free Full-Text | Advanced Biomedical Applications of Multifunctional Natural and Synthetic Biomaterials [Internet]. [cited 2024 Jun 23]. Available from: https://www.mdpi.com/2227-9717/11/9/2696

45. Mohamed Alshangiti D, K. El-damhougy T, Zaher A, Madani M, Ghobashy MM. Revolutionizing biomedicine: advancements, applications, and prospects of nanocomposite macromolecular carbohydrate-based hydrogel biomaterials: a review. RSC Adv. 2023;13(50):35251–91.

46. Pharmaceutics | Free Full-Text | Emerging Role of Hydrogels in Drug Delivery Systems, Tissue Engineering and Wound Management [Internet]. [cited 2024 Jun 23]. Available from: https://www.mdpi.com/1999-4923/13/3/357

47. Atia GAN, Shalaby HK, Ali NG, Morsy SM, Ghobashy MM, Attia HAN, et al. New Challenges and Prospective Applications of Three-Dimensional Bioactive Polymeric Hydrogels in Oral and Craniofacial Tissue Engineering: A Narrative Review. Pharmaceuticals. 2023 May 5;16(5):702.

48. Muzzio N, Moya S, Romero G. Multifunctional Scaffolds and Synergistic Strategies in Tissue Engineering and Regenerative Medicine. Pharmaceutics. 2021 May 26;13(6):792.

49. Chew SA, Danti S. Biomaterial-Based Implantable Devices for Cancer Therapy. Adv Healthc Mater. 2017;6(2):1600766.

50. Matrix-binding checkpoint immunotherapies enhance antitumor efficacy and reduce adverse events | Science Translational Medicine [Internet]. [cited 2024 Jun 7]. Available from: https://www.science.org/doi/full/10.1126/scitranslmed.aan0401

51. Kennedy S, Roco C, Déléris A, Spoerri P, Cezar C, Weaver J, et al. Improved magnetic regulation of delivery profiles from ferrogels. Biomaterials. 2018 Apr 1;161:179–89.

CHAPTER SIX

# ADVANCE BIOMATERIALS IN CANCER IMMUNOTHERAPY

**Mani Sharma**[a]

[a] CSIR-Indian Institute of Chemical Technology, Tarnaka, Hyderabad, Secunderabad-500007, Telangana , India

## Introduction

Cancer immunotherapy has emerged as a groundbreaking approach for treating cancer by harnessing the power of the immune system to recognize and eliminate cancerous cells. Biomaterials play a crucial role in advancing cancer immunotherapy by serving as carriers for immunomodulatory agents, facilitating targeted delivery to the tumor microenvironment, and enhancing therapeutic efficacy. This chapter explores the recent advancements and applications of biomaterials in cancer immunotherapy, focusing on key strategies, challenges, and future directions in this rapidly evolving field.

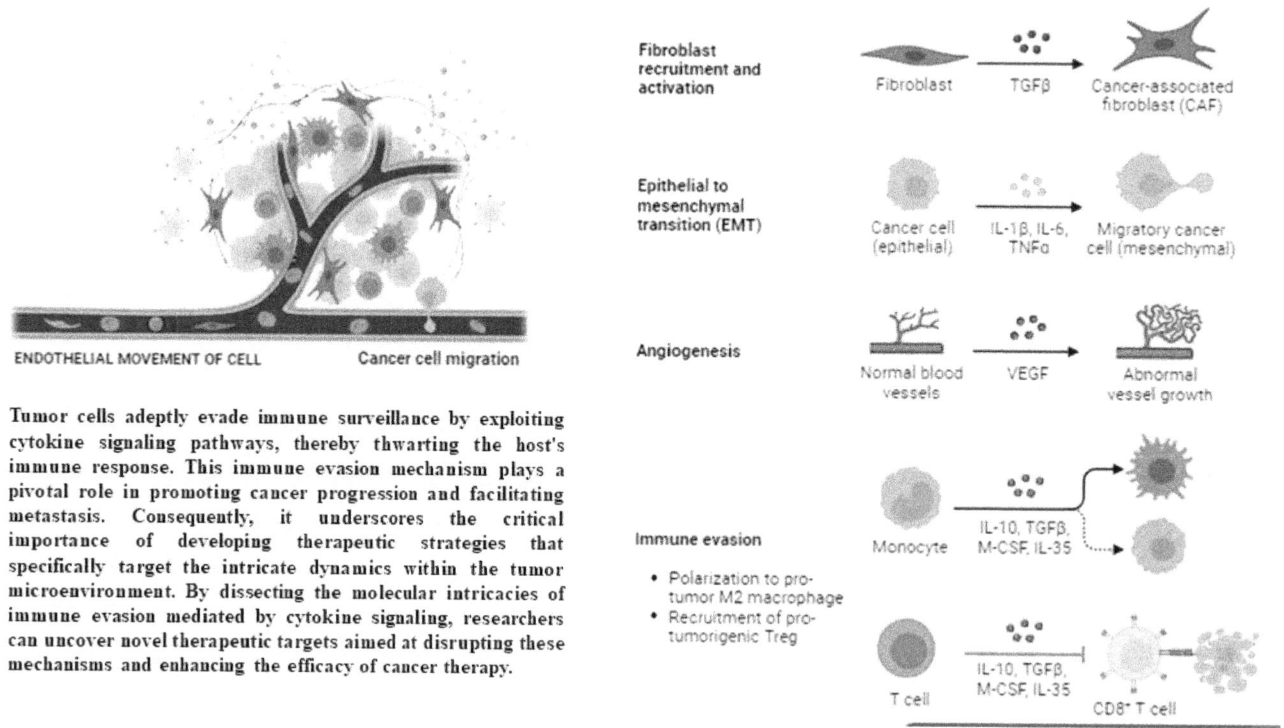


Enter Caption

Cancer remains a formidable challenge in modern medicine, with conventional treatments often failing to achieve durable responses and cure. In recent years, cancer immunotherapy has emerged as a revolutionary approach, leveraging the power of the immune system to recognize and eliminate cancerous cells. While immunotherapy has shown remarkable success in some patients, challenges such as immune evasion, off-target effects, and limited efficacy in certain cancer types persist. Advanced biomaterials offer promising solutions to overcome these challenges, enabling precise delivery of immunomodulatory agents, enhancing immune cell activation, and promoting sustained antitumor immune responses within the tumor microenvironment.

The immune system plays a central role in surveilling and eradicating abnormal cells, including cancer cells. However, tumors often develop mechanisms to evade immune detection and suppression, enabling them to proliferate and metastasize. Cancer immunotherapy aims to overcome these immune evasion mechanisms and activate the immune system to recognize and attack cancer cells. Biomaterial-based approaches in cancer immunotherapy focus on enhancing immune cell activation, modulating immune responses, and promoting sustained antitumor immunity within the tumor microenvironment.

**Harnessing the Immune System**

Harnessing the immune system represents a groundbreaking approach in cancer treatment, aiming to leverage the body's natural defense mechanisms to recognize and eliminate cancerous cells. The immune system is equipped with a sophisticated network of cells, tissues, and molecules that work together to defend against foreign invaders, including pathogens and abnormal cells. Among the key players in this defense system are T cells, B cells, natural killer (NK) cells, dendritic cells, and various cytokines and chemokines. These immune cells collaborate to identify, target, and destroy cancer cells through a process known as immunosurveillance.

However, cancer cells have evolved multiple strategies to evade immune detection and destruction, allowing them to proliferate and spread unchecked. These mechanisms include downregulation of major histocompatibility complex (MHC) molecules, secretion of immunosuppressive cytokines, and expression of immune checkpoint proteins that inhibit T cell activation and function. Cancer immunotherapy seeks to overcome these immune evasion mechanisms and reinvigorate the immune response against cancer cells.

One of the most successful approaches in cancer immunotherapy is the use of checkpoint inhibitors, which block inhibitory pathways that suppress T cell activation and function. Checkpoint molecules such as programmed cell death protein 1 (PD-1) and cytotoxic T-lymphocyte-associated protein 4 (CTLA-4) act as brakes on the immune system, preventing excessive activation and autoimmunity. However, tumors exploit these checkpoints to evade immune surveillance. Checkpoint inhibitors release these brakes, allowing T cells to recognize and attack cancer cells more effectively.

Biomaterials play a crucial role in enhancing the efficacy of checkpoint inhibitors by enabling localized and sustained delivery to the tumor microenvironment. Nanoparticle-based delivery systems, for example, can encapsulate checkpoint inhibitors and target them specifically to tumor-infiltrating immune cells, such as T cells and dendritic cells. This targeted delivery minimizes systemic exposure and off-target effects while maximizing therapeutic efficacy within the tumor.

In addition to checkpoint inhibitors, cytokines also play a vital role in regulating immune responses and orchestrating antitumor immunity. Interleukin-2 (IL-2) and interferon-alpha (IFN-α), for example, stimulate the activation and proliferation of T cells and NK cells, enhancing their cytotoxic activity against cancer cells. However, systemic administration of cytokines can lead to dose-limiting toxicities. Biomaterial-based delivery systems offer a solution by enabling localized and controlled release of cytokines directly to the tumor site, thereby enhancing immune cell activation and effector functions within the tumor microenvironment.

Furthermore, biomaterials can be engineered to deliver tumor antigens and adjuvants to antigen-presenting cells, such as dendritic cells, promoting their activation and antigen presentation to T cells. This antigen presentation primes T cells to recognize and attack cancer cells bearing the same antigens, thus enhancing the antitumor immune response. Particulate carriers, such as liposomes or polymeric nanoparticles, can encapsulate tumor antigens and adjuvants, enhancing their uptake by antigen-presenting cells and triggering robust immune responses.

In conclusion, harnessing the immune system represents a promising approach in cancer treatment, with biomaterials playing a crucial role in enhancing the efficacy and safety of immunotherapeutic agents. By enabling precise delivery of checkpoint inhibitors, cytokines, and tumor antigens to the tumor microenvironment, biomaterial-based approaches offer new opportunities for targeted and personalized cancer treatment. Further research and development in this field hold the potential to revolutionize cancer therapy and improve patient outcomes.

Checkpoint Inhibitor Delivery:

Checkpoint inhibitors, such as programmed cell death protein 1 (PD-1) and cytotoxic T-lymphocyte-associated protein 4 (CTLA-4) inhibitors, have revolutionized cancer treatment by blocking immune checkpoint pathways and unleashing antitumor immune responses. Biomaterials offer a versatile platform for delivering checkpoint inhibitors to the tumor site while minimizing systemic toxicity. Nanoparticle-based delivery systems can encapsulate checkpoint inhibitors and target them to tumor-infiltrating immune cells, such as T cells and dendritic cells, within the tumor microenvironment. Surface modification of nanoparticles with targeting ligands or stimuli-responsive moieties enables precise control over drug release kinetics and enhances therapeutic efficacy.

**Cytokine Delivery Systems**

Cytokines are essential signaling molecules that play a pivotal role in regulating immune responses and orchestrating the complex interactions between immune cells. In the context of cancer immunotherapy, cytokines serve as potent immunomodulators that can enhance antitumor immune responses and promote tumor regression. However, the systemic administration of cytokines often leads to dose-limiting toxicities and off-target effects, limiting their clinical utility. Cytokine delivery systems offer a promising solution by enabling localized and controlled release of cytokines directly to the tumor microenvironment, thereby enhancing immune cell activation and effector functions while minimizing systemic toxicity.

One of the primary challenges in cytokine delivery is achieving precise spatiotemporal control over cytokine release kinetics. Biomaterial-based delivery systems provide a versatile platform for achieving this goal by encapsulating cytokines within biocompatible carriers and modulating their release properties. For example, hydrogels, microparticles, and nanoparticles can be engineered to release cytokines in a sustained and controlled manner, thereby prolonging their biological activity and enhancing their therapeutic efficacy within the tumor microenvironment.

In addition to controlling release kinetics, biomaterial-based cytokine delivery systems can also improve the targeting specificity of cytokines to tumor tissues. By functionalizing biomaterial carriers with targeting ligands or antibodies that recognize tumor-specific antigens or receptors, cytokines can be selectively delivered to cancer cells while sparing healthy tissues. This targeted delivery minimizes off-target effects and systemic toxicity, thereby improving the safety profile of cytokine-based immunotherapy.

Moreover, biomaterial carriers can protect cytokines from degradation and clearance by the immune system, prolonging their circulation time and enhancing their bioavailability at the tumor site. This prolonged exposure to cytokines enhances immune cell activation and effector functions within the tumor microenvironment, leading to more potent antitumor immune responses. Furthermore, biomaterial carriers can be engineered to respond to specific stimuli present within the tumor microenvironment, such as pH, enzymes, or temperature, enabling triggered release of cytokines in response to local cues.

Particulate carriers, such as liposomes or polymeric nanoparticles, represent promising platforms for cytokine delivery due to their versatility in encapsulating and delivering a wide range of cytokines with varying physicochemical properties. These particulate carriers can be engineered to encapsulate cytokines either alone or in combination with other immunomodulatory agents, such as checkpoint inhibitors or tumor antigens, to achieve synergistic effects and enhance therapeutic outcomes.

In conclusion, cytokine delivery systems based on biomaterial carriers offer a promising approach for enhancing the efficacy and safety of cytokine-based cancer immunotherapy. By providing precise control over release kinetics, improving targeting specificity, and protecting cytokines from degradation, biomaterial-based cytokine delivery systems hold the potential to revolutionize cancer treatment by enhancing antitumor immune responses and promoting tumor regression. Further research and development in this field are essential to optimize the design and performance of cytokine delivery systems for clinical translation and widespread adoption in cancer therapy

**Antigen Delivery and Presentation**

Antigen-presenting cells (APCs), notably dendritic cells (DCs), are key orchestrators of the adaptive immune response and play a crucial role in initiating and regulating antitumor immune responses. DCs are specialized immune cells that possess a unique ability to capture, process, and present antigens to T cells, thereby initiating an adaptive immune response against foreign invaders, including cancer cells. In the context of cancer immunotherapy, DCs serve as crucial mediators in the activation of cytotoxic T lymphocytes (CTLs) and the generation of tumor-specific immune responses.

Dendritic cells are highly efficient in capturing antigens derived from cancer cells through various mechanisms, including phagocytosis, receptor-mediated endocytosis, and uptake of apoptotic bodies. Once internalized, cancer-derived antigens are processed within the DCs' endosomal compartments, where they are degraded into peptide fragments. These peptide fragments are then presented on the surface of DCs bound to major histocompatibility complex (MHC) molecules, forming peptide-MHC complexes that are recognized by T cell receptors (TCRs) on T cells.

The presentation of tumor antigens by DCs to T cells is essential for the activation and expansion of tumor-specific T cell responses. Upon encountering peptide-MHC complexes on the surface of DCs, naive T cells undergo activation and differentiation into effector T cells, including cytotoxic CD8+ T cells and helper CD4+ T cells, which are capable of recognizing and eliminating cancer cells. Dendritic cells also provide essential co-stimulatory signals to T cells through interactions between co-stimulatory molecules, such as CD80/86 on DCs and CD28 on T cells, further enhancing T cell activation and effector functions.

In addition to priming T cell responses, dendritic cells play a critical role in regulating immune tolerance and preventing autoimmunity. DCs possess the ability to induce immune tolerance by presenting self-antigens to T cells in the absence of co-stimulatory signals, leading to T cell anergy or deletion. However, in the context of cancer immunotherapy, DCs can be manipulated to overcome immune tolerance and induce robust antitumor immune responses.

Various strategies have been developed to harness the immunostimulatory properties of dendritic cells for cancer immunotherapy, including DC-based vaccines, adoptive cell transfer therapies, and ex vivo manipulation of DCs. DC-based vaccines involve the ex vivo generation and activation of DCs from patient-derived blood or bone marrow precursors, followed by loading with tumor antigens or tumor lysates and reinfusion into the patient to stimulate antitumor immune responses.

Furthermore, biomaterial-based approaches offer innovative strategies for enhancing the efficacy of dendritic cell-based immunotherapies by providing a controlled and localized delivery of tumor antigens and adjuvants to DCs within the tumor microenvironment. Particulate carriers, such as liposomes or polymeric nanoparticles, can encapsulate tumor antigens and adjuvants and target them to DCs, promoting their uptake and activation. This targeted delivery enhances the presentation of tumor antigens by DCs and stimulates potent antitumor immune responses.

In conclusion, dendritic cells play a pivotal role in initiating and regulating antitumor immune responses by presenting tumor antigens to T cells. Harnessing the immunostimulatory properties of dendritic cells holds great promise for enhancing the efficacy of cancer immunotherapy. Biomaterial-based approaches offer innovative strategies for delivering tumor antigens and adjuvants to DCs within the tumor microenvironment, thereby promoting robust antitumor immune responses and improving patient outcomes in the fight against cancer. Continued research and development in this field are essential to optimize the design and performance of dendritic cell-based immunotherapies for clinical translation and widespread adoption in cancer therapy.

**Combination Therapies and Multifunctional Biomaterials**

Combination therapies, encompassing the concurrent administration of multiple therapeutic agents with complementary mechanisms of action, have emerged as a promising strategy for enhancing treatment outcomes in various disease conditions, including cancer. By targeting multiple pathways involved in disease progression, combination therapies can achieve synergistic effects that surpass the efficacy of individual drugs alone. In the context of cancer treatment, combination therapies aim to overcome drug resistance, minimize off-target effects, and improve overall therapeutic efficacy. Multifunctional biomaterials, capable of integrating diagnostic, therapeutic, and targeting functionalities into a single platform, play a pivotal role in enabling effective combination therapies.

One of the key advantages of combination therapies is their ability to target heterogeneous cell populations within tumors, thereby minimizing the emergence of drug-resistant clones and improving overall treatment response. Biomaterial-based delivery systems provide an ideal platform for delivering combination therapies, allowing for precise control over drug release kinetics and spatial distribution. By encapsulating multiple therapeutic agents within a single carrier, biomaterials enable simultaneous delivery of synergistic drug combinations to the tumor site while minimizing systemic toxicity.

Moreover, multifunctional biomaterials can be engineered to respond to specific physiological cues or disease microenvironments, enabling spatiotemporal control over drug release kinetics. For example, stimuli-responsive biomaterials can be designed to release therapeutic agents in response to changes in pH, temperature, or enzymatic activity within the tumor microenvironment, thereby enhancing therapeutic efficacy and minimizing off-target effects. Additionally, biomaterial carriers can be surface-functionalized with targeting ligands or antibodies to selectively deliver drugs to tumor cells or specific cellular subsets within the tumor microenvironment, further enhancing treatment specificity.

Combination therapies can involve various classes of therapeutic agents, including chemotherapeutic drugs, targeted therapies, immunomodulators, and gene therapy vectors. By combining agents with complementary mechanisms of action, such as chemotherapy with immunotherapy or targeted therapy with anti-angiogenic agents, combination therapies aim to exploit the vulnerabilities of cancer cells while minimizing resistance mechanisms. Biomaterial-based delivery systems enable precise tuning of drug ratios and release kinetics, optimizing the synergistic effects of combination therapies and enhancing therapeutic outcomes.

Furthermore, integration of diagnostic imaging modalities into biomaterial-based delivery systems allows for real-time monitoring of treatment response and disease progression, facilitating adaptive therapy regimens. By incorporating imaging agents, such as fluorescent dyes or contrast agents, into multifunctional biomaterial carriers, researchers can visualize drug distribution, tumor targeting, and therapeutic response non-invasively, enabling personalized treatment optimization and timely intervention.

In conclusion, combination therapies and multifunctional biomaterials hold great promise for improving treatment outcomes in various disease conditions, particularly cancer. By enabling precise delivery of synergistic drug combinations, enhancing treatment specificity, and facilitating real-time monitoring of therapeutic response, biomaterial-based approaches offer new opportunities for personalized and targeted therapy. Continued research and development in this field are essential to optimize the design and performance of multifunctional biomaterials for clinical translation and widespread adoption in disease management

Challenges and Future Directions

The field of advanced biomaterials in cancer immunotherapy holds tremendous promise for revolutionizing cancer treatment by harnessing the power of the immune system to recognize and eradicate cancer cells. However, several challenges must be addressed to fully realize the potential of biomaterial-based approaches in enhancing the efficacy and safety of cancer immunotherapy. Additionally, identifying future directions and opportunities for advancement is essential for guiding research efforts and translating innovative technologies into clinical applications.

One of the primary challenges facing advanced biomaterials in cancer immunotherapy is optimizing the pharmacokinetics and pharmacodynamics of biomaterial carriers. Achieving a balance between controlled release and sustained therapeutic effect while minimizing off-target effects and systemic toxicity remains a complex task. Biomaterial carriers must be carefully designed to ensure optimal drug loading, release kinetics, and stability in physiological conditions. Furthermore, understanding the interactions between biomaterials and the immune system is critical for predicting and mitigating potential immune responses to biomaterial carriers.

Enhancing targeting specificity represents another significant challenge in biomaterial-based cancer immunotherapy. While biomaterials can be engineered to selectively target immune cells or tumor cells within the tumor microenvironment, achieving uniform distribution and penetration throughout the tumor remains a challenge. Overcoming biological barriers such as the extracellular matrix and the blood-brain barrier is essential for ensuring effective drug delivery to tumor cells while minimizing damage to healthy tissues. Additionally, biomaterial carriers must be designed to evade clearance by the reticuloendothelial system and enhance accumulation within the tumor through passive or active targeting mechanisms.

Long-term safety and biocompatibility are critical considerations in the development of biomaterial-based cancer immunotherapy. Biodegradable polymers, while advantageous in facilitating controlled drug release and minimizing the need for device removal, must be carefully designed to avoid adverse inflammatory reactions or immune responses. Furthermore, concerns regarding the potential accumulation of degradation byproducts and their impact on systemic physiology necessitate thorough preclinical evaluation and long-term monitoring. Strategies for enhancing the biocompatibility of biomaterial carriers, such as surface modification with biocompatible coatings or incorporation of immunomodulatory agents, are actively being explored to mitigate potential adverse effects.

Scalability and regulatory considerations pose additional challenges to the clinical translation and widespread adoption of biomaterial-based cancer immunotherapy. Achieving reproducibility and standardization in manufacturing processes while complying with regulatory requirements for safety and efficacy represents a formidable task. Moreover, the cost-effectiveness of biomaterial-based therapies must be carefully evaluated to ensure accessibility and affordability for patients. Collaborations between academia, industry, and regulatory agencies are essential for navigating the regulatory landscape and facilitating the translation of innovative biomaterial technologies from bench to bedside.

Despite these challenges, the future of advanced biomaterials in cancer immunotherapy holds immense promise. Continued research efforts focused on optimizing biomaterial design, enhancing targeting specificity, and improving biocompatibility will drive innovation in this field. Furthermore, interdisciplinary collaborations and advances in materials science, immunology, and oncology will facilitate the development of novel biomaterial-based therapies with improved therapeutic outcomes and reduced adverse effects. By addressing these challenges and leveraging emerging technologies, biomaterial-based approaches have the potential to transform cancer treatment and improve patient outcomes in the years to come.

## References


1. Wang, C., Ye, Y., Hochu, G. M., Sadeghifar, H., & Gu, Z. (2016). Enhanced cancer immunotherapy by microneedle patch-assisted delivery of anti-PD1 antibody. Nano letters, 16(4), 2334-2340.
2. Stephan, S. B., Taber, A. M., Jileaeva, I., Pegues, E. P., Sentman, C. L., & Stephan, M. T. (2015). Biopolymer implants enhance the efficacy of adoptive T-cell therapy. Nature biotechnology, 33(1), 97-101.
3. He, Q., & Gao, H. (2017). Tumor-specific self-degradable hybrid nanogels for combined chemotherapy and immunotherapy. Nanoscale, 9(1), 1-10.
4. Riley, R. S., June, C. H., Langer, R., & Mitchell, M. J. (2019). Delivery technologies for cancer immunotherapy. Nature reviews. Drug discovery, 18(3), 175-196.
5. Zhu, G., Lynn, G. M., Jacobson, O., Chen, K., Liu, Y., Zhang, H., ... & Chen, X. (2017). Albumin/vaccine nanocomplexes that assemble in vivo for combination cancer immunotherapy. Nature communications, 8, 1954.
6. Roy, S., & Mehta, R. N. (2020). Nanomedicine in cancer immunotherapy: Beyond immune checkpoint inhibition. Nanomedicine: Nanotechnology, Biology and Medicine, 27, 102178.
7. Fan, Y., Kuai, R., Xu, Y., Ochyl, L. J., & Moon, J. J. (2017). Therapeutic peptide-based nanovaccines for cancer immunotherapy. Advanced Drug Delivery Reviews, 114, 195-210.
8. Kranz, L. M., Diken, M., Haas, H., Kreiter, S., Loquai, C., Reuter, K. C., ... & Sahin, U. (2016). Systemic RNA delivery to dendritic cells exploits antiviral defense for cancer immunotherapy. Nature, 534(7607), 396-401.
9. Ali, O. A., Lewin, S. A., Dranoff, G., & Mooney, D. J. (2015). Vaccines combined with immune checkpoint antibodies promote cytotoxic T-cell activity and tumor eradication. Cancer immunology research, 4(2), 95-100.
10. Hu, Q., Li, H., Archibong, E., Chen, Q., Ruan, H., Ahn, S., ... & Gu, Z. (2018). In vivo delivery of nanopleX-loaded immuno-modulating therapeutics for synergistic cancer immunotherapy. ACS nano, 12(9), 9021-9032.

11. Zhou, X., Yang, X., Yang, Y., Zhang, H., & Gu, Z. (2020). Nanomaterials for cancer immunotherapy. View, 1(1), e9.
12. Chen, Q., Wang, C., Chen, G., Hu, Q., Gu, Z., & Bomba, H. N. (2016). Liposomes coated with low molecular weight heparin for high-efficiency cancer immunotherapy. Journal of the American Chemical Society, 138(20), 7056-7062.
13. Tang, J., Zhang, L., Gao, H., Liu, Y., & Zhang, Q. (2019). Nanoparticles co-loaded with doxorubicin and interleukin-2 for cancer immunotherapy. RSC advances, 9(56), 32877-32885.
14. Rodell, C. B., Ahmed, M. S., Garris, C. S., Pittet, M. J., & Weissleder, R. (2019). Development of adamantane-conjugated TLR7/8 agonists for supramolecular delivery and cancer immunotherapy. ACS nano, 13(6), 7394-7407.
15. Kuai, R., Ochyl, L. J., Bahjat, K. S., Schwendeman, A., & Moon, J. J. (2017). Designer vaccine nanodiscs for personalized cancer immunotherapy. Nature materials, 16(4), 489-496.

CHAPTER SEVEN

# Therapeutic Approach for Organ Transplantation Utilizing Biomaterials

**Mani Sharma**[a], **Mohini Rawat**[b]
[a] CSIR-Indian Institute of Chemical Technology, Tarnaka, Hyderabad, Secunderabad-500007, Telangana , India
[b] Himalayan Institute of Pharmacy and Research,Atak farm,Rajawala, Dehradun-248007, Uttarakhand, India

## 1. Introduction

Organ transplantation has long been a critical medical procedure for patients with end-stage organ failure, offering them a chance for renewed health and extended life. Despite significant advancements in surgical techniques and immunosuppressive therapies, challenges such as organ rejection, donor organ shortages, and post-transplant complications persist. Traditional immunosuppressive drugs, while effective in reducing acute rejection, often come with severe side effects, including increased susceptibility to infections and malignancies. Given these limitations, innovative approaches are being explored to enhance the success rates and overall outcomes of organ transplantation. One such promising avenue is the use of biomaterials in transplantation therapy.

Biomaterials, which are natural or synthetic materials compatible with living tissue, have revolutionized various fields of medicine, including regenerative medicine, tissue engineering, and drug delivery systems. In the context of organ transplantation, biomaterials offer several potential benefits. They can be engineered to create scaffolds for organ regeneration, deliver immunomodulatory agents precisely to the transplant site, and even promote tolerance by modulating the immune response. This chapter delves into the emerging therapeutic applications of biomaterials in organ transplantation, highlighting their potential to address current challenges and improve patient outcomes.

One of the foremost applications of biomaterials in transplantation is in the development of bioengineered organs. The shortage of suitable donor organs is a significant hurdle in transplantation medicine, leading to long waiting lists and high mortality rates among patients awaiting transplants. Bioengineered organs, created using scaffolds made from biomaterials, offer a potential solution to this problem. These scaffolds can be seeded with a patient's own cells to grow functional tissues and organs, thereby eliminating the need for donor organs and reducing the risk of rejection. For instance, decellularized matrices, which retain the extracellular structure of organs but lack cellular components, can be repopulated with recipient cells to create personalized organs. This approach not only addresses the issue of organ shortage but also ensures better biocompatibility and integration with the recipient's body.

A critical area where biomaterials are making an impact is in the delivery of immunosuppressive and immunomodulatory therapies. Traditional systemic administration of immunosuppressive drugs often leads to adverse side effects due to the high doses required to achieve therapeutic levels at the transplant site. Biomaterials can be designed to release these drugs in a controlled manner directly at the site of the transplanted organ, enhancing the efficacy of the drugs while minimizing systemic toxicity. For example, hydrogels and nanoparticles can be engineered to encapsulate immunosuppressive agents and release them in response to specific triggers, such as changes in pH or temperature, at the site of inflammation. This localized delivery system ensures that the drugs are concentrated where they are most needed, reducing the overall dosage required and limiting side effects[1].

Biomaterials can play a pivotal role in promoting immune tolerance, which is the ultimate goal in transplantation therapy. Achieving immune tolerance would eliminate the need for lifelong immunosuppression, significantly improving the quality of life for transplant recipients. Biomaterials can be used to create a local microenvironment that Favors regulatory immune responses and suppresses harmful immune reactions against the transplanted organ. For instance, biomaterial scaffolds can be functionalized with molecules that promote the development and activation of regulatory T cells, which are essential for inducing and maintaining tolerance. These scaffolds can be loaded with cytokines or other signalling molecules that modulate the immune response to be more tolerant and less aggressive.

Biomaterials are being explored for their ability to enhance the regeneration and repair of transplanted tissues. The integration of growth factors, extracellular matrix proteins, and other bioactive molecules into biomaterial scaffolds can facilitate tissue repair and regeneration at the site of transplantation. For example, incorporating vascular endothelial growth factor (VEGF) into scaffolds can promote angiogenesis, ensuring an adequate blood supply to the transplanted tissue and enhancing its survival and function. Similarly, the use of biomaterials that mimic the natural extracellular matrix can provide the necessary structural support and biochemical cues to guide the regeneration of functional tissue[2].

Advances in biomaterial science have led to the development of "smart" biomaterials that can respond dynamically to the physiological environment. These materials can adapt their properties in response to changes in the local environment, such as inflammation or mechanical stress, providing a more tailored and effective therapeutic approach. For example, stimuli-responsive hydrogels can change their swelling behaviour and drug release profiles in response to inflammatory signals, ensuring that therapeutic agents are released precisely when and where they are needed most.

The application of biomaterials in organ transplantation represents a novel and promising therapeutic approach that addresses several critical challenges in the field. By leveraging the unique properties of biomaterials, researchers and clinicians can enhance the success rates of transplantation, reduce the reliance on donor organs, minimize adverse side effects of immunosuppressive therapy, and promote long-term tolerance and tissue regeneration. As the field of biomaterials continues to evolve, it holds the potential to transform organ transplantation into a more effective, safer, and patient-friendly therapy, ultimately improving the lives of countless individuals with organ failure[3].

## 1. Organ transplantation

Organ transplantation stands as a monumental achievement in 20$^{th}$-century medicine. Presently, ailing organs are being substituted with healthy ones sourced from living donors, cadavers, and animals. Successful transplantations of bone marrow, kidney, liver, cornea, pancreas, heart, and nerve cells underscore the breadth of this medical advancement. However, the paramount limitations stem from organ availability and cost. The emergence of effective immunosuppressive drugs in the late 1970s played a pivotal role in bolstering the success rate of organ transplants. Consequently, this development has transformed organ transplantation into a customary medical practice in the 21$^{st}$ century[4].

Organ donation involves the generous gift of biological tissue or an organ from a living or deceased person to a recipient in need of a transplant. According to the Encyclopaedia Britannica (2013), organ donation refers to the selfless act of giving one or more organs, without compensation, for transplantation into another individual. This decision is deeply personal and multifaceted, encompassing medical, legal, religious, cultural, and ethical considerations. In today's context, organ donation includes the donation and transplantation of vital organs such as the heart, intestines, kidneys, liver, lungs, and pancreas (including the islets of Langerhans). Additionally, it encompasses corneas, bones, skin, joints, and blood[5].

### 2.1 Types of Transplants

**Autograft**: Autograft, also known as auto transplantation, involves the transfer of organs or tissues from one part of the body to another within the same individual. This procedure is called an "autologous" transplant, and the transplanted tissue is referred to as an autograft.

**Allograft:** Allograft refers to the transplantation of an organ or tissue between two individuals of the same species who are not genetically identical. The majority of human tissue and organ transplants fall into this category.

**Xenograft:** Xenograft is the transplantation of organs or tissue from one species to another. A common and successful example of this is the transplant of porcine (pig) heart valves into humans[6].

### 2.2 Types of Organs Donors

There are several sources of organs for transplantation, including living donors (related and non-related), cadaveric donors, and brain-dead patients. In established transplantation systems, organs are obtained from both living and deceased (cadaveric) donors using various strategies, such as opt-in (explicit consent), opt-out (presumed consent), and donation after brain death.

**Systems of "Opt-in" and "Opt-out"**

The United States and many other countries use the "opt-in" organ donation system, where individuals must actively sign up to become a donor before their death. The final decision to use the organs from the individual's body rests with the potential donor's family after their death. In contrast, some European countries, including France, Belgium, Finland, Denmark, Italy, Spain, Norway, and Sweden, have adopted the opt-out system. The opt-out system presumes that all individuals would consent to have their organs used for transplant unless they explicitly opt-out. For example, in Belgium, only 3–4% opt out, leaving 96–97% of the population as potential donors, as compared with the roughly 30% of Americans who are organ donors in the opt-in system. The opt-in systems place a higher emphasis on the requirement of consent compared to the opt-out systems[7].

## 3. Role of Biomaterial in Organ Transplantation

Biopolymers play a crucial role in enhancing the outcomes of organ transplantation through various innovative approaches that address the limitations and challenges associated with traditional transplantation methods. These natural and synthetic polymers contribute significantly to the fields of stem cell transplantation, tissue engineering, and regenerative medicine. Below is an expanded discussion on their roles:

### 3.1 Enhancing Stem Cell Transplantation through Biopolymers

In the realm of stem cell transplantation, biopolymers provide essential structural support and biochemical signals that enhance the survival, proliferation, and differentiation of transplanted cells. For instance, hydrogels and other biopolymer-based scaffolds mimic the extracellular matrix (ECM), offering a conducive environment for cell growth and tissue regeneration. These scaffolds help in maintaining the viability of stem cells during transplantation, ensuring they remain functional and integrate effectively into the host tissue. Additionally, biopolymers can be engineered to release growth factors and cytokines that promote the differentiation of stem cells into the desired cell types, thereby enhancing the overall efficacy of the transplant[8].

### 3.2 Advancing Tissue Engineering with Biopolymer Scaffolds

Biopolymer scaffolds are integral to tissue engineering efforts aimed at repairing or replacing damaged tissues and organs. They can be engineered to possess specific mechanical and biochemical properties that match those of the target tissue. For example, in cardiac tissue engineering, biopolymer scaffolds like gelatin methacrylate (GelMA) and polyethylene glycol diacrylate (PEGDA) have been used to create constructs that support the maturation and integration of cardiomyocytes, leading to improved cardiac function post-transplantation. These scaffolds not only provide the necessary structural support but also deliver biochemical cues that facilitate the formation of functional tissue, thereby enhancing the success of tissue engineering applications in organ transplantation[9].

### 3.3 Biopolymers in Advanced Drug Delivery Systems

Biopolymers are also utilized in the development of advanced drug delivery systems that enhance the therapeutic efficacy of transplanted tissues. These systems can be designed to release bioactive molecules, such as growth factors and cytokines, in a controlled manner, thereby promoting tissue repair and regeneration[10]. The use of biopolymers in drug delivery helps in reducing inflammation and preventing immune rejection of the transplanted organ. For instance, biopolymer-based nanoparticles can be engineered to deliver immunosuppressive drugs directly to the site of transplantation, minimizing systemic side effects and improving the localized immune response[11].

### 3.4 Immunomodulation and Biocompatibility of Biopolymers

One of the significant challenges in organ transplantation is the immune response against the transplanted tissue. Biopolymers can be engineered to modulate the immune system, creating a more favorable environment for the graft[12]. For instance, specific biopolymer coatings can be applied to transplanted tissues to reduce their immunogenicity and prevent rejection, thereby improving the long-term success of the transplant. These coatings can be designed to release immunomodulatory agents that suppress the host's immune response, allowing the transplanted tissue to integrate more seamlessly with the host's body[13].

### 3.5 Clinical Applications and Innovations with Biopolymers

In clinical settings, biopolymers have been used to develop bioartificial organs and tissues, such as bioengineered corneas and retinal tissues. These biopolymer-based constructs not only replace the damaged tissues but also promote endogenous tissue regeneration, reducing the dependence on donor organs. The use of biopolymers in creating bioartificial tissues has shown promising results in restoring function and improving the quality of life for patients with organ failure. Additionally, biopolymers are being explored for their potential in creating whole organ scaffolds that can be seeded with patient-specific cells, paving the way for personalized organ transplants[14].

## 4. Classification of Biomaterial in Contrast of Organ Transplantation

The role of biomaterials in the medical field has significantly evolved with scientific and technological advancements. The growing and diverse needs in healthcare have been a major driving force behind the progress in the development and application of biomaterials. These materials can be categorized in various ways, often based on their function within the human body and their material properties.

One way to classify biomaterials is by considering the level of the human body they interact with, such as organs and systems. For instance, at the system level, the skeletal system can benefit from joint replacements and bone plates. At the organ level, the heart can be repaired or replaced with devices like artificial heart valves, complete heart valves, and cardiac pacemakers. Another method of classification is by the specific body parts they treat. For example, artificial hip joints and kidney dialysis machines are used to replace or support failing body parts, while screws, sutures, and bone plates aid in the healing of wounds. (Table no.1)

A third way to classify biomaterials is based on their material properties, dividing them into bioceramics, polymers, and metals. This broad range of biomaterials allows for selecting the most appropriate material for specific treatments. For instance, chemically inert metals with high electroconductivity are ideal for use as electrodes in artificial organs and for durable restoration of lost body functions. On the other hand, biodegradable materials, such as sutures, serve as temporary scaffolds for tissue regeneration. Additionally, some biomaterials, like coronary and peripheral stents used in cardiovascular implants, are bioabsorbable and gradually dissolve in the body after completing their intended function[15].

### 4.1 Bioceramics

Bioceramic biomaterials are composed of non-metallic and metallic elements bonded through covalent and/or ionic bonds. These materials include oxides like aluminum oxide (Al2O3), magnesium oxide (MgO), and silicon dioxide (SiO2), which combine non-metallic and metallic elements. Ionic salts can form polycrystalline structures, such as ZnS, CsCl, and NaCl, while diamond and carbon-based structures are examples of covalently bonded ceramics. The strong covalent and ionic bonds in ceramics make them hard, brittle, and stiff, preventing the easy movement of atomic or ionic planes within the material.Advances in science and technology have enabled the use of ceramics and their composites in medical devices to enhance or restore various body parts[16]. This has led to the development of bioceramic implants and devices like hip prostheses, bone grafts, and artificial tendons. For a material to be classified as a bioceramic, it must possess several crucial properties when implanted in the body: it should be non-inflammatory, non-allergic, biofunctional, biocompatible, non-carcinogenic, and non-toxic.Ceramics are also frequently used in dentistry due to their relative inertness to bodily fluids such as saliva, their aesthetically pleasing appearance, and their excellent compressive strength. Recently, bioceramics have found significant applications in controlled drug delivery, gene therapies, and cancer treatments.

Bioceramics like black pyrolytic carbons are used in cardiovascular implants, particularly in blood-interfacing applications such as heart valves. While their dark color is a disadvantage in dental applications, pyrolytic carbons are easy to produce and exhibit good biocompatibility with the human body. They are also utilized in composite implant materials and components for tensile loading applications, such as artificial ligaments and tendons, due to their excellent biocompatibility and high specific strength as fibers[17].

There are three types of ceramics used to make implants:

1. **Resorbable or Biodegradable (Non-Inert) Ceramics:** Examples include calcium phosphate and calcium aluminate.
2. **Surface Reactive or Bioactive (Semi-Inert) Ceramics:** Examples include glass ceramics and hydroxyapatites.
3. **Non-Absorbable (Relatively Inert) Ceramics:** Examples include alumina, zirconia, and carbons.

### 4.2 Polymeric Biomaterials

Polymers in biomaterials include both naturally occurring and synthetic types, and they can be either biodegradable or non-biodegradable. Naturally derived polymers such as starch, collagen, and chitin are widely used due to their biodegradability and easy availability. In contrast, synthetic polymers are extensively applied in various medical fields, including prosthetics, dental materials, disposable medical products, and implants.Many synthetic polymers that are non-biodegradable were initially created for non-medical purposes. However, their physical and mechanical properties, which mimic those of human soft tissues, have led to their broad adoption in biomedical applications. Common examples of synthetic polymers in the medicalfield include polypropylene, polyethylene, polymethylmethacrylate, polyethylenterephthalate, and polyurethane[15], [18].

Polymers are often chosen over metals and ceramics for biomaterials due to their versatility in manufacturing into different forms such as fibers, films, sheets, and synthetic latex. They are also easy to process, cost-effective, and can be tailored to have specific physical and mechanical properties. However, polymeric biomaterials also have drawbacks. They tend to absorb water and proteins in the body, their surfaces can become easily contaminated and are difficult to sterilize, they may release leachable substances, they are prone to biodegradation, and they can wear down and degrade. Additionally, the widespread use of non-biodegradable polymers poses challenges for environmental pollution and waste management[19].

### 4.3 Metallic Biomaterials

Metals are among the most widely used biomaterials due to their excellent thermal and electrical conductivity. They are commonly utilized in artificial heart valves, pacemaker leads, and vascular stents. Metallic biomaterials are also favored for load-bearing implants like hip and knee replacements due to their exceptional corrosion resistance and mechanical properties. In addition to pure metals, metal alloys, which combine two or more elements, are frequently used. These alloys often undergo surface modifications, such as coating with bioactive ceramics or polymeric thin films, to enhance corrosion resistance and increase material strength. The main groups of metallic biomaterials include pure titanium (Ti) and titanium alloys like Ti-6Al-4V, stainless steel, and cobalt-chromium (Co-Cr) alloys[20].

Several factors influence the selection of metals and alloys for medical applications, including their physical and mechanical properties, cost-effectiveness, corrosion resistance, and biocompatibility. Among these, Ti-6Al-4V is one of the most widely used metallic biomaterials due to its superior strength, light weight, and excellent corrosion resistance. However, Ti-6Al-4V has some drawbacks, such as less elasticity and higher wear and tear in articulation surfaces of human bones. Additionally, the presence of vanadium in the alloy can lead to adverse tissue reactions and cytotoxicity. Over time, leached vanadium and aluminum ions can cause long-term health issues such as neurodegenerative diseases (e.g., Alzheimer's and Parkinson's) and affect the respiratory and reproductive systems. Recent research has focused on developing various coatings for Ti-6Al-4V alloys to enhance their biocompatibility and corrosion resistance.Metals offer several advantages as biomaterials, including corrosion resistance, wear resistance, high strength, ease of sterilization, fabrication, and shape memory capabilities. However, their use in the human body also presents challenges, such as high modulus, potential cytotoxicity, susceptibility to corrosion, and metal ion sensitivity[21].

| **Bioceramics Biomaterials** | **Uses** |
|---|---|
| Calcium aluminate | dental restoration supplies, orthopedic uses |
| Calcium phosphate | artificial hips, knees, tendons, ligaments, teeth, and bones |
| Glass-ceramic | Bone repair and augmentation |
| Hydroxyapatite | fillers, coatings for metal implants, and bone grafts |
| Alumina | implants for the teeth and bones, hip prosthesis |
| Carbon | Cartilage regeneration, scaffolds made of bone, and heart valves |
| Silicon nitride | Spinal fusion implants |
| Zirconia | hip replacement, dental implants |
| **Polymeric Biomaterials** | **Uses** |
| Polypropylene | Hernia repair, artificial vascular grafts, blood oxygenator membranes, and biodegradable sutures |
| Polyethylene | Acetabular liners, tendon, tubing for drainage and catheters, and surgical implants |
| Polymethylmethacrylate | Provisional crowns, artificial teeth, and bone cement |
| Polyethylenterephthalate | Artificial heart valves and vascular grafts |
| Polyurethane | bandages, breast implants, and cardiac patches |
| **Metallic Biomaterials** | **Uses** |
| Pure titanium (Ti) and titanium alloys (Ti-6Al-4V | Joint prostheses, screws, and conductive leads |
| Stainless stee | Guide wires, fracture plates, and vascular stents |
| Cobalt-chromium (Co-Cr) alloys | Dental apparatus, artificial cardiac valves, joint replacement |

**Table no.1** Classification of biomaterial

### 4.4 Inorganic Biomaterials

Gold nanoparticles are a type of inorganic biomaterial that has been extensively researched for disease treatments. According to Li et al., using gold nanorods in photothermal therapy combined with chemotherapy improves cancer treatment efficacy and modulates the tumor microenvironment. Another study discovered that radioisotope-labeled gold nanoclusters can activate dendritic cells, leading to long-term anti-cancer immunity in mouse models by eliminating primary tumors and preventing the development of distant tumors[22]. Additionally, gold nanoparticles have been shown to enhance imaging by being coated with cancer-specific T-cell receptors, serving as a contrast agent in computed tomography. This coating allows for easy observation of T-cell migration, distribution, and kinetics during imaging. Although most research is still in the animal trial stage, gold nanoparticles show significant potential for human cancer treatment.Another inorganic biomaterial, silica nanoparticles, also exhibit anti-cancer properties when doped with elements like calcium, magnesium, and zinc. These doped mesoporous silica nanospheres have been shown to increase CD4+ and CD8+ T-cells in the spleen, thereby stimulating an anti-cancer immune response. Additionally, Kakizawa et al. found that silica nanoparticles coated with specific amino acids and incubated with dendritic cells and ligands can induce the production of important cytokines such as IL-1 and IFN, suggesting their potential use as carriers for cellular immunotherapy. Furthermore, silica nanoparticles have been widely utilized in developing vaccines against various bacteria and viruses, including Mycoplasma hyopneumoniae, hepatitis B[23].

### 3D Printing Technology

3D printing, particularly 3D bioprinting, represents a transformative approach in the field of regenerative medicine and tissue engineering. This technology addresses the critical shortage of organs available for transplantation by enabling the creation of patient-specific tissues and organs. Recent advancements have made it possible to not only replicate the structure but also the functionality of these biological systems. By combining living cells with biomaterials, 3D bioprinting offers the potential to create complex tissue constructs that can be used for transplantation, drug testing, and disease modelling [24].

### Current Approaches in Tissue and Organ Engineering

The development of bioartificial organs requires careful consideration of several factors, including scaffold design, cell types, immunological barriers, and methods for maintaining vascular networks. Tissue engineering typically involves creating a scaffold that provides a framework for cell attachment and tissue development. These scaffolds are made from biomaterials like polymers, biocomposites, and bioceramics. Effective scaffold design must ensure biocompatibility, mechanical strength, and the ability to mimic the properties of the original tissue. Additionally, the scaffold must support vascularization, which is critical for the survival and integration of the engineered tissue once implanted in the body.

Recent advances in computer-aided design (CAD) and manufacturing techniques have enabled the creation of highly precise and customizable scaffolds. These technologies allow for the incorporation of intricate features such as microchannels and pores that facilitate nutrient and oxygen transport, essential for cell survival and function. Furthermore, the integration of bioactive molecules within the scaffold can enhance cell attachment, proliferation, and differentiation, leading to more functional tissue constructs.

### Scaffold Designing and Decellularization

Scaffold designing involves using computer-aided design (CAD) software to create biomedically relevant structures. The decellularization process, which removes cellular components from donor organs while preserving the extracellular matrix (ECM), is a crucial method. This ECM serves as a natural scaffold that can be repopulated with stem cells in a process known as recellularization, ultimately producing functional tissues and organs. Decellularized scaffolds retain the complex architecture and biochemical cues of the native tissue, providing an ideal environment for cell growth and tissue development. Decellularization techniques include the use of physical, chemical, and enzymatic methods to remove cellular components without damaging the ECM. Physical methods may involve freeze-thaw cycles or mechanical agitation, while chemical methods use detergents or acids. Enzymatic methods employ enzymes like trypsin to break down cellular components. The choice of decellularization method depends on the tissue type and the intended application of the scaffold[25].

### Recellularization and 3D Bioprinting

Recellularization involves repopulating decellularized ECM with stem cells. Factors such as cell number, infusion route, growth factors, and oxygen supply are crucial in this process. Following recellularization, the printed tissue is assessed for functional characteristics and cell survival. 3D bioprinting uses bioinks, which are mixtures of living cells and biomaterials, to create tissue constructs layer by layer. This technology allows for precise modeling and printing of tissues using CAD software.The process of recellularization typically begins with the selection of appropriate cell types, such as autologous stem cells derived from the patient, to minimize immune rejection. These cells are seeded onto the decellularized scaffold and cultured under controlled conditions to promote cell growth and tissue maturation. Bioreactors are often used to provide the necessary mechanical and biochemical stimuli to enhance tissue development and function[26].

### Types of 3D Bioprinters

Different types of 3D bioprinters are utilized based on the specific requirements of the tissue or organ being printed:

**Extrusion-Based Bioprinters:**

**Microextrusion Printing:** Utilizes mechanical pressure to extrude bioink through a heated nozzle, creating continuous strands of material. This method is versatile and used for printing various structures including cells, tissues, and microfluidic devices. Microextrusion printing allows for the deposition of high-viscosity materials and can produce large, complex structures with multiple cell types and biomaterials.

**Pneumatic Extrusion:** Uses air pressure to extrude bioink. This method is suitable for printing high-viscosity materials and is often used for creating complex tissue constructs. Pneumatic extrusion offers precise control over the extrusion process, allowing for the creation of detailed and accurate tissue structures.

**Inkjet Bioprinters:**

**Thermal Inkjet Printing**: Employs heat to vaporize bioink, forming droplets that are ejected through a nozzle. This technique allows for high-resolution printing but can cause cell damage due to heat exposure. Thermal inkjet printing is commonly used for creating patterns of cells and biomolecules on substrates, making it suitable for applications like tissue patterning and drug screening.

**Piezoelectric Inkjet Printing**: Uses a piezoelectric actuator to generate pressure pulses that force droplets out of the nozzle. This method provides better cell viability compared to thermal inkjet printing. Piezoelectric inkjet printing is versatile and can handle a wide range of bioink viscosities, making it suitable for printing complex tissues and organ models.

**Laser-Based Bioprinters:**

**Laser-Assisted Bioprinting (LAB):** Utilizes a laser to create high-resolution patterns of bioink on a substrate. The laser causes a precise deposition of bioink droplets, minimizing cell damage and maintaining high resolution. LAB is ideal for printing tissues with intricate structures and fine details, such as vascular networks and neural tissues.

**Stereolithography (SLA):** Uses UV light to polymerize photosensitive resins layer by layer, creating highly detailed and complex 3D structures. SLA is known for its precision and ability to produce intricate designs. SLA bioprinters are particularly useful for creating scaffolds with complex geometries and high-resolution features.

**Droplet-Based Bioprinters**

Continuous Inkjet Printing: Produces a continuous stream of bioink droplets that can be directed onto a substrate to form patterns. This method is suitable for printing cells in a highly controlled manner. Continuous inkjet printing is effective for applications requiring high throughput and precise cell placement, such as tissue arrays and microtissues.

Microvalve Inkjet Printing: Uses microvalves to control the deposition of bioink droplets, allowing for precise placement of cells and materials. Microvalve inkjet printing offers flexibility in droplet size and placement, making it suitable for creating heterogeneous tissue constructs with multiple cell types.

**Bio-ink**

Bioinks are the foundational materials used in 3D bioprinting to create tissue constructs and organs. These inks are composed of living cells mixed with compatible biomaterials that provide a suitable environment for cell growth and differentiation. The development of bioinks is a crucial aspect of 3D bioprinting technology, as they must fulfil a range of functional requirements to ensure the successful creation of viable, functional tissues. The use of bioinks allows for the precise placement of cells in predefined architectures, closely mimicking the natural structure of tissues and organs.The significance of bioinks lies in their ability to replicate the complex microenvironment of the body's tissues. This includes not only providing a scaffold for cells to adhere to but also supplying essential nutrients, signalling molecules, and mechanical support. The integration of bioinks into 3D bioprinting processes enables the creation of customized tissue constructs that can be tailored to the specific needs of individual patients, enhancing the potential for successful implantation and integration with the patient's own tissues[27].

**Types of Bioinks**

Bioinks can be categorized based on their composition and functionality into several types:

1. **Hydrogels:**

    - **Natural Hydrogels**: Derived from biological sources, such as alginate, gelatin, collagen, and fibrin. They provide a favorable environment for cell growth and mimic the natural extracellular matrix. Natural hydrogels are widely used in tissue engineering due to their biocompatibility and ability to support cell functions. They are often used in applications requiring soft, flexible tissues, such as skin and cartilage.

- **Synthetic Hydrogels**: Engineered to have precise mechanical and chemical properties. Examples include polyethylene glycol (PEG) and polyacrylamide. Synthetic hydrogels offer tunable properties and can be customized for specific applications. They provide consistent and predictable behavior, making them suitable for applications requiring precise control over the tissue microenvironment.

2. **Decellularized Extracellular Matrix (dECM):**
   - Derived from decellularized tissues or organs, retaining the complex composition of natural ECM. This type provides a highly biomimetic environment for cells, promoting better integration and function. dECM bioinks are used to create scaffolds that closely resemble the native tissue environment, enhancing cell behavior and tissue development. They are particularly useful for applications requiring complex tissue structures, such as liver and heart tissues.

3. **Composite Bioinks:**
   - Combine different materials to leverage the advantages of each. For example, a composite bioink might include both natural and synthetic polymers, providing a balance of biocompatibility and mechanical strength. Composite bioinks can be tailored to achieve specific mechanical and biological properties required for different tissues. They are used in applications requiring both structural support and biological functionality, such as bone and cartilage.

4. **Cell Aggregates and Spheroids:**
   - Use cell aggregates or spheroids as building blocks. These bioinks rely on the natural self-assembly of cells into tissue-like structures, eliminating the need for synthetic materials. Scaffold-free bioinks offer a more natural approach to tissue engineering by using cells' inherent ability to organize and form functional tissues. They are suitable for applications requiring high cell density and natural tissue organization, such as liver and cardiac tissues.

**Characteristics of Ideal Bioinks**

**Biocompatibility:** Must be compatible with living cells and not elicit immune responses or cytotoxic effects. Ensuring biocompatibility is crucial for maintaining cell viability and function during and after the printing process. Bioinks should support the attachment, proliferation, and differentiation of the encapsulated cells without causing adverse reactions.

**Printability:**Bioink Should have suitable rheological properties to be extruded smoothly through the printer's nozzle without clogging. Printability is essential for achieving precise and accurate tissue structures. The bioink must be able to flow through the printing nozzle and solidify in a controlled manner to maintain the integrity of the printed construct.

**Mechanical Properties:** Should provide adequate mechanical strength to support the tissue structure. The mechanical properties of the bioink must match those of the target tissue to ensure proper function and integration. This includes properties such as elasticity, stiffness, and compressive strength, which are critical for the structural stability of the printed tissue.

**Degradability:** Should degrade at a rate that matches the formation of new tissue. The degradability of the bioink ensures that the scaffold provides temporary support while the new tissue matures and integrates. Ideally, the bioink should degrade into non-toxic byproducts that can be safely absorbed or excreted by the body.

**Biological Activity:** Should include bioactive molecules that promote cell attachment, growth, and differentiation. Bioactive molecules such as growth factors, cytokines, and adhesion proteins enhance the biological functionality of the printed tissue. These molecules can guide cell behaviour and tissue development, leading to more effective and functional tissue constructs[28].

**Organ Development using Biomaterial**

Developing organs using biomaterials is a highly intricate process that integrates expertise across multiple scientific disciplines to create viable substitutes for damaged or dysfunctional organs. This approach is driven by the critical need to address various medical conditions such as injuries, diseases, congenital defects, or age-related degeneration that compromise organ function.(Figure.1)

The process begins with identifying the specific organ or tissue requiring replacement or augmentation. This initial step is crucial as it sets the foundation for subsequent design and planning phases. Engineers, medical professionals, and biologists collaborate closely to meticulously design the structure, shape, and functional requirements of the organ or tissue replacement. This phase involves considering anatomical compatibility, mechanical properties, and the desired biological functionality to ensure the biomaterial-based organ can effectively mimic natural organs.Once the design is finalized, the next critical stage involves selecting appropriate biomaterials. These biomaterials can vary widely and may include bioceramics such as hydroxyapatite for bone applications, polymers like polyethylene for flexibility in joint replacements, metals such as titanium alloys known for their strength and durability in load-bearing implants, and even inorganic materials like silica nanoparticles for specialized applications such as drug delivery systems[29].

Fabrication techniques play a pivotal role in shaping these biomaterials into the desired organ structure. Advanced manufacturing methods such as 3D printing, molding, or machining are employed to achieve precise dimensions and configurations. This precision is essential to ensure the biomaterials meet exacting standards for anatomical fit and functional integration within the body.Integration of functional elements is often necessary for more complex organs. For instance, artificial hearts may require embedded electrical components or vascular networks to replicate natural cardiac function. These additions enhance the organ's ability to perform essential physiological tasks once implanted[22].

Rigorous testing and validation follow fabrication to assess the biomaterial-based organ's safety, efficacy, and durability. Mechanical testing evaluates structural integrity and load-bearing capabilities, while biocompatibility tests ensure the biomaterial interacts harmoniously with biological tissues without triggering adverse reactions or immune responses.Before human trials, extensive preclinical studies using animal models provide crucial insights into the organ's performance in vivo. These studies evaluate factors such as integration with surrounding tissues, long-term stability, immune responses, and potential complications that may arise post-implantation.Upon successful completion of preclinical studies, clinical trials commence to evaluate the biomaterial-based organ's safety and effectiveness in human patients. Data gathered from these trials informs regulatory bodies such as the FDA or EMA, which review comprehensive clinical trial data to grant approval for market distribution.Once approved, the biomaterial-based organ enters clinical implementation, where it is used to treat patients in need. Ongoing monitoring and studies are conducted to assess long-term outcomes, address any complications that may arise, and further refine the biomaterial's performance based on real-world feedback and patient experiences[30].

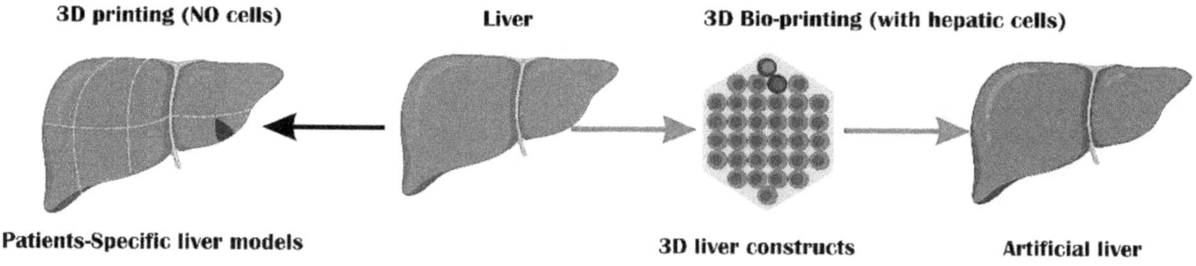


**Figure 1:** Organ Development using Biomaterial

### Challenges

A novel therapeutic approach for organ transplantation using biomaterials presents a promising avenue for addressing current limitations in traditional organ transplantation methods. However, it also faces several significant challenges that must be carefully navigated to realize its full potential.One of the primary challenges is ensuring biocompatibility and minimizing immunogenicity. Biomaterials used in organ transplantation must interact harmoniously with the recipient's immune system to prevent rejection reactions and promote integration with host tissues. Achieving this requires meticulous selection of biomaterials that are non-toxic, non-inflammatory, and capable of supporting cellular integration without triggering immune responses.Another critical aspect is functional integration. Biomaterial-based organs or tissues need to replicate the complex structure and functions of natural organs. This includes considerations for vascularization, electrical conductivity (in cases like cardiac tissue), or the functional aspects specific to each organ type. Developing biomaterials that can support these functionalities and ensuring they perform effectively in vivo poses significant technical challenges.Long-term stability and durability of biomaterial-based organs are essential for their clinical viability. These organs must withstand mechanical stresses, biological degradation, and environmental factors over extended periods without compromising their structural integrity or functionality. Enhancing the longevity of biomaterial-based implants involves optimizing material properties, surface modifications, and biofunctionalization strategies.Safety and regulatory approval are paramount in translating biomaterial-based therapies from research to clinical practice. Rigorous preclinical and clinical studies are necessary to demonstrate safety, efficacy, and reliability according to regulatory standards. Obtaining regulatory approval involves comprehensive data on biocompatibility, effectiveness in restoring organ function, and long-term outcomes in patient populations.

Scalability and cost-effectiveness are additional challenges in biomaterial-based organ transplantation. Developing manufacturing processes that can produce biomaterials on a large scale while managing costs is crucial for widespread adoption. Optimizing production methods, sourcing materials efficiently, and minimizing production complexities are essential steps towards making these therapies economically viable and accessible.Ethical considerations such as patient consent, equitable access to advanced therapies, and societal acceptance also play a pivotal role. Addressing these ethical concerns involves ensuring transparency, respecting patient autonomy, and promoting equitable distribution of innovative treatments.Technological innovation remains fundamental in overcoming current challenges. Advancements in biomaterial science, tissue engineering techniques, and bioengineering solutions are pivotal for enhancing the performance and applicability of biomaterial-based organ transplantation therapies.Educational efforts and public awareness are essential to facilitate acceptance and adoption of biomaterial-based organ transplantation. Educating healthcare providers, patients, and the public about the benefits, risks, and ethical implications of these therapies fosters informed decision-making and promotes acceptance within society.

### Clinical Significance

The clinical significance of biomaterial-based approaches in organ transplantation is profound, offering innovative solutions to several critical challenges and significantly advancing patient care. By mimicking the natural properties of human tissues, biomaterials enhance biocompatibility, reducing the risk of immune rejection and potentially minimizing the need for lifelong immunosuppressive drugs. This improvement allows for more successful integration of transplanted organs with the recipient's body, promoting better long-term outcomes.Biomaterials also facilitate the creation of complex organ structures that closely resemble natural tissues. This includes the development of vascular networks, electrical conductivity in cardiac tissues, and functional bile duct systems in the liver, among other advancements. Such detailed replication of essential physiological functions leads to enhanced restoration of organ functionality, greatly benefiting the overall effectiveness of organ transplantation procedures.Moreover, the robustness of biomaterials ensures long-term durability and mechanical strength, crucial for maintaining structural integrity within the dynamic environment of the human body. This durability reduces the frequency of re-transplantations and associated risks, providing patients with more stable and lasting solutions. Some biomaterials also possess regenerative properties or can be engineered to promote tissue regeneration and repair, enhancing organ function post-transplantation and supporting the body's natural healing processes.

The precision medicine approach enabled by biomaterials tailors the composition and design of the biomaterial to match individual patient needs. This customization optimizes compatibility and functionality, leading to better treatment outcomes by addressing each patient's specific physiological requirements. Furthermore, the use of advanced biomaterials facilitates minimally invasive surgical techniques, reducing surgical risks and recovery times, thus improving patient recovery and overall quality of life post-transplantation.

**Advantage and Disadvantage**

Biomaterial-based organ transplantation presents a range of advantages and disadvantages that highlight its potential while also underscoring the challenges that need to be addressed.

One of the primary advantages is the enhanced biocompatibility of biomaterials, which are engineered to mimic the natural properties of human tissues. This characteristic reduces the risk of immune rejection, a common issue in traditional organ transplants, and minimizes the necessity for lifelong immunosuppressive drugs that can have severe side effects. Additionally, biomaterials allow for the detailed replication of complex organ structures, such as vascular networks and electrical pathways, ensuring that the transplanted organ can perform its intended functions effectively. This functional restoration is crucial for improving patient outcomes and quality of life.

Another significant advantage is the long-term durability of biomaterials. Their high mechanical strength and robustness ensure that transplanted organs can withstand physiological stresses, thereby reducing the need for re-transplantations. Furthermore, some biomaterials possess regenerative properties or can be engineered to promote tissue regeneration and repair. This regenerative potential enhances the body's natural healing processes and improves the functionality of the transplanted organ over time. The customization capabilities of biomaterials also allow for precision medicine approaches, tailoring the biomaterial composition and design to match the specific needs of individual patients, optimizing compatibility, and functionality.

Moreover, biomaterials facilitate minimally invasive surgical techniques, reducing surgical risks, shortening recovery times, and improving overall patient outcomes. The increased availability of biomaterial-based organs also addresses the critical shortage of donor organs, providing more patients with access to life-saving treatments. In the long term, these innovations can lead to economic benefits by reducing healthcare costs associated with complications, rejections, and prolonged hospital stays.

Despite these significant advantages, biomaterial-based organ transplantation also faces several disadvantages. Ensuring perfect biocompatibility remains a challenge, as immune responses, inflammation, or other adverse reactions can still occur, potentially compromising the success of the transplant. Additionally, replicating the intricate functions of natural organs, such as neural connections or biochemical signaling pathways, is complex and poses significant technical challenges. This complexity can limit the functionality of some biomaterial-based organs.

Long-term stability and degradation are also concerns, as some biomaterials may degrade or lose functionality over time, necessitating further interventions or replacements. The regulatory and safety hurdles are substantial, with extensive testing and long validation processes required to gain approval for new biomaterials. These regulatory requirements, while essential for ensuring safety and efficacy, can delay clinical application and increase development costs. The initial costs associated with the development and implementation of biomaterial-based organs can be high, posing financial challenges for healthcare systems and potentially limiting accessibility for some patients.

Ethical and social considerations are also significant. There are ethical concerns related to the use of biomaterials, including issues of consent, equitable access, and societal acceptance. These must be carefully navigated to ensure fair and ethical use of the technology. Current technological limitations mean that not all organs can be fully replicated to their natural complexity and functionality, limiting the effectiveness of biomaterial-based solutions for some medical conditions. Additionally, the production and disposal of some biomaterials can have environmental implications, necessitating the development of sustainable practices and materials. The long-term effects of many biomaterials are still not fully understood, and unforeseen complications may arise years after transplantation, requiring ongoing research and monitoring.

**Conclusive remark**

In conclusion, biomaterial-based organ transplantation represents a groundbreaking advancement in medical science, offering promising solutions to many of the challenges associated with traditional organ transplantation. The enhanced biocompatibility and functional restoration provided by these materials hold significant potential for improving patient outcomes and quality of life. By replicating complex organ structures and ensuring long-term durability, biomaterials pave the way for more effective and lasting treatments.

However, several challenges need to be addressed to fully realize the potential of this innovative approach. Issues related to immune responses, the complexity of replicating natural organ functions, long-term stability, regulatory approval, and high initial costs remain significant hurdles. Continued research, technological innovation, and interdisciplinary collaboration are essential to overcoming these obstacles.

Ethical considerations, including equitable access and societal acceptance, must also be navigated carefully to ensure the fair and ethical application of biomaterial-based organ transplantation. As the field progresses, addressing these challenges will be crucial for the successful integration of biomaterial-based therapies into clinical practice, ultimately revolutionizing patient care and expanding the possibilities of modern medicine.

**Reference**


[1] X. Zhao, K. Cui, and Z. Li, "The Role of Biomaterials in Stem Cell-Based Regenerative Medicine," *Future Med Chem*, vol. 11, no. 14, pp. 1779–1792, 2019, doi: 10.4155/FMC-2018-0347.

[2] A. Petrosyan *et al.*, "Regenerative medicine technologies applied to transplant medicine. An update," *Front BioengBiotechnol*, vol. 10, p. 1015628, Sep. 2022, doi: 10.3389/FBIOE.2022.1015628/BIBTEX.

[3] M. E. Scarritt, N. C. Pashos, and B. A. Bunnell, "A review of cellularization strategies for tissue engineering of whole organs," *Front BioengBiotechnol*, vol. 3, no. MAR, 2015, doi: 10.3389/FBIOE.2015.00043/FULL.

[4] P. Pei *et al.*, "Radionuclide labeled gold nanoclusters boost effective anti-tumor immunity for augmented radio-immunotherapy of cancer," *Nano Today*, vol. 38, Jun. 2021, doi: 10.1016/J.NANTOD.2021.101144.

[5] M. A. Al-Bar and H. Chamsi-Pasha, "Contemporary Bioethics Islamic Perspective."

[6] D. Bezinover and F. Saner, "Organ transplantation in the modern era," *BMC Anesthesiol*, vol. 19, no. 1, Mar. 2019, doi: 10.1186/S12871-019-0704-Z.

[7] H. R. Etheredge, "Assessing Global Organ Donation Policies: Opt-In vs Opt-Out," *Risk Manag Healthc Policy*, vol. 14, p. 1985, 2021, doi: 10.2147/RMHP.S270234.

[8] C. Zhang *et al.*, "Construction of tissue-engineered full-thickness cornea substitute using limbal epithelial cell-like and corneal endothelial cell-like cells derived from human embryonic stem cells," *Biomaterials*, vol. 124, pp. 180–194, Apr. 2017, doi: 10.1016/J.BIOMATERIALS.2017.02.003.

[9] S. M. Willerth and S. E. Sakiyama-Elbert, "Combining Stem Cells and Biomaterial Scaffolds for Constructing Tissues and Cell Delivery," *StemJournal*, vol. 1, no. 1, pp. 1–25, Jan. 2019, doi: 10.3233/STJ-180001.

[10] C. Vilela, A. R. P. Figueiredo, A. J. D. Silvestre, and C. S. R. Freire, "Multilayered materials based on biopolymers as drug delivery systems," *Expert Opin Drug Deliv*, vol. 14, no. 2, pp. 189–200, Feb. 2017, doi: 10.1080/17425247.2016.1214568.

[11] J. Jacob, J. T. Haponiuk, S. Thomas, and S. Gopi, "Biopolymer based nanomaterials in drug delivery systems: A review," *Mater Today Chem*, vol. 9, pp. 43–55, Sep. 2018, doi: 10.1016/j.mtchem.2018.05.002.

[12] F. Ah. Fouad, D. G. Youssef, F. A. Refay, and F. E.-T. Heakal, "Biocompatibility of Nanomaterials Reinforced Polymer-Based Nanocomposites," *Handbook of Biodegradable Materials*, pp. 1–41, 2022, doi: 10.1007/978-3-030-83783-9_17-1.

[13] M. Rezaei, F. Davani, M. Alishahi, and F. Masjedi, "Updates in immunocompatibility of biomaterials: applications for regenerative medicine," *Expert Rev Med Devices*, vol. 19, no. 4, pp. 353–367, 2022, doi: 10.1080/17434440.2022.2075730.

[14] S. Talebian*et al.*, "Biopolymers for Antitumor Implantable Drug Delivery Systems: Recent Advances and Future Outlook," *Advanced Materials*, vol. 30, no. 31, Aug. 2018, doi: 10.1002/ADMA.201706665.

[15] E. T. J. Chong, J. W. Ng, and P. C. Lee, "Classification and Medical Applications of Biomaterials–A Mini Review," *BIO Integration*, vol. 4, no. 2, pp. 54–61, 2023, doi: 10.15212/BIOI-2022-0009.

[16] D. Shekhawat, A. Singh, M. K. Banerjee, T. Singh, and A. Patnaik, "Bioceramic composites for orthopaedic applications: A comprehensive review of mechanical, biological, and microstructural properties," *Ceram Int*, vol. 47, no. 3, pp. 3013–3030, Feb. 2021, doi: 10.1016/J.CERAMINT.2020.09.214.

[17] H. Jodati, B. Yılmaz, and Z. Evis, "A review of bioceramic porous scaffolds for hard tissue applications: Effects of structural features," *Ceram Int*, vol. 46, no. 10, pp. 15725–15739, Jul. 2020, doi: 10.1016/J.CERAMINT.2020.03.192.

[18] M. A. Velazco-Medel, L. A. Camacho-Cruz, and E. Bucio, "Modification of relevant polymeric materials for medical applications and devices," *Med Devices Sens*, vol. 3, no. 6, Dec. 2020, doi: 10.1002/MDS3.10073.

[19] A. J. T. Teo, A. Mishra, I. Park, Y. J. Kim, W. T. Park, and Y. J. Yoon, "Polymeric Biomaterials for Medical Implants and Devices," *ACS Biomater Sci Eng*, vol. 2, no. 4, pp. 454–472, Apr. 2016, doi: 10.1021/ACSBIOMATERIALS.5B00429.

[20] R. M. Pilliar, "Metallic Biomaterials," *Biomedical Materials: Second Edition*, pp. 1–47, Jan. 2020, doi: 10.1007/978-3-030-49206-9_1.

[21] C. Morsiya, "A review on parameters affecting properties of biomaterial SS 316L," *Australian Journal of Mechanical Engineering*, vol. 20, no. 3, pp. 803–813, 2022, doi: 10.1080/14484846.2020.1752975.

[22] K. D'Costa, M. Kosic, A. Lam, A. Moradipour, Y. Zhao, and M. Radisic, "Biomaterials and Culture Systems for Development of Organoid and Organ-on-a-Chip Models," *Ann Biomed Eng*, vol. 48, no. 7, pp. 2002–2027, Jul. 2020, doi: 10.1007/S10439-020-02498-W.

[23] D. Li *et al.*, "Biomimetic albumin-modified gold nanorods for photothermo-chemotherapy and macrophage polarization modulation," *Acta Pharm Sin B*, vol. 8, no. 1, pp. 74–84, Jan. 2018, doi: 10.1016/j.apsb.2017.09.005.

[24] S. Dai *et al.*, "Application of three-dimensional printing technology in renal diseases," *Front Med (Lausanne)*, vol. 9, Dec. 2022, doi: 10.3389/FMED.2022.1088592.

[25] V. S. Reddy, B. Ramasubramanian, V. M. Telrandhe, and S. Ramakrishna, "Contemporary standpoint and future of 3D bioprinting in tissue/organs printing," *Curr Opin Biomed Eng*, vol. 27, Sep. 2023, doi: 10.1016/j.cobme.2023.100461.

[26] S. Agarwal, S. Saha, V. K. Balla, A. Pal, A. Barui, and S. Bodhak, "Current Developments in 3D Bioprinting for Tissue and Organ Regeneration–A Review," *Front Mech Eng*, vol. 6, 2020, doi: 10.3389/FMECH.2020.589171.

[27] S. Ji and M. Guvendiren, "Recent Advances in Bioink Design for 3D Bioprinting of Tissues and Organs," *Front BioengBiotechnol*, vol. 5, no. APR, Apr. 2017, doi: 10.3389/FBIOE.2017.00023.

[28] S. KholghiEshkalak, E. Kowsari, and S. Ramakrishna, "3D printing of graphene-based composites and their applications in medicine and health care," *Innovations in Graphene-Based Polymer Composites*, pp. 463–485, Jan. 2022, doi: 10.1016/B978-0-12-823789-2.00011-X.

[29] K. D'Costa, M. Kosic, A. Lam, ... A. M.-A. of biomedical, and undefined 2020, "Biomaterials and culture systems for development of organoid and organ-on-a-chip models," *Springer*, Accessed: Jun. 22, 2024. [Online]. Available: https://link.springer.com/article/10.1007/s10439-020-02498-w

[30] E. K. Hendow, P. Guhmann, B. Wright, P. Sofokleous, N. Parmar, and R. M. Day, "Biomaterials for hollow organ tissue engineering," *Springer*, vol. 9, no. 1, 2016, doi: 10.1186/s13069-016-0040-6.

CHAPTER EIGHT

# Therapeutic Strategies Utilizing Biomaterials in the Field of Neuroscience

**Sahil Hussain[1], Badruddeen*[1], Alina Khan[2], Vani Shukla[3]**

[1]*Department of Pharmacy, Integral University, Lucknow – 226026.*

[2]*Department of Toxicology and Medical Elementology, JamiaHamdard, New Delhi – 110062.*

[3]*Department of Food and Nutrition, Era University, Lucknow – 226003.*

**Highlights**

- Biomaterials, traditionally non-living materials in medical devices, are evaluated for safety and effectiveness, requiring biocompatibility, biofunctionality, bioinertness, biodegradability, and sterilization.
- Neurological disorders, especially those affecting the nervous system (NS), present significant health challenges due to the inability of neurons to regenerate. Spinal cord injury (SCI) leads to severe complications, affecting 27 million people globally.
- Glioblastoma treatment is hindered by poor drug transport through the BBB. Biomaterials enable innovative therapies like gene therapy, photodynamic therapy, anti-angiogenic therapy, and thermotherapy for brain tumors.
- The chapter explores cutting-edge research on developing biomaterials to enhance nervous system functionality, focusing on improving treatments for neurological disorders and brain tumors.

## Introduction

The science and engineering of biomaterials is an emerging field. Traditionally, biomaterials were defined as "non-living materials used in medical devices to interact with biological systems,"and they were primarily associated with the realm of medical devices. The evaluation of biomaterials is centred on their safety and effectiveness. Biomaterials must be biocompatible, biofunctional, bioinert, biodegradable, and capable of being sterilized to prevent irritation and rejection (1).

Neurological disorders continue to pose significant threats to both physical and mental health, primarily due to the inability of neurons in the nervous system (NS) to regenerate. Conventional therapies, such as surgery and medication, struggle to repair NS damage effectively. Consequently, repairing the damaged NS remains a major challenge in the field of neurology(2). Spinal cord injury (SCI) is a debilitating neurological condition that results in the loss of sensory and motor functions. It can also cause significant complications, including bladder and bowel dysfunction, infections, chronic pain, and cardiac and respiratory problems. SCI affects the lives of many individuals globally, with an estimated 27 million people living with this condition (3). Specifically, delivering drugs to the brain remains a major challenge in treating neurodegenerative (ND) disorders. Nanotechnology offers a potential solution to these limitations due to nanomaterials' very small size and high surface area, which distinguish nanoscience from other classical technologies. Currently, nearly all macromolecular drugs and over 98% of small drug molecules fail to cross the blood-brain barrier (BBB), and drug candidates often exhibit poor biopharmaceutical and pharmacokinetic properties. Thus, there is a strong need for suitable drug delivery systems that can distribute drug molecules without harming healthy organs and tissues. Although nanoparticles administered systemically are more chemically stable, they present challenges related to large-scale industrial production and quality control. Additionally, the safety of nanoparticles when injected and their effects on the central nervous system after crossing the BBB need further investigation. Modern treatment options for ND diseases include implanting therapy and using anticancer drug-loaded biomaterials, such as hydrogels (4). Notably, collagen-based hydrogels have been successfully used in clinical trials as conduits, replicating the native physiological environment of neural tissues, controlling cell behavior, and supporting the regeneration of damaged nerve tissue (5).

The incidence of neurodegenerative diseases is rising due to shifting age demographics, and sports-related traumatic brain injuries are becoming more common over time. Currently approved medicines for neurodegenerative diseases only temporarily alleviate symptoms and do not cure or delay disease progression. Cell transplantation strategies present an alternative approach for central nervous system repair. However, their effectiveness is hindered by the low survival rates of cells injected in suspension. Enhancing cell survival in vivo can be achieved by transplanting cells attached to or encapsulated within suitable biomaterial constructs.

Various biomaterials have been used to create constructs such as nanoparticles, nanotubes, microspheres, microscale fibrous scaffolds, and scaffolds made of gels and micro-columns(6).Neural interfaces (NIs) are neuroengineering tools that establish a bidirectional communication pathway with the nervous system. The major technical and scientific challenge remains probing neurons over a long-term period with high precision and accuracy. Smart biomaterials (SBMs), such as stimuli-responsive and shape-memory biomaterials, have emerged as innovative materials with exceptional properties. SBMs improve the biointegration and performance of neural implants, enabling the development of stable, implantable, minimally invasive, and untethered NIs with controllable spatial resolution. These materials can reduce biological inflammatory responses and open numerous future possibilities in neuroscience research and neuromodulation therapies. SBMs can intelligently respond to electrical, optical, mechanical, and magnetic stimuli to power NIs implanted deep within the brain and/or facilitate reciprocal communication with neurons (7). Treating malignant brain tumours is one of the most formidable challenges in oncology. Current brain tumour treatments are hindered by the difficulty of delivering drugs across the BBB to the tumour site. Biomaterials are increasingly crucial in developing more effective treatments for brain tumours. Specifically, polymer (nano)particles can provide sustained drug delivery directly to the tumour via intracerebral injection, be designed to cross the BBB or be functionalized with peptides and ligands to enable systemic administration while still targeting the tumour endothelium or tumour cells. Furthermore, nanoparticles have the potential to revolutionize the diagnosis and imaging of brain tumours by enhancing both preoperative and intraoperative detection, enabling early identification of precancerous cells, and offering real-time, non-invasive monitoring and imaging of treatment effects(8).Glioblastoma (GB) commonly arises in the cerebral hemispheres of the frontal and temporal lobes and can significantly infiltrate surrounding tissue, making maximum surgical resection impossible due to its high vascularization. Current brain tumour therapy is hindered by the inadequate transport of medication through the BBB to the tumour site. Biomaterials have significantly enhanced the ability to investigate, diagnose, and treat brain tumors by improving preoperative and intraoperative tumour detection. Nanostructured -based biomaterials can deliver drugs directly to the tumour bed for extended periods. Additionally, biomaterials can be utilized to provide innovative therapies such as gene therapy, photodynamic therapy, anti-angiogenic therapy, and thermotherapy(9).In this chapter, we explore cutting-edge research on the development of various types of biomaterials designed to improve and enhance the functionality of the nervous system.

**Pathophysiology of neurodegenerative disorders (ND)**

## *Parkinson's*

Parkinson's disease is the second most serious neurodegenerative disorder, characterized by the pathological decline of dopaminergic neurons. This decline leads to reduced dopamine levels in the striatum, which may result in motor impairments. Parkinson's disease is a chronic and progressive neurodegenerative disorder that affects motor function, leading to symptoms such as resting tremors, postural instability, bradykinesia, and muscle stiffness(10). The condition originates due to the gradual decline of dopaminergic nigrostriatal neurons. Symptoms of Parkinson's disease is illustrated in figure 1.

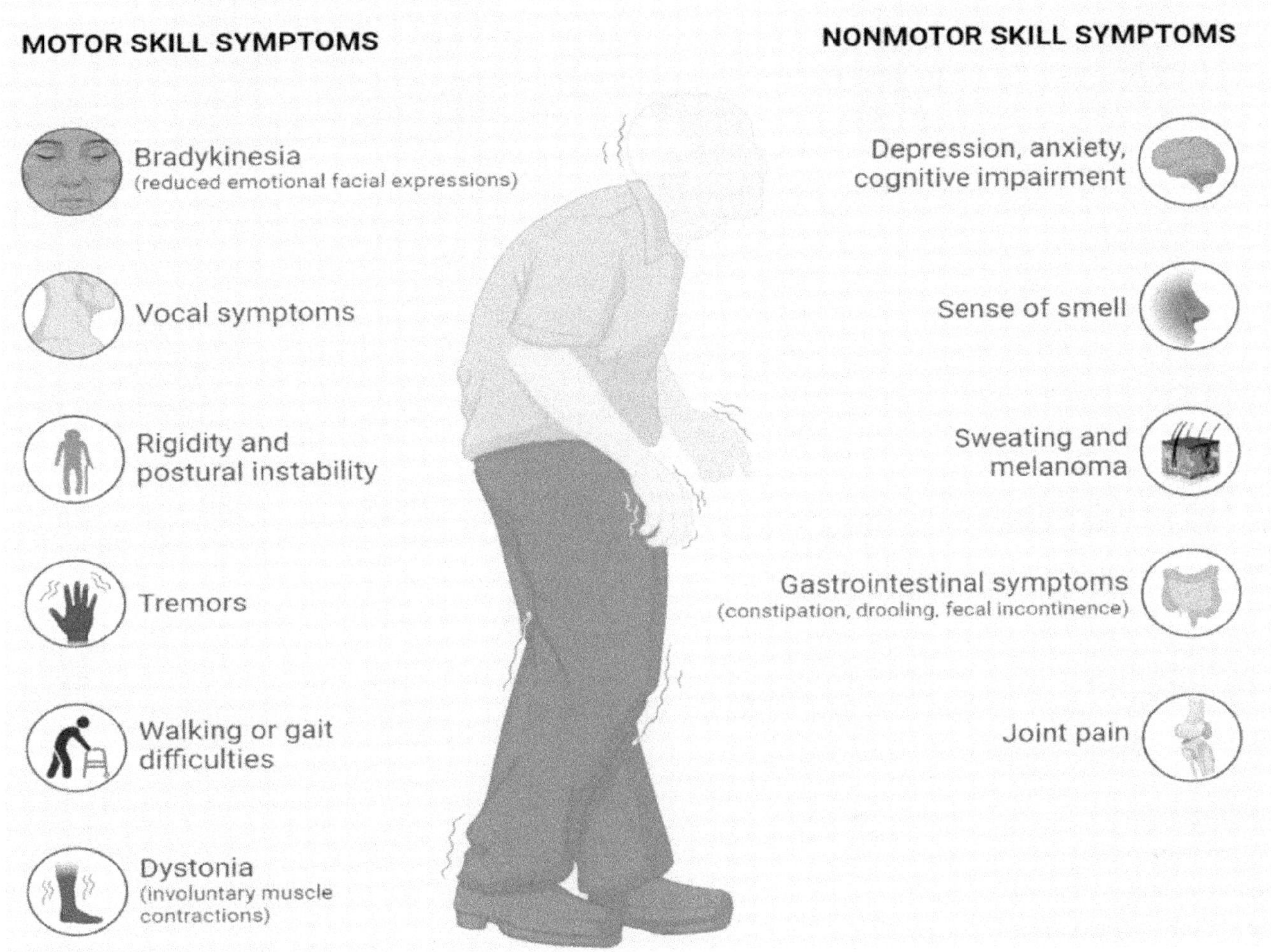


**Figure 1: Symptoms of Parkinson's Disease (10).** Sourec:*https://doi.org/10.1016/j.ipha.2023.09.006*

**Alzheimer's Disease**

Alzheimer's disease is characterized by cognitive issues related to memory, learning, and synapse function, along with behavioral disturbances. The amygdala and hippocampus are the primary brain regions responsible for memory regulation. Among the most notable neurodegenerative disorders associated with tau protein aggregation, which manifest with both motor and mental abnormalities, is Alzheimer's disease. Tauopathies are marked by abnormal intracellular tau protein aggregation in the brain due to hyperphosphorylation, leading to oxidative damage, increased intracellular calcium levels, and inflammation. Hyperphosphorylated tau, which is insoluble, can form paired cytotoxic helical structures. According to the amyloid hypothesis, another key feature of Alzheimer is the extracellular accumulation of beta-amyloids, which are also considered cytotoxic and a critical mediator of the disease (11). Figure 2 illustrates the difference between a normal brain and the brain of an Alzheimer's disease patient.

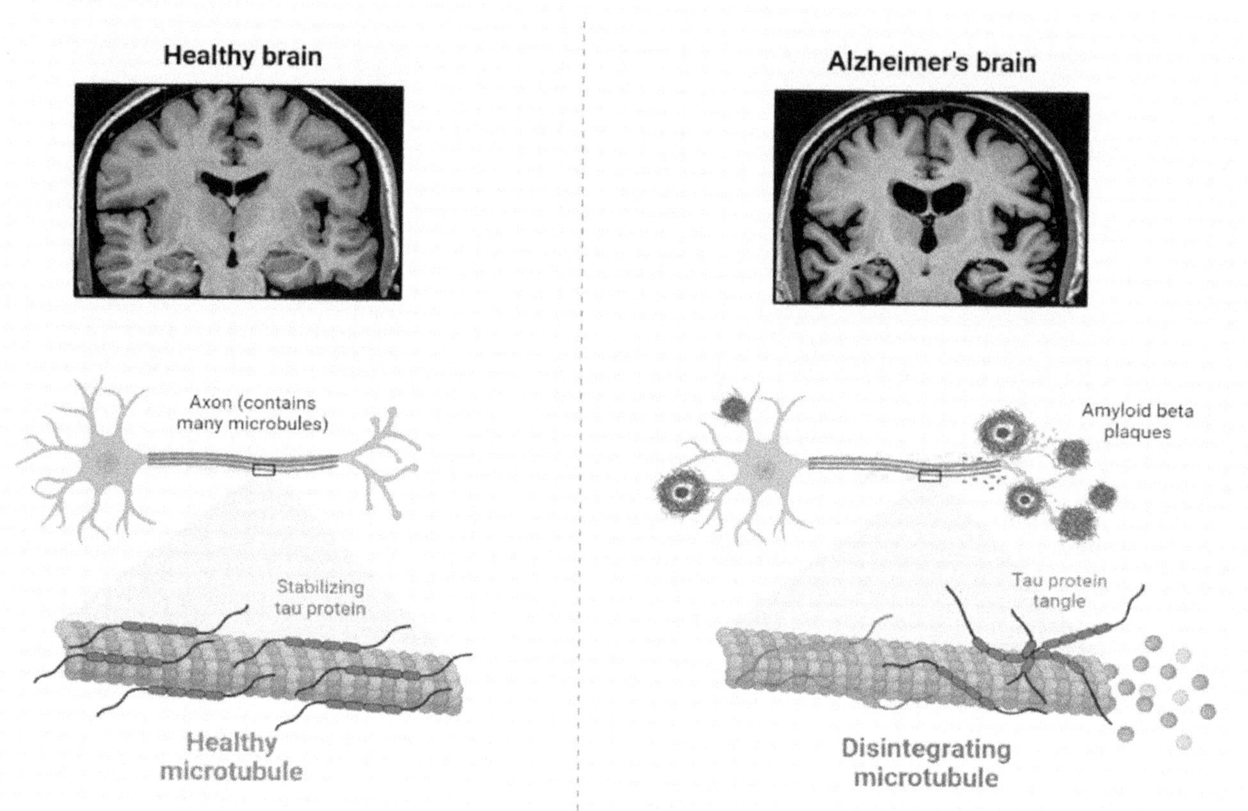


**Figure 2: Difference between a normal brain and the brain of an Alzheimer's disease patient.***Figure adapted from: https://doi.org/10.1016/j.ipha.2023.09.006*

**Glioblastoma**

Glioblastoma multiforme (GBM), also known simply as glioblastoma (GB), is the most common invasive, obstructive, and generally fatal primary or secondary brain tumor, affecting 1 in 100,000 people annually (12).

**Function of Blood Brain Barrier**

The blood-brain barrier (BBB) is a critical endothelial membrane within the brain's microvasculature, formed by tight junctions between brain capillary endothelial cells (BCECs). These cells are surrounded by mural cells and astrocytic end-feet, which effectively separate the central nervous system (CNS) from the systemic blood circulation (Figure 1). The BBB serves to safeguard the brain by selectively permitting the passage of nutrients while preventing the entry of substances such as neurotoxins and blood-borne pathogens, thus maintaining brain homeostasis. Comprising a continuous layer of BCECs tightly interconnected by junction proteins, the BBB also includes mural cells (pericytes in microcapillaries and vascular smooth muscle cells in larger vessels), a basement membrane, and glial cells (astrocytes, microglia, and oligodendrocytes), collectively known as the neurovascular unit (NVU). These NVU components interact synergistically to uphold the integrity of the microvasculature, including the BBB, and regulate cerebral blood flow. In contrast to peripheral microvasculature, CNS microvasculature is notably thinner (~200 nm), and BCEC junctions are significantly tighter (~50–100 times) with virtually no fenestrations and minimal pinocytotic vesicles, necessitating an energy-dependent active transport mechanism for nutrient passage. BCECs also possess a higher density of mitochondria (~5–6 times) to support these energy demands. Moreover, BCECs contain proteolytic enzymes that can degrade neuroactive substances and drugs, adding an enzymatic barrier. Pericytes, found within the vascular basement membrane, cover approximately 20% of the BBB's abluminal surface. These cells are equipped with contractile proteins that enable them to regulate blood flow in brain capillaries through contraction and relaxation. The BBB is further reinforced by two basement membranes: the inner vascular basement membrane, formed by ECM secreted by BCECs and pericytes, and the outer parenchymal basement membrane, secreted by astrocytic processes. These basement membranes serve as anchoring points for signaling processes and provide an additional barrier. Astrocytes, a predominant type of glial cell, play a crucial role in maintaining BBB structure and function. Their endfeet form an intricate network surrounding BCECs, enhancing tight junctions and enveloping brain endothelial capillaries to preserve BBB integrity. Astrocytes also facilitate intercellular communication between BCECs and neurons, regulating vascular dynamics and blood flow in response to neuronal activity.

Additionally, astrocytes contribute significantly to CNS homeostasis by clearing synaptic debris, protecting against injury, and fulfilling various essential roles. Microglia, another type of glial cell, participate in immune regulation within the brain and contribute to CNS homeostasis. Recent studies suggest that activated microglia can increase the expression of tight junction proteins, further supporting BBB integrity.(13)

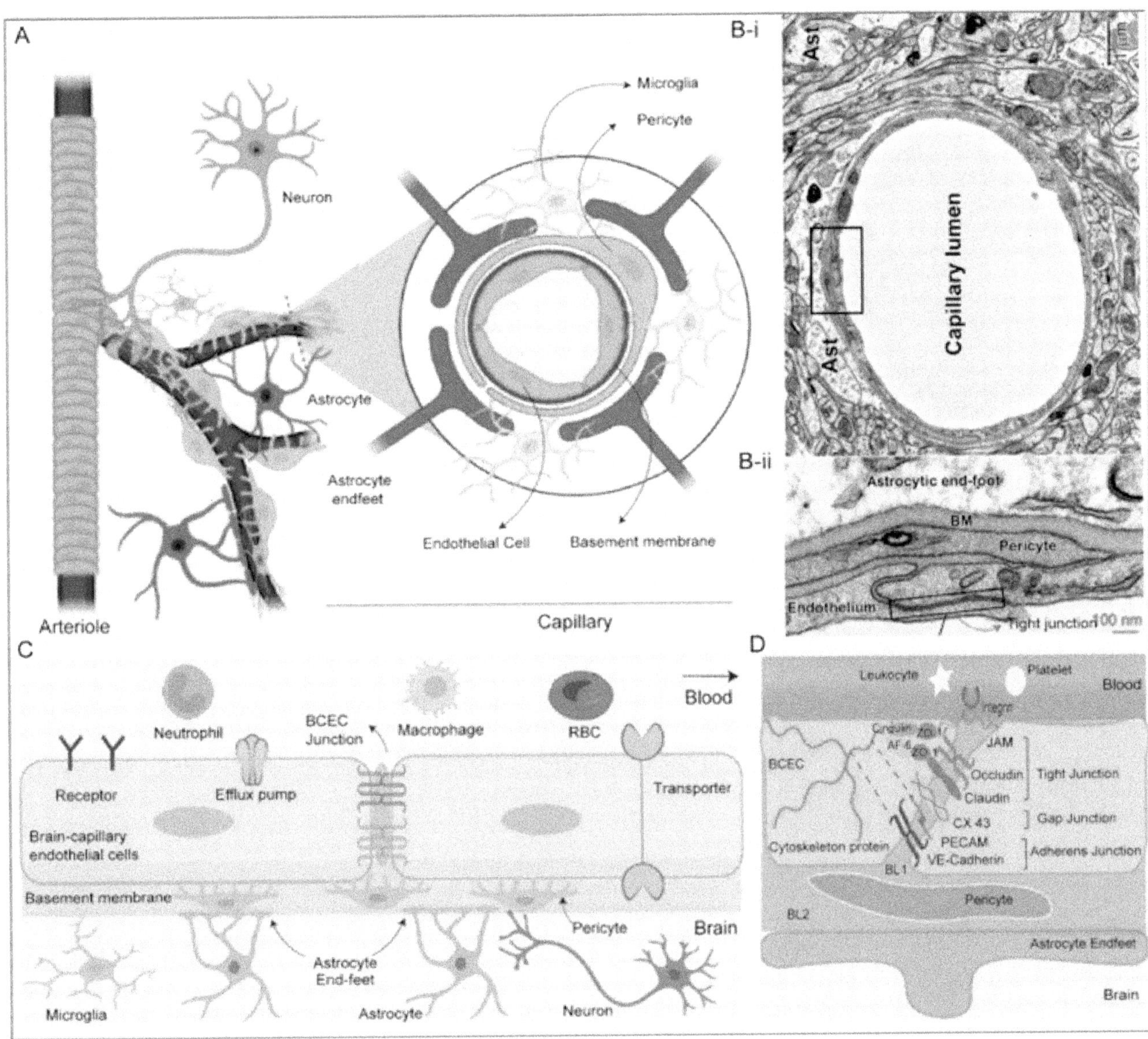


***Figure:3***(A) Schematic of the neurovascular unit (NVU) includes neurons, vascular cells (EC, SMC at arterioles, PC at capillaries), and glial cells (Ast, microglia). EC is covered by PC and astrocyte end-feet in the basement membrane (BM). Neurons regulate blood flow with adjacent mural cells (PC, SMC) in brain microvasculature. Microglia are located around open areas of brain capillaries without astrocyte coverage. (B-i) TEM of brain tissue shows NVU components: EC, PC, Ast, tight junctions (B-ii). (C) Schematicof the blood-brain barrier with interconnected brain capillary endothelial cells via junction proteins (D) and other NVU components.(14)

| Material classifications | Nanocarrier approach | Therapeutics agents | Structure | References |
|---|---|---|---|---|
| Metal Elemental | Gold Nanoparticle | Gold-Poly-L-Lysine nano complexes | Nanosphere | (14) |
| Metal Oxide | Iron Oxide Nanoparticle | Alpha-Synuclein RNAi | Nanosphere | (15) |
| Inorganic Compound | Quantum Dots | palmitoylated peptide WGDap(Palmitoyl)VKIKKP9G GH6 | Nano Tube | (16) |
| Metalloid Elemental | Silica Nanoparticle (SiNPs) | Nootropics | Nanosphere | (17) |
| Lipid | Liposomes | Drug loaded Nanoparticle | Nanosphere with Bilayer Surface | (18) |
| Cationic Lipid | Solid Lipid Nanoparticle (SLN) | - | Nanosphere with Monolayer Surface | (19) |
| Polymer | Polylactic Acid (PLA) | (methylaminomethyl)anthracene (MAMA) and procaine hydrochloride (PrHy) | Porous Nanosphere | (20) |

**Table 1.** Summary of popular biomaterials used in neurodegenerative diseases and related classification.

**Natural Biomaterials**

1. **Chitosan:**Chitosan is a natural polymer derived from chitin, the main structural carbohydrate found in shellfish and crustaceans. Chitosan has several intriguing properties, including gel formation, high conductivity, and biocompatibility. This biomaterial is exceptionally biodegradable and non-cytotoxic, and it possesses antibacterial, antifungal, and anticancer properties(21).Ananthanarayanan et al.(22) demonstrated that human GB and glioblastoma multiforme (GBM) cells propagate based on structural rigidity, with greater growth observed on tougher surfaces. This partly explains the disparity in growth between U-118 MG cells on polystyrene 2D in vitro propagation and 3D chitosan scaffolds with a drastically reduced Young's modulus. In 2D standards, the cells formed smooth monolayers, whereas in the chitosan scaffolds, the cells formed tumor spheroids that more closely mimic the shape of GB/GBM tumors in cell culture. The chitosan scaffold environment enabled the cells to establish more cell-cell and cell-extracellular matrix (ECM) interactions. These findings underscore the importance of using 3D scaffolds to accurately replicate the development and morphology of in vivo malignancies(9).

2. **Alginate**

Alginate hydrogel, a polysaccharide derived from brown seaweed, has been extensively researched and used in a wide range of medical applications due to its biocompatibility, low toxicity, cost-effectiveness, and moderate gelation induced by the accumulation of divalent cations such as $Ca^{2+}$(23). This hydrogel can be synthesized through various crosslinking processes, and its structural similarity to the ECM of human tissue makes it suitable for a wide range of applications, including skincare, delivery of bioactive agents like small molecule drugs and proteins, and cell implantation. Alginate is a class of linear copolymers composed of (1,4)-linked β-D-mannuronate (M) and α-L-guluronate (G) residue blocks. These blocks consist of alternating M and G residues (GMGMGM) and consecutive G residues (GGGGGG).Research by Sharma et. al reported Cisplatin, at higher doses, killed the cells after 48 hours, with an $IC_{50}$ value estimated at 4 μg/mL. However, at a moderate concentration of silver nanoparticles (Ag NPs), the cells were destroyed after 12 hours, indicating that this approach is more effective. Cell viability studies revealed that Ag NPs-Alg-Chi nanocomposites (NCs) were also effective against human cancer cell lines (HT-29) and non-malignant hematopoietic stem and progenitor cells (HEK-293).

## *Synthetic biomaterials*

**3. Poly lactic-co-glycolic acid (PLGA)**

One of the most widely used and promising synthesized biodegradable polymers is an FDA-approved copolymer, poly(lactide-co-glycolide) (PLGA). PLGA is a co-polymer formed from glycolic acid and lactic acid. Due to its biocompatibility and biodegradability, it has been utilized and approved for various medical devices. It has been applied in numerous delivery systems for different diseases, including cancer treatments. PLGA is also used in tissue engineering and vaccine development, often in the form of microparticles. By adjusting the ' 'copolymer's lactic-to-glycolic acid ratio, molecular weight, and end-group compounds, the degradation rate of PLGA can be controlled. When exposed to moisture, the ester linkages in PLGA hydrolyze, breaking down the hydrocarbon chains into smaller fragments that eventually produce lactic and glycolic acid, which can be naturally metabolized(24).

**4. Poly-lactic acid (PLA)**

During metabolism, lactic acid evolves, resulting in the conversion of poly(lactic acid) (PLA) into a hydrophobic and biodegradable polymer capable of serving as a transport medium for hydrophobic chemical medicines. In antitumor clinical trials, this polymer has been introduced and has already shown positive outcomes. For instance, Genexol®-PM, formed by monomethoxy PEG-block-poly(D,L-lactide) (mPEG-PDLLA), has been developed into a paclitaxel-loaded formulation(25).

**5. Poly-ethylene imine (PEI)**

PEI with various molecular weights has been extensively studied for the in vitro and in vivo delivery of nucleic acids. However, only specific PEIs are suitable for DNA or siRNA transfer within or outside laboratory settings. PEIs are water-soluble linear or branched polymers that enhance effective gene delivery into tumour cells. PEI holds a prominent position among polycationic polymers due to its high gene transfer efficiency, altered pharmacokinetic properties, improved biocompatibility, and the potential for tailored administration(26, 27). Animal tests showed that the combination treatment significantly reduced median tumour growth compared to the standards and resulted in a longer generation diurnal cycle. When combined with an anticancer drug, this medical technology demonstrated increased antitumor effectiveness in treating GBM/GB cells (28).

**6. Poly-B-amino ' 'Ester's (PBAEs)**

PBAEs have been utilized as gene delivery vectors within a group of biodegradable polymers. Under acidic conditions, the β-amino ester bonds undergo hydrolytic cleavage, causing the polymer to degrade rapidly and efficiently (29). This ' 'polymer's unique characteristics enable effective gene transport and release for both in vitro and in vivo studies, as demonstrated by Rahman et al. In a malignant glioblastoma model, PBAEs were tested as carriers for HSVtk (Herpes Simplex Virus type 1 thymidine kinase) to deliver DNA. The distinctive properties of PBAEs enhanced cellular uptake and facilitated the endosomal escape of antitumor gene therapies. However, individual nanoparticles of the gene were insufficient to completely eradicate the malignant tumours(30).

**7. PEG – DMA**

An injectable hydrogel made from polyethylene glycol dimethacrylate (PEG-DMA) was deemed suitable for delivering TMZ consistently and locally. This gel polymerized rapidly upon exposure to light and exhibited a high viscosity modulus of approximately 10 kPa in under two minutes (31). A scheme involving a photo-polymerizable PEG-DMA hydrogel for delivering TMZ locally could offer several benefits. In brain tumour beds, PEG-DMA can be injected and quickly photo-polymerized using visible or ultraviolet (UV) and, therefore, should be absorbed well by the vascular endothelium (32). The properties of hydrogels based on PEG-DMA, characterized by their small pore size, can prevent cell invasion and avoid creating an environment conducive to cancer cell proliferation (33).

**8. Gliadel wafers**

Gliadel Wafer is a biomaterial composed of 1,3-bis-(p-carboxyphenoxy) propane (pCPP) and sebacic acid (SA) (polifeprosan 20) used to deliver various chemotherapy drugs, including BCNU, a chemotherapeutic agent for treating recurrent gliomas. The development of interstitial BCNU Gliadel wafers has shown promising results in treating glioblastoma tumours. BCNU was one of the first systemic chemotherapies approved by the FDA for treating brain tumours. However, its systemic use has been limited due to only marginally increased survival rates, prolonged myelosuppression, and potentially fatal pulmonary toxicity. The advent of BCNU treatments marked a significant advancement by enabling direct delivery to the tumor bed with minimal systemic effects. BCNU-polifeprosan 20 wafers have been well tolerated, with an acceptable rate of complications in phase I and II clinical trials. BCNU has demonstrated efficacy against newly diagnosed and recurrent malignant gliomas compared to patients who did not receive placebo wafers (34).

**9. Vesicular phospholipid gels (VPGs)**

Vesicular Phospholipid Gels (VPGs) are characterized as semisolid droplets and membranous nanostructures. Recent studies have highlighted several desirable features of VPGs, demonstrating their potential in various applications (35). In xenografts, VPG formulations containing various cytostatic drugs have been evaluated and shown to be effective. Research indicates that the vesicles protect the drugs from early metabolic inactivation and direct them to solid tumours with increased vascular permeability (36).

**Challenges**

When it comes to treating neuroscience, biomaterials are crucial. In research and development, nanoparticles in particular have been utilized more often. Several biomaterials that are nanoparticles have been thoroughly studied for their benefits and drawbacks.Numerous problems remain unanswered for scientists and medical professionals creating biomaterials for tissue creation and regenerative medicine.

As of right now, implantable tissue creation can be done at a much larger scale. Large implantable structures, for instance, may now be made more easily thanks to 3D bioprinting technology (37). On the other hand, inadequate vascularization during regeneration of tissue is linked to subpar healing results. Thus, it's critical to increase the post-implantation vascularization and integration as well as the biocompatibility of created constructions. Investigating workable strategies to promote the development of new vasculature inside synthetic tissues is necessary. The ability to layer many tissues at once is restricted in the tissue production technologies now in use. However, since human tissues constantly come into touch with other or distinct tissue types, tissue interfaces are crucial to the functional restoration of injured organs. New strategies are required to facilitate the spatial transition between different tissue types (such as tendon-muscle, bone-cartilage, and bone-neuro).

Progress in biomaterial science, tissue engineering, and neuroscience is crucial for improving the effectiveness and use of biomaterial-based neurological therapies. Raising awareness and educating the public iskey to encouraging these therapies' acceptance and adoption. Informing healthcare providers, patients, and the general public about thes treatments' benefits, risks, and ethical considerations supports informed decision-making and societal acceptance.

**Clinical Significance**

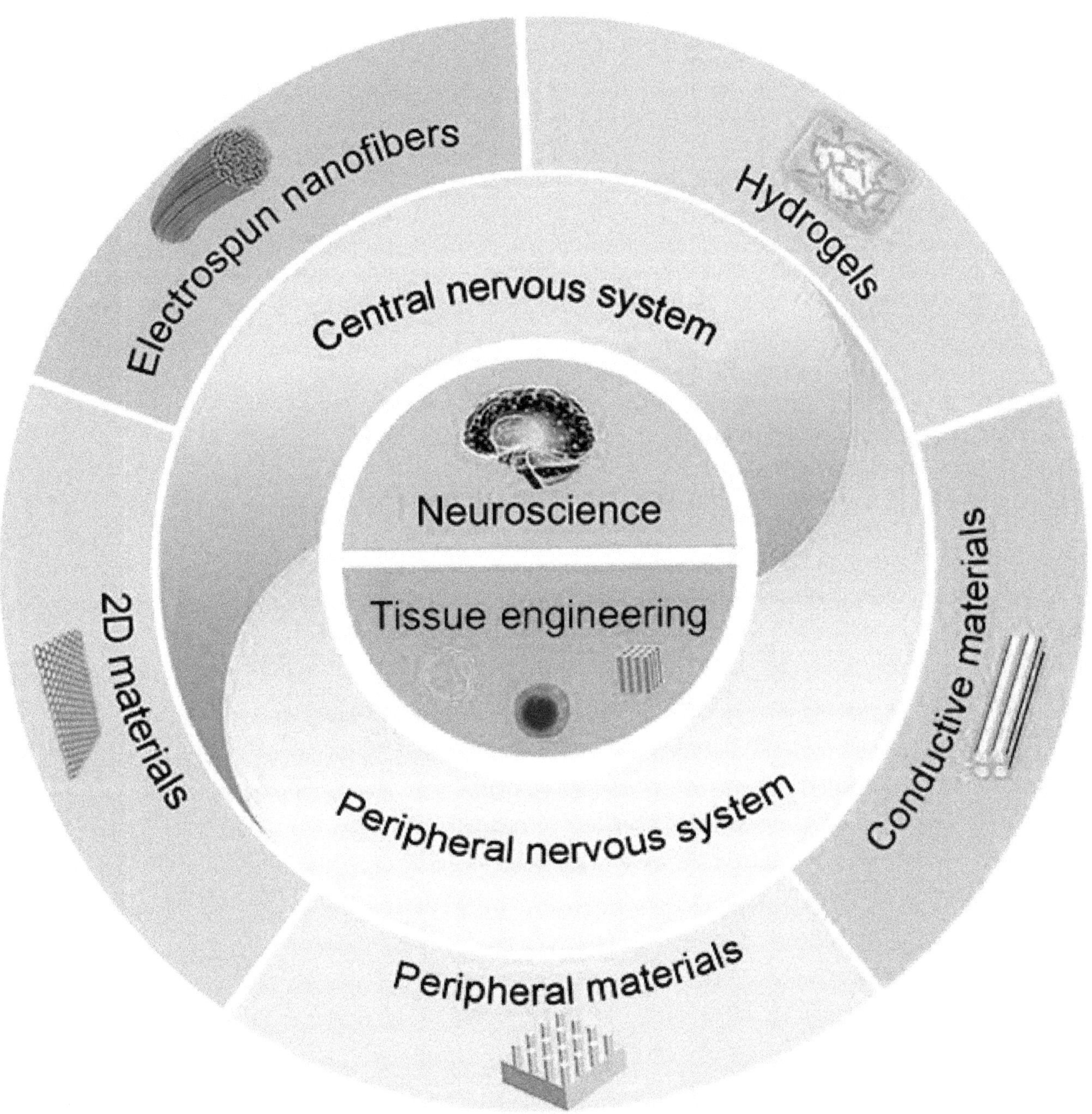


**Figure 4**: Clinical significance of biomaterials in the field of neuroscience(2) Figure credits : Xiaoge Zhang et. al

**Utilizing Tissue engineering in Neurosciences**

Regulating sensory and motor activities, as well as transmitting physiological information between limbs and organs, all depend on the nervous system (2). People with nerve damage, including those with SCI, TBI, PNI, and neurodegenerative disorders, may lose their ability to move or sense things. In order to reconstruct the disrupted brain tissue architecture, implantable or injectable bioengineered nanomaterials have been developed in response to the advancement of TE in the neuroscience field (38).

## *Nanofibers produced by electrospinning*

Electrospinning has been accessible for the past 20 years to produce nanofiber-based scaffolds for the treatment of SCI. Due to its straightforward manufacturing, wide range of applications, and significant manufacturing potential, electrically spinning is still regarded as one of the most adaptable methods for creating nanofibers with diameters that vary from just a few to a few hundred nanometers, even though many fabrication techniques, including assembling themselves, super drawing, and phase separation, have been documented for nanofiber fabrication (39). Due to their capacity to replicate the fundamental makeup of fibrillar ECM, nanofibers have found widespread use in the creation of nerve-guiding conduits (40).

**Advantage and Disadvantage**

**Polyethyleneimine(PEI)**

*In vivo/ Invitro*

1. Non-cytotoxicity and blood compatibility.

2. PEI creates tiny complexes by electrostatically interacting with negatively charged DNA. Influenced by dose cytotoxicity brought on by proteins within the cell that get aggregated and become negatively charged as a consequence of the substance's inability to biodegrade within the cells. (26, 42)

**Poly (Lactic-co-Glycolic Acid) (PLGA)**

*In vivo/ In vitro*

1. Throughout 60 days, tumor removal dramatically improved the mice's survival rates.

2. There are PLGAs with a wide range of physicochemical characteristics; the mechanism of release may be customized by choosing PLGAs having the right lactide:glycolide ratio (L:G) and molecular weight (Mw). As with many other polymers that decompose, the drawback of PLGA is that it breaks down to produce acids.(24)

**Chitosan**

*In vitro*

Possesses intriguing qualities, including being able to form gels, an elevated capacity for adhesion, and biodegradable.

2. Exceptionally non-cytotoxic and biodegradable, with antimicrobial, antimicrobial, and anticancer properties.

3. A flexible biopolymer, chitosan may be treated to create sponges, gels, membranes, beads, and scaffolds with ease.

1. Not stable; there may be an uncontrollable disintegration

2. Minimal resistance to mechanical action.

3. It's challenging to regulate pore size.

4. Chitosan's inherent characteristics may be impacted by crosslinking. (43-45)

Gliadel wafers (polifeprosan 20) with BCNU and Temozolomide

*In vivo*

Enabling administration straight to the cancer bed without requiring passage via the blood-brain barrier

With almost negligible toxicities throughout the system.

The chloroethyl moieties of BCNU operate as a mediating agent, causing reactive sites on nucleic acids to get alkylated and disrupting DNA synthesis and repair.

RNA and protein production may also be inhibited by the carbonylation of nucleoprotein lysine residues.

1. Brain edema, irregular healing, cerebral spinal fluid leaks, intracranial infections, seizures, hydrocephalus, and cyst development are among the risks associated with Gliadel wafer implantation.

2. Increased toxicity incidence.

3. Interstitial pneumonia brought on by high alkylating activity of BCNU and DNA damage to the alveolar epithelial cells. (46, 47)

**Vesicular phospholipid gels (VPGs)**

*In vivo/ Invitro*

The hydrogel shows excellent stability when subjected to autoclaving, meeting sterility standards.It is biocompatible and biodegradable.Lipid-based gels are cost-effective and simple to produce.VPGs have been evaluated for effectiveness using a human subcutaneous GBM model, showing promising results.This hydrogel can adapt to any shape or size of the surgical cavity.VPGs face challenges such as their semisolid nature, the need for high injection forces, and difficulties with sterilization, necessitating aseptic production.Additional in vivo studies are required to confirm their safety for clinical applications.While natural phospholipids are inexpensive, maintaining their purity is difficult, and they are less stable than synthetic phospholipids, which are more expensive.(35, 48, 49)

**Alginates**

*In vivo/In vitro*

A natural polysaccharide obtained from seaweed and algae serves as a biocompatible implant, offering low toxicity and affordability.It can be easily processed into various three-dimensional scaffolding materials, including hydrogels, microspheres, microcapsules, sponges, foams, and fibers.This biomaterial is biodegradable, and its degradation can be regulated through gelation.Alginate can limit cell migration, causing cells to proliferate in specific areas and form clusters.Cell survival decreases due to its chemical crosslinking with calcium chloride, and the viscosity of alginate can also adversely affect cell survival.To avoid adverse effects in the body, alginate needs to be purified of impurities such as heavy metals and endotoxins through a multi-step extraction process.(50-52)

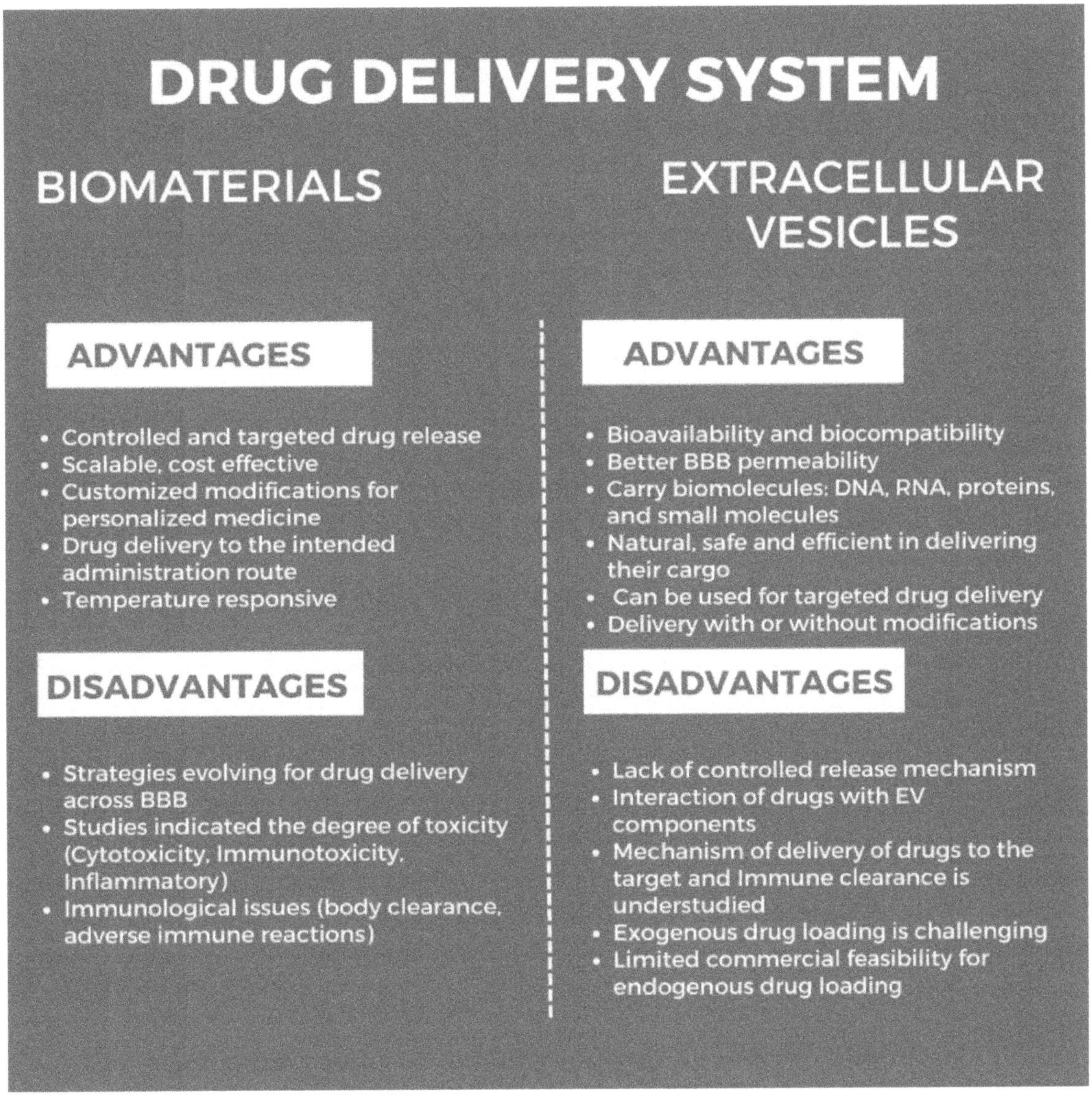

**Figure 5: Advantages and disadvantages of drug delivery system.**

**Conclusive remark**

This chapter focuses on various biomaterials used in neurological disorders specifically glioblastoma treatment. Despite aggressive treatment, standard chemotherapy and radiation are often ineffective, leading to inevitable tumour persistence. The GB environment typically hinders many tumours and malignant cells; specialized niches within it play vital roles in sustaining various glioma stem cells (GSCs) that contribute to tumour recurrence. Additionally, increasing evidence suggests that these environments and microenvironments facilitate mechanisms to overcome and control plasticity through a complex array of subtle interactions. In vitro research using three-dimensional scaffolds has become a well-established tool for identifying and isolating environmental and microenvironmental processes that influence GB and GSC behaviour. Consequently, further development of these models may enhance our understanding of the microenvironmental mechanisms that support GSCs. In various tissue engineering applications that have not yet reached clinical use, the distribution of nanomedicines on biomaterial scaffolds and gene-activated scaffolds has shown potential. Treating glioblastoma is particularly challenging due to difficulties in delivering therapeutics to the brain, along with the tumor's heterogeneity, aggressiveness, and recurrence. While the prognosis for glioblastoma patients remains poor, recent advancements in drug delivery methods offer hope for more effective treatment. However, the use of biomaterials for glioblastoma treatment as a tissue engineering approach remains largely unexplored. Given the diverse biomaterials and techniques used in numerous in vitro models, there might already be a technique within these experiments that could help combat this deadly disease. These novel therapeutic approaches could successfully overcome numerous limitations or obstacles, such as crossing the BBB, reducing off-tumour effects, and releasing therapeutic agents at the specific site with minimal concentration.

Overall, further studies and advancements are necessary to develop safe biomaterials and effective methods for controlling drug release at specific sites in the brain. It is hoped that these developments will lead to better therapeutic approaches that can enhance the quality of life for neuro-oncology patients.

**Reference**

1.Bordoni M, Scarian E, Rey F, Gagliardi S, Carelli S, Pansarasa O, et al. Biomaterials in Neurodegenerative Disorders: A Promising Therapeutic Approach. International Journal of Molecular Sciences. 2020;21(9):3243.

2.Zhang X, Liu F, Gu Z. Tissue Engineering in Neuroscience: Applications and Perspectives. BME Front. 2023;4:0007.

3.Elliot L, Melissa RA, Elizabeth JB, Heather E, Penny H, Ronaldo MI, et al. Refining rodent models of spinal cord injury. Experimental Neurology. 2020;328:113273.

4.Amna A, Anisa A, Tayyba Sher W, Masoomeh B, Ali-Reza M, Nasir Raza A, et al. Neurodegenerative diseases and effective drug delivery: A review of challenges and novel therapeutics. Journal of Controlled Release. 2021;330:1152-67.

5.Amna A, Vahideh, Ali-Reza M, Muhammad Y, Masoomeh B. Emerging polymeric biomaterials and manufacturing-based tissue engineering approaches for neuro regeneration-A critical review on recent effective approaches. Smart Materials in Medicine. 2023;4:337-55.

6.Martinez B, Peplow PV. Biomaterial and tissue-engineering strategies for the treatment of brain neurodegeneration. Neural Regeneration Research. 2022;17(10):2108-16.

7.Sadeghi A, Afshari E, Hashemi M, Kaplan D, Mozafari M. Brainy biomaterials: Latest advances in smart biomaterials to develop the next generation of neural interfaces. Current Opinion in Biomedical Engineering. 2023;25:100420.

8.Orive G, Ali OA, Anitua E, Pedraz JL, Emerich DF. Biomaterial-based technologies for brain anti-cancer therapeutics and imaging. Biochimica et Biophysica Acta (BBA) - Reviews on Cancer. 2010;1806(1):96-107.

9.Abdul-Al M, Saeinasab M, Zare A, Barati M, Shakeri S, Keykhosravi E, et al. Application of biomaterials for glioblastoma treatment: Promises, advances, and challenges. Materials Today Communications. 2022;33:104562.

10.Mursal M, Kumar A, Hasan SM, Hussain S, Singh K, Kushwaha SP, et al. Role of natural bioactive compounds in the management of neurodegenerative disorders. Intelligent Pharmacy. 2024;2(1):102-13.

11.Apostolova LG. Alzheimer disease. Continuum: Lifelong Learning in Neurology. 2016;22(2):419-34.

12.Stupp R, Hegi ME, Mason WP, Van den Bent M, Taphoorn M, Janzer R, et al. European Organisation for Research and Treatment of Cancer Brain Tumour and Radiation Oncology Groups; National Cancer Institute of Canada Clinical Trials Group. Effects of radiotherapy with concomitant and adjuvant temozolomide versus radiotherapy alone on survival in glioblastoma in a randomised phase III study: 5-year analysis of the EORTC-NCIC trial. Lancet Oncol. 2009;10(5):459-66.

13.Bhunia S, Kolishetti N, Vashist A, Yndart Arias A, Brooks D, Nair M. Drug Delivery to the Brain: Recent Advances and Unmet Challenges. Pharmaceutics. 2023;15(12).

14.Nahirney PC, Tremblay M-E. Brain Ultrastructure: Putting the Pieces Together. Frontiers in Cell and Developmental Biology. 2021;9.

15.Niu S, Zhang L-K, Zhang L, Zhuang S, Zhan X, Chen W-Y, et al. Inhibition by Multifunctional Magnetic Nanoparticles Loaded with Alpha-Synuclein RNAi Plasmid in a Parkinson's Disease Model. Theranostics. 2017;7(2):344-56.

16.Agarwal R, Domowicz MS, Schwartz NB, Henry J, Medintz I, Delehanty JB, et al. Delivery and tracking of quantum dot peptide bioconjugates in an intact developing avian brain. ACS Chem Neurosci. 2015;6(3):494-504.

17.Jampilek J, Zaruba K, Oravec M, Kunes M, Babula P, Ulbrich P, et al. Preparation of Silica Nanoparticles Loaded with Nootropics and Their In Vivo Permeation through Blood-Brain Barrier. BioMed Research International. 2015;2015(1):812673.

18.Tam VH, Sosa C, Liu R, Yao N, Priestley RD. Nanomedicine as a non-invasive strategy for drug delivery across the blood brain barrier. International Journal of Pharmaceutics. 2016;515(1):331-42.

19.Mehnert W, Mäder K. Solid lipid nanoparticles: Production, characterization and applications. Advanced Drug Delivery Reviews. 2001;47(2):165-96.

20.Xiong XY, Tam KC, Gan LH. Release kinetics of hydrophobic and hydrophilic model drugs from pluronic F127/poly(lactic acid) nanoparticles. J Control Release. 2005;103(1):73-82.

21.Dash M, Chiellini F, Ottenbrite RM, Chiellini E. Chitosan—A versatile semi-synthetic polymer in biomedical applications. Progress in Polymer Science. 2011;36(8):981-1014.

22.Ananthanarayanan B, Kim Y, Kumar S. Elucidating the mechanobiology of malignant brain tumors using a brain matrix-mimetic hyaluronic acid hydrogel platform. Biomaterials. 2011;32(31):7913-23.

23.Gombotz WR, Wee S. Protein release from alginate matrices. Advanced Drug Delivery Reviews. 1998;31(3):267-85.

24.Chew SA, Danti S. Biomaterial-based implantable devices for cancer therapy. Advanced healthcare materials. 2017;6(2):1600766.

25.Kim T-Y, Kim D-W, Chung J-Y, Shin SG, Kim S-C, Heo DS, et al. Phase I and pharmacokinetic study of Genexol-PM, a cremophor-free, polymeric micelle-formulated paclitaxel, in patients with advanced malignancies. Clinical cancer research. 2004;10(11):3708-16.

26.Höbel S, Aigner A. Polyethylenimines for siRNA and miRNA delivery in vivo. Wiley Interdisciplinary Reviews: Nanomedicine and Nanobiotechnology. 2013;5(5):484-501.

27.Neu M, Fischer D, Kissel T. Recent advances in rational gene transfer vector design based on poly (ethylene imine) and its derivatives. The Journal of Gene Medicine: A cross-disciplinary journal for research on the science of gene transfer and its clinical applications. 2005;7(8):992-1009.

28.Zhan C, Wei X, Qian J, Feng L, Zhu J, Lu W. Co-delivery of TRAIL gene enhances the anti-glioblastoma effect of paclitaxel in vitro and in vivo. Journal of controlled release. 2012;160(3):630-6.

29.Kozielski KL, Tzeng SY, Hurtado De Mendoza BA, Green JJ. Bioreducible cationic polymer-based nanoparticles for efficient and environmentally triggered cytoplasmic siRNA delivery to primary human brain cancer cells. ACS nano. 2014;8(4):3232-41.

30.Jackson P, Kim M, Hawkins-Daarud A, Singleton K, Mohammad A, Burns T, et al. SCIDOT-16. T2-WEIGHTED IMAGING MAY BE INDICATIVE OF DRUG DISTRIBUTION IN GLIOBLASTOMA PATIENTS. Neuro-Oncology. 2019;21(Supplement_6):vi274-vi5.

31.Fourniols T, Randolph LD, Staub A, Vanvarenberg K, Leprince JG, Préat V, et al. Temozolomide-loaded photopolymerizable PEG-DMA-based hydrogel for the treatment of glioblastoma. Journal of Controlled Release. 2015;210:95-104.

32.Leprince JG, Palin WM, Hadis MA, Devaux J, Leloup G. Progress in dimethacrylate-based dental composite technology and curing efficiency. Dental Materials. 2013;29(2):139-56.

33.Bryant SJ, Vernerey FJ. Programmable hydrogels for cell encapsulation and neo-tissue growth to enable personalized tissue engineering. Advanced healthcare materials. 2018;7(1):1700605.

34.Bota DA, Desjardins A, Quinn JA, Affronti ML, Friedman HS. Interstitial chemotherapy with biodegradable BCNU (Gliadel®) wafers in the treatment of malignant gliomas. Therapeutics and clinical risk management. 2007;3(5):707-15.

35.Brandl M. Vesicular phospholipid gels. Liposomes: Methods and Protocols, Volume 1: Pharmaceutical Nanocarriers. 2010:205-12.

36.Brandl M. Vesicular phospholipid gels: a technology platform. Journal of liposome research. 2007;17(1):15-26.

37.Kim Y-H, Vijayavenkataraman S, Cidonio G. Biomaterials and scaffolds for tissue engineering and regenerative medicine. BMC Methods. 2024;1(1):2.

38.Zhou X, He X, Ren Y. Function of microglia and macrophages in secondary damage after spinal cord injury. Neural Regen Res. 2014;9(20):1787-95.

39.Jassam YN, Izzy S, Whalen M, McGavern DB, El Khoury J. Neuroimmunology of Traumatic Brain Injury: Time for a Paradigm Shift. Neuron. 2017;95(6):1246-65.

40.Liebner S, Dijkhuizen RM, Reiss Y, Plate KH, Agalliu D, Constantin G. Functional morphology of the blood-brain barrier in health and disease. Acta Neuropathol. 2018;135(3):311-36.

41.Petralito S, Spera R, Pacelli S, Relucenti M, Familiari G, Vitalone A, et al. Design and development of PEG-DMA gel-in-liposomes as a new tool for drug delivery. Reactive and Functional Polymers. 2014;77:30-8.

42.Fischer D, Bieber T, Li Y, Elsässer H-P, Kissel T. A novel non-viral vector for DNA delivery based on low molecular weight, branched polyethylenimine: effect of molecular weight on transfection efficiency and cytotoxicity. Pharmaceutical research. 1999;16:1273-9.

43.Hsu S-H, Kuo W-C, Chen Y-T, Yen C-T, Chen Y-F, Chen K-S, et al. New nerve regeneration strategy combining laminin-coated chitosan conduits and stem cell therapy. Acta biomaterialia. 2013;9(5):6606-15.

44.Huang YC, Huang CC, Huang YY, Chen KS. Surface modification and characterization of chitosan or PLGA membrane with laminin by chemical and oxygen plasma treatment for neural regeneration. Journal of Biomedical Materials Research Part A: An Official Journal of The Society for Biomaterials, The Japanese Society for Biomaterials, and The Australian Society for Biomaterials and the Korean Society for Biomaterials. 2007;82(4):842-51.

45.Yu LM, Kazazian K, Shoichet MS. Peptide surface modification of methacrylamide chitosan for neural tissue engineering applications. Journal of Biomedical Materials Research Part A. 2007;82(1):243-55.

46.De Bonis P, Anile C, Pompucci A, Fiorentino A, Balducci M, Chiesa S, et al. Safety and efficacy of Gliadel wafers for newly diagnosed and recurrent glioblastoma. Acta neurochirurgica. 2012;154:1371-8.

47.Jones T, Zhang B, Major S, Webb A. All-trans retinoic acid eluting poly (diol citrate) wafers for treatment of glioblastoma. Journal of Biomedical Materials Research Part B: Applied Biomaterials. 2020;108(3):619-28.

48.Qi N, Tang X, Lin X, Gu P, Cai C, Xu H, et al. Sterilization stability of vesicular phospholipid gels loaded with cytarabine for brain implant. International journal of pharmaceutics. 2012;427(2):234-41.

49.Breitsamer M, Winter G. Vesicular phospholipid gels as drug delivery systems for small molecular weight drugs, peptides and proteins: State of the art review. International journal of pharmaceutics. 2019;557:1-8.

50.Lee KY, Mooney DJ. Alginate: properties and biomedical applications. Progress in polymer science. 2012;37(1):106-26.

51.Lee J, Lee KY. Local and sustained vascular endothelial growth factor delivery for angiogenesis using an injectable system. Pharmaceutical research. 2009;26:1739-44.

52.Vigués N, Pujol-Vila F, Marquez-Maqueda A, Muñoz-Berbel X, Mas J. Electro-addressable conductive alginate hydrogel for bacterial trapping and general toxicity determination. Analytica Chimica Acta. 2018;1036:115-20.

CHAPTER NINE

# IMPLEMENTATION OF BIOMATERIALS FOR CONSTRUCTING A 3D TUMOR MODEL TO BUILD UNDERSTANDING FOR ANTICANCER DRUG DISCOVERY

**Shivang Shukla[1], Neeraj Sharma[2], Abhiram Kumar[3]***

[1]*Para Medical and Allied Health Sciences, Jagannath University, Jaipur Rajasthan 30390, India*

[2]*Department of Pharmacy, BanasthaliVidyapith, Jaipur, Rajasthan, 304022, India.*

[3]*Laboratory of Molecular Medicine,Birla Institute of Technology and Sciences, Pilani Hyderabad Campus, 500078, India*

**Highlights**

- Emphasize the significance of using biomaterials and microfluidics to create more accurate and personalized 3D tumor models, enhancing research in cancer treatment.
- Highlight the potential impact of these models on clinical applications, particularly in developing personalized medicine and improving patient outcomes.
- Discuss how these advanced models can unlock new insights into cancer biology, potentially leading to breakthroughs in understanding tumor behavior and progression.
- The development of more sophisticated models and their integration into clinical practice for better diagnosis and treatment strategies.

## Introduction

One of the largest barriers to developing useful anticancer therapies is the inadequacy of proper in vitro models that are able to mimic the tumor microenvironment. The complex interplay between cancer cells, stromal cells, and the extracellular matrix is largely not replicated in traditional two-dimensional (2D) cell culture models and animal models (1). This discrepancy accounts for a significant number of failed clinical trials and reflects the poor knowledge of cancer biology. As a result, such limitations strongly hinder the efficacy of many novel therapeutic candidates and lead to a high attrition rate in drug discovery and low translation efficiency into the clinic, hence requiring costly and time-consuming clinical trials. Furthermore, the inadequate understanding of cancer biology and the absence of effective in vitro models have impeded the development of personalized cancer therapies, leaving a significant medical need unmet(2).

Biomaterial-based construction of in vivo-like 3-D tumor models is one such approach that holds promise for the treatment of this major frontier. Through the engineering of biologically relevant mechanical cues, biochemical signals, and other tumor-specific properties within materials, these improved detection technologies employ biomaterials to simulate realistic cell behavior and therapeutic responses. These biomimetic properties can be embraced by researchers to engineer 3D tumor models that better mimic the TME, thereby enhancing our understanding of cancer progression and more accurately predicting the efficacy of potential anticancer therapies.The use of biomaterials for constructing bioengineered 3D tumors may be useful for identifying differences between in vitro and in vivo investigations(3). These biomaterial-based biomimetic models also enable HCSs and prevent the use of animal models in drug screening, providing an efficient way to discover drugs.

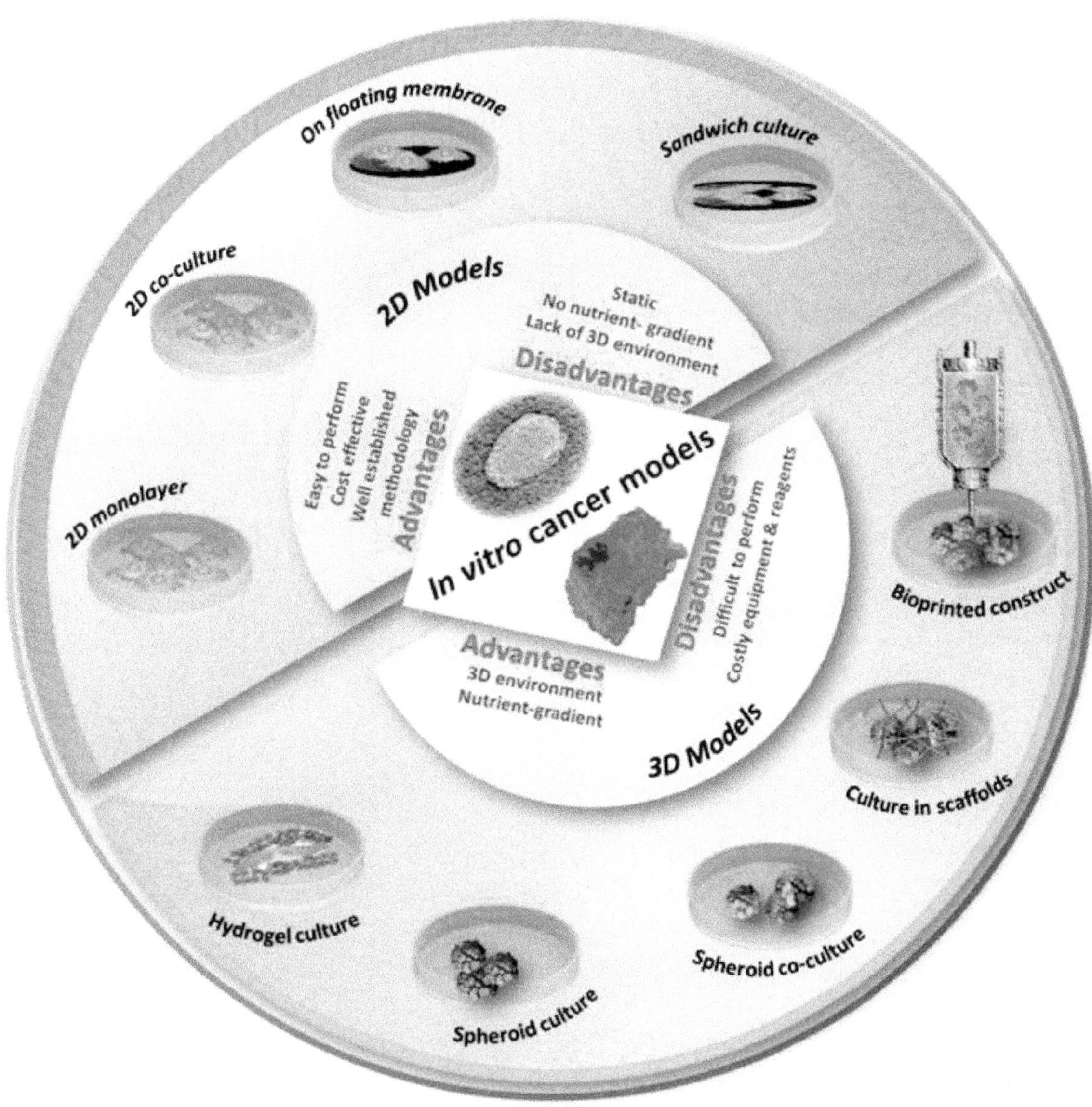


**Figure 1.** Various in vitro cancer models used in chemotherapeutic screening. Evolution of cellculture models from simple 2D to complex 3D bioprinted models. Conventional 2D monolayer culture, monolayer coculture, cèlls grown over floating membranes, and cell monolayers sandwiched between membranes are commonly used 2D cancer models in research and drug screening.Cancer cells cultured in hydrogels, spheroid monocultures, spheroid cocultures, cancer/stromal cells cultured in porous 3D scaffolds, and advanced bioprinted constructs are among the available 3D cancer models. (4)

### Applications of Biomaterials for 3D Tumor Models

1. **Cancer Stem Cells and Cancer Progression Study:** These biomaterials could be used to construct 3D models that imitate the tumor microenvironment, allowing for the extensive study of cancer stem cells and their role in cancer development, progression, and metastasis. These models can therefore assist in identifying unique properties and actions pertaining to cancer stem cells that are frequently unresponsive to normal cancer treatments, thus leading to the reoccurrence of tumors. For instance, by understanding how specific mechanisms control the functions of cancer stem cells within a three-dimensional tumor environment, researchers will be able to develop more selective drugs that can eradicate these important subsets of cells(5).
2. **Estimation of Efficacy and Identification of Possible Cancer Diagnosis and Treatment Biomarkers:** Three-dimensional biomaterial-based tumor models can serve as more physiologically relevant platforms for assessing the effectiveness of novel anticancer agents and identifying possible cancer biomarkers for diagnosis and personalized therapy. These models are capable of mimicking the intricate environment within tumors, which includes interactions among cancer cells, stromal cells and the extracellular matrix, thus influencing drug reactions. Before advancing to extensive animal trials that are not only expensive but also time consuming, researchers can gain useful information about the way these drugs work and their potential toxicities by trying them in these improved 3D systems(6).
3. **Research on Tumor Heterogeneity and the Spatial Interactions between Cell Types:** 3D tumor models that mimic the cellular and spatial heterogeneity present in actual tumors can be created using biomaterials. These models enable scientists to study the three-dimensional interactions between different cell types in a tumor microenvironment, including stromal cells, immune cells, and cancer cells. Understanding these complex cell–cell and cell-matrix interactions is crucial if we are to develop treatments that specifically target distinct cell subpopulations inside a given tumor.
4. **Identification of Potential Biomarkers for Cancer Diagnosis and Treatment:**

By building three-dimensional tumor models using biomaterials and patient-derived cells, researchers may be able to find novel biomarkers that potentially improve cancer diagnosis, prognosis, or treatment choices. By examining unique molecular and cellular signatures in these customized 3D models, it is possible to identify potential biomarkers that were overlooked in conventional 2D cell culture or animal models, which could result in the development of more accurate and reliable diagnostic instruments (6).

1. **Personalized Cancer Therapy and Tailored Therapy Development:**

Using biomaterials and 3D personalized tumor models created from patient cells, it is now possible to create tailored cancer treatments that are specific to each patient's tumor. These models can also be used to evaluate various drug combinations, determine the best treatment plans, and occasionally even forecast how a patient will respond to therapy, which can improve treatment outcomes and reduce toxicity or lack of response (7).

6. **Measuring Cancer Progression and Identifying Potential Therapeutic Targets:**

Using biomaterials to create three-dimensional tumor models allows researchers to examine various stages of cancer progression, from early transformation to metastasis. Through the longitudinal observation of alterations in cellular behavior, signalingpathways, and the tumor microenvironment, scientists might discern pivotal agents that propel cancer advancement and plausible targets for novel drug discovery.

7. **Innovation in Targeted Treatments and Novel Cancer Therapies:**

Biomaterials are used to establish the complex three-dimensional environment of a tumor, including its matrix, extracellular angiogenesis, and immune cell function. This serves as a platform for the development of novel cancer therapies that are directed toward particular elements within the tumor niche, such as immune cell functions, the extracellular matrix, or angiogenesis itself.

8. **Enhanced Cancer Diagnosis and Creation of New Diagnostic Instruments:**

3D tumor models made of biomaterials can be utilized to create biomarkers and new diagnostic instruments that increase the sensitivity and accuracy of cancer detection. Through examination of the distinct cellular and molecular characteristics of these sophisticated in vitro models, scientists are able to find new diagnostic markers that may help identify cancer early and track the course of the illness more successfully(8).

9. **Research on Cancer Invasion and Metastasis:** Biomaterials can be utilized to construct three-dimensional tumor models that replicate the intricate process of cancer metastasis, from distant organ colonization to local invasion. These models can assist in clarifying the mechanisms that underlie the metastatic cascade, such as the function of the tumor microenvironment, the transition between epithelial and mesenchymal cells, and the development of premetastatic niches. By examining metastasis in these sophisticated three-dimensional (3D) systems, scientists can pinpoint possible therapeutic targets and create novel approaches to stop or slow the progression of cancer(9).
10. **Development of Biomaterial-Based Cancer Medicines:**

Biomaterials are so adaptable that it is possible to develop novel cancer medications that incorporate these materials into therapeutic approaches. Through the use of hydrogels or biomaterial scaffolds, therapeutic agents—such as drugs, genes, or immune cells—can be delivered directly to the site of the tumor. These biomaterial-based treatments can improve the targeted distribution and retention of the therapeutic payload by imitating the tumor microenvironment and affecting cellular activity (10).

11. **Scaffolds in Cancer Immunotherapy:**

Advanced in vitro 3D cancer models have been created using scaffold-based tissue engineering techniques to investigate the interplay between tumor and immune cells and assess new immunotherapies. In regard to accurately capturing the intricate tumor microenvironment, these 3D scaffold-based platforms outperform conventional 2D cell culture models by a wide margin. The in vivo tumor microenvironment can be closely mimicked by these scaffolds by incorporating different cell types, extracellular matrix components, and signaling cues. This allows researchers to examine the intricate interactions between different cell populations and assess the effectiveness of new immunotherapies in a more physiologically relevant setting(11).

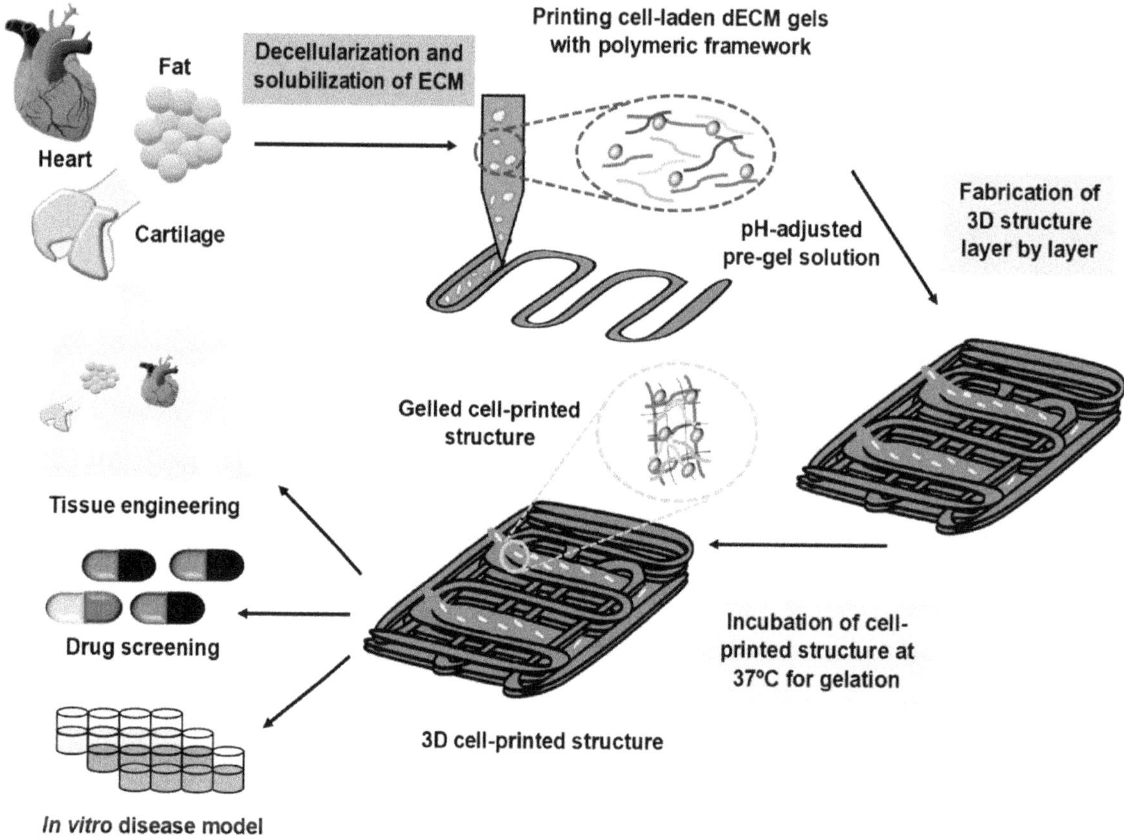


**Figure 2.** 3D printing process and its application. (12)

**Advanced 3D scaffolding techniques for cancer research and tissue engineering**

1. **Scaffolds for Polyhydroxyalkanoates (PHA):**

Microorganisms that yield the biopolymer polyhydroxyalkanoates are used to create PHA scaffolds. Particulate leaching, a technique that includes the removal of particles to generate interconnected pores within the scaffold, is then used to convert this material into 3D porous structures. The ability of these porous structures to permit nutrient diffusion and cell penetration across the scaffold makes them very helpful for the culture of breast and colon cancer cells. Unlike conventional two-dimensional cultures, this arrangement allows researchers to analyze the behavior of cancer cells in a three-dimensional environment that more closely reflects real tissue architecture(13).

2. **3D Aligned Microfiber Scaffolds:**

Melt electrowriting is a process used to generate scaffolds that imitate the complex structures present in brain tissue by producing fine, aligned microfibers. Through orientation-specific fiber alignment, topographical cues of the extracellular matrix of the brain can be mimicked by researchers. This is particularly relevant to the study of metastatic brain cancer since the topology of the scaffold affects the behavior, migration, and environmental interactions of cancer cells. These models offer important insights into the processes underlying brain metastasis and suggest new treatment avenues(14).

3. **3D-Printed Polyurethane Scaffolds:**

The porosity and mechanical characteristics of polyurethane scaffolds can be precisely controlled via 3D printing technology. The scaffolds can be tuned to maximize cell colonization and osteogenic differentiation, two important processes involved in the production and repair of bones. These scaffolds offer a platform for researching the interactions between bone cancer cells and their microenvironment in an in vitro osteosarcoma model, which can aid in understanding tumor formation and lead to the development of novel treatments(15).

4. **Fibronectin coating:**

The glycoprotein fibronectin is an essential component of cell adhesion, proliferation, and differentiation. Fibronectin coating of scaffolds facilitates the creation of in vitro models that approximate the hypoxic (low oxygen) environments frequently observed in malignancies, especially pancreatic cancer. It is well known that these hypoxic environments affect the behavior of tumors and their resistance to therapies such as radiation. Through controlled replication of these conditions, scientists may investigate how hypoxia affects cancer cells and assess the effectiveness of various treatment approaches.

5. **Hydrogel-Based 3D Cancer Models:**

Three-dimensional models that closely resemble the tumor microenvironment are made using hydrogels. These models are very useful for determining how the immune system and malignancies interact, as well as for evaluating the efficacy of immunotherapies.Hydrogels offer a biocompatible and hydrated matrix that promotes cell proliferation and function, enabling scientists to mimic the intricate milieu of the tumor microenvironment in vitro(16).

6. **Optical Barcoding:**

Optical barcoding involves tagging cells with unique optical markers that allow for the tracking and monitoring of individual cells within a 3D in vitro model. This technique is used to study intratumoral cell heterogeneity, particularly in colorectal cancer models. By observing how different cell populations behave and interact within tumors, researchers can gain insights into the diversity and dynamics of cancer cells, which is crucial for understanding tumor progression and resistance to therapies(17).

7. **3D Disease Modeling Using PHA-Based Scaffolds:**

PHA-based scaffolds are employed to model both hard (e.g., bone) and soft (e.g., breast) cancers in a three-dimensional context. These models enable the study of cancer biology in a more physiologically relevant setting, helping researchers to understand how tumors grow, invade, and respond to treatments. By mimicking the physical and biochemical properties of native tissue, these scaffolds provide a valuable tool for cancer research(18).

8. **Patient-Derived Cancer Cells:**

Researchers can use cancer cells obtained directly from patients to create personalized 3D in vitro models. These models reflect the unique characteristics of an individual's tumor, allowing for the study of personalized treatment approaches. By testing how these patient-specific cells respond to different therapies, researchers aim to develop more effective and tailored treatment plans, advancing the field of personalized medicine(19).

9. **Biomimetic Cues:**

Scaffolds precoated with bone-like extracellular matrix (ECM) are used to mimic the natural bone environment. This is achieved by using osteoinduced mesenchymal stem cells to generate the ECM on the scaffold before introducing other cells. Such biomimetic cues are critical for creating realistic models of bone tissue and can be used to study bone regeneration, disease, and the interaction of cancer cells with the bone microenvironment(20).

10. **Mechanical Cues:**

The mechanical properties of scaffolds, such as stiffness and elasticity, are fine-tuned to create an optimal environment for cell colonization and differentiation. These mechanical cues are essential for directing cell behavior and ensuring that the scaffold can support tissue development. By adjusting these properties, researchers can create scaffolds that more accurately replicate the physical conditions of the native tissue, improving the relevance of in vitro models(21).

11. **Chemical/Biological Cues:**

Certain extracellular matrix (ECM) components can be added to scaffolds to assist them in mimicking the metabolic conditions of living tissues. To replicate the intricate relationships that exist between cells and their environment, these chemical and biological cues are essential. Researchers can develop more precise in vitro models for examining the behavior of cancer cells and evaluating possible therapies by accurately mimicking the makeup of the extracellular matrix(22).

12. **Methodical Comparative Evaluations:**

Evaluating the response of ovarian cancer cells to different scaffold designs and biomaterials is a crucial step in conducting systematic comparative studies. Researchers can determine which combinations of materials and scaffold features work best for fostering desired biological responses by comparing them. These evaluations are essential for improving scaffold designs and accelerating the creation of more potent instruments and therapies for cancer research(23).

| Type of scaffolds | Advantages | Disadvantages |
|---|---|---|
| Hydrogels | Tissue-like responsiveness<br>Water-soluble factors are easily supplied to cells<br>Generally, biocompatible<br>Low immunogenicity | Mechanical resistance is minimal<br>Physically cross-linked gels are weak |
| 3D Bioprinted scaffolds | High-reproducibility of biomimetic microenvironments<br>Homogeneous distribution of cells | Low-concentration solutions can be a limiting factor when building up material into a 3D structure. |
| Decellularized scaffolds | Provides ECM environment<br>High bioactivity,<br>Low immunogenicity<br>Promotes cell-material interactions | Decellularization of thick tissues can be difficult.<br>The number of cell adhesion sites is limited. |
| Fibrous scaffolds | Characterized by high surface-area-to-volume favoring cell proliferation, migration, adhesion and differentiation of cells | Low structural stability<br>Limited by cell seeding<br>Scaffold morphology is difficult to regulate.<br>Limited in thickness and small pore size. |
| Microsphere scaffolds | Cumulative release of encapsulated bioactive substances<br>Long-time maintenance of cancer cells in culture<br>Excellent mechanical properties | May results in loss of bioactivity of encapsulated factors<br>Residual solvent toxicity<br>Expensive |
| Nanoparticle incorporated scaffolds | High penetration ability<br>Tunable surface properties | Particle aggregation |

**Table 1.**Advantages and disadvantages of different scaffolds in tissue engineering. (11)

**Advanced Techniques for Creating 3D Tumor Models for Personalized Medicine**

1. **Hydrogel Bioprinting:** Using hydrogels, this technique produces complex, three-dimensional constructs that closely mimic the tumor microenvironment (TME). These biocompatible materials are perfect for creating patient-specific tumor models using cells generated from individual patients since they are designed to mimic the mechanical and chemical characteristics of the TME. This method is essential for the advancement of personalized medical strategies (24).
2. **Electrospinning:** Electrospinning is the process of producing porous scaffolds that are three-dimensional and mimic the extracellular matrix (ECM) and vasculature of tumors. These scaffolds replicate the intricacy of particular malignancies by supporting the culture of different cell types. For instance, colon and breast cancer cells are cultured on scaffolds produced from polyhydroxyalkanoates (PHA) via particle leaching. Within the three-dimensional framework, these scaffolds promote cell infiltration and the transport of nutrients(25).
3. **3D Printing:** Using 3D printing, complex constructs that mimic the morphology and architecture of the TME are created. For example, three-dimensional models of brain metastasis and osteosarcoma have been made using polyurethane (PU) scaffolds. The development of patient-specific tumor models is made possible by this technology, and these models are essential for researching the biology of tumors and creating novel treatment approaches(25).
4. **Particulate Leaching:** Using polyhydroxyalkanoates (PHA), particulate leaching is a technique for creating three-dimensional porous scaffolds. By cultivating breast and colon cancer cells on these scaffolds, researchers are able to observe efficient nutrient flow and cell penetration inside the three-dimensional structure of the biomaterial(25).
5. **Optical Barcoding:** In three-dimensional in vitro models of colorectal cancer, optical barcoding is utilized to track intratumoral cell heterogeneity. This method enables noninvasive, real-time monitoring of cell heterogeneity and

behavior. In a 3D in vitro colorectal cancer model, Castro et al. devised a technique for the optical barcoding of cancer cells taken from patients(26).

6. **Melt Electrowriting:** In this technique, three-dimensionally aligned microfiber scaffolds that imitate brain architecture are created. Using these scaffolds, researchers may examine how topography affects cell behavior in models of metastatic brain disease. Melt electrowriting was used, for example, by Peiffer et al. to create aligned microfiber scaffolds that mimic brain architecture and show how topography affects cell behavior in a metastatic brain environment (27).
7. **Fibronectin Coating:** To create in vitro models that mimic hypoxic conditions in three-dimensional pancreatic cancer models, a fibrin coating on polyurethane (PU) scaffolds was utilized. More precise research on the effects of radiation in physiologically appropriate settings is possible with this method. ContessiNegrini et al. emphasized the importance of fibronectin coating on polyurethane scaffolds to establish a hypoxic three-dimensional pancreatic cancer model for examining the effects of radiation therapy(28).
8. **In vitro Models Assisted by Biomaterials:** Biomaterials are used in biomaterial-assisted in vitro models to construct intricate, three-dimensional structures that resemble the TME. These models are able to replicate the intricacy of certain tumors by cultivating several cell populations. For example, Prem Ananth et al.used particle leaching to create 3D porous scaffolds using polyhydroxyalkanoates produced by microorganisms. They were able to cultivate breast and colon cancer cells, showing that the 3D structure of the biomaterial effectively allowed for cell penetration and nutrient dispersion(29).

**Biomaterial- and Microfluidic-Based 3D Tumor Models**

In an effort to close the gap between conventional 2D cell culture and in vivo studies, biomaterial- and microfluidic-based 3D tumor models have become increasingly useful for cancer research and drug development. These models offer more accurate and representative in vitro representations of tumor biology and therapeutic responses. These models generate three-dimensional (3D) cancer models that replicate the tumor microenvironment by using synthetic biomaterials such as hydrogels, e-spun materials, and nanoparticles(30).

In particular, hydrogels are employed to construct more representative tumor models by enabling the self-assembly of cell-filled 3D structures. This is accomplished using a variety of methods, including 3D bioprinting, electrospinning, and photolithography. Moreover, tissue-like microenvironments and intricate cellular structures can be recapitulated using microfluidic technologies. Organ-on-a-chip platforms facilitate the study of normal physiology and the course of illness by constructing dynamic and regulated microenvironments that replicate the vital functions of particular organs(31). Enhanced drug screening, tailored therapy, and better representation of the tumor microenvironment are the main benefits of these 3D tumor models. To better understand cancer biology and therapeutic responses, more realistic simulations of the tumor microenvironment can be produced using biomaterials and microfluidics. These models can be used to investigate the mechanisms of chemoresistance and evaluate the effectiveness of treatment interventions. More precise targeted cancer treatments as well as individualized medical approaches can be developed with the aid of advanced biomaterials and microfluidics(32).

For example, biomaterials can be engineered to replicate the mechanical and metabolic characteristics of native tissues, enabling more precise tumor-stroma interaction modeling. By using microfluidics, one may replicate the dynamic environment of tumors by creating intricate gradients and flow patterns. These models can also be used to investigate how cancer cells behave and react to treatment in relation to hypoxia, nutrient deprivation, and other microenvironmental variables. However, there are issues to be resolved and directions for the future. Further advancements in fabrication methods, such as self-assembly and 3D bioprinting, are required to produce elaborate and physiologically accurate models. Combining several biofabrication techniques can result in more complete models that more accurately reflect the intricacies of cancer biology and treatment reactions(32).

Furthermore, to produce models that can precisely predict patient outcomes and guide therapeutic decision-making, more sophisticated biomaterials and microfluidic systems must be developed.

**3D Chitosan-Alginate (CA) Scaffolds for Tumor Spheroids**

The potential of 3D chitosan-alginate (CA) scaffolds to enhance the growth and enrichment of cancer stem-like cells (CSCs) has been thoroughly investigated. These scaffolds are intended to replicate the microenvironment of a tumor and offer a more realistic depiction of the intricate relationships that exist between cancer cells and their surroundings(33).

Research has demonstrated that 3D CA scaffolds can enhance CSCs in a variety of cancer cell lines, such as those from the breast, liver, and prostate. Reduced proliferation, the development of tumor spheroids, and elevated expression of CSC-associated markers such as CD133 and NANOG are the characteristics of this enrichment. The distinct characteristics of CA scaffolds are assumed to be the cause of the enrichment of CSCs. Tumor spheroids, which are a hallmark of CSCs, can form because of the porous structure that is produced when chitosan and alginate are combined. Furthermore, the behavior of cancer cells can be influenced by scaffold stiffness; more aggressive cell development is promoted by stiffer scaffolds. Studies have also examined how prostate cancer cells react to CA scaffolds. The proliferation and phenotypic expression of prostate cancer cells, including the creation of cell clusters and multicellular spheroids, have been demonstrated to be supported by these scaffolds. Knowledge of how prostate cancer progresses requires knowledge of how the stiffness of the scaffold affects the mineralization of prostate cancer cells(34).

There are various benefits to using 3D CA scaffolds in cancer research. By offering a more realistic depiction of the tumor microenvironment, researchers have examined the intricate relationships that exist between cancer cells and their surroundings. These scaffolds can also be used to screen chemotherapies and assess how well they target CSCs. In conclusion, 3D chitosan-alginate scaffolds are useful for stimulating the growth and enrichment of cancer stem-like cells. These scaffolds are potentially useful tools for deciphering cancer cell behavior and developing more potent therapies(35).

**Unlocking the Secrets of Cancer Biology**

When creating and utilizing three-dimensional (3D) tumor models, it is important to consider the many benefits and drawbacks associated with this method. To produce precise and useful 3D tumor models that can improve our knowledge of cancer biology and speed up the discovery of new treatments, researchers must be aware of the subtleties of these benefits and drawbacks(36).

**Advantages:**

1. **Tissue-like Flexibility:** Hydrogels, which include collagen, fibrin, and alginate, can imitate the dynamic nature of tumors by offering a flexible and tissue-like environment. Because of its flexibility, a more accurate representation of the tumor microenvironment can be achieved by easily supplying cells with water-soluble substances such as cytokines and growth factors(37).
2. **Biomechanical Properties:** The mechanical strength of solid scaffolds, such as porous polymers or decellularized extracellular matrix (ECM), can be tailored to closely resemble the biomechanical characteristics of natural tumor tissues. Understanding the significance of mechanical forces in tumor development, invasion, and metastasis is vital(38).
3. **Complex biochemistry:** Decellularized native tumor tissue improves cellular activities and signaling pathways by offering complex biochemical and biomechanical effects akin to those of the initial tumor microenvironment. More precise modeling of tumor behavior and therapeutic response may be needed(28).
4. **Better Cellular Functions:** Compared to conventional 2D cultures, cells grown in a 3D microenvironment with ECM components have more realistic shapes and gene expression patterns. This may lead to improved knowledge of the biology of tumor cells and the creation of preclinical models with increased predictive power(37).
5. **Enhanced ECM Synthesis:** By mimicking the dynamic interaction between tumor cells and the surrounding matrix, cells in 3D cultures create an extracellular matrix, as they do in vivo. This is especially relevant to research on the role of the extracellular matrix (ECM) in tumor progression, invasion, and metastasis (38).
6. **Customizable Matrix Composition:** State-of-the-art 3D bioprinting techniques enable local customization of the matrix composition and stiffness within the tumor construct, resulting in multicellular, complex, and highly reproducible models that can help clarify the impact of particular matrix components and mechanical properties

on tumor behavior.

7. **Reproducibility:**Cancer models with high reproducibility can be generated using bioprinted materials, guaranteeing consistent outcomes and facilitating more trustworthy comparisons between various experimental conditions or treatments. This is essential for preclinical research and the development of personalized therapies(38).
8. **Multicellular Constructs:** To more closely resemble the tumor microenvironment, 3D bioprinting can combine several cell types, such as immune, stromal, and tumor cells, into a single construct. This can shed light on the intricate relationships between various cell populations, their functions in the development of tumors, and how those relationships affect the effectiveness of treatments(28).

**Disadvantages:**

1. **Low Mechanical Resistance:** Although hydrogels offer a flexible and tissue-like environment, their mechanical resistance is frequently low. This can restrict their usage in some applications, especially those that investigate tumor invasion and metastasis(39).
2. **Difficulty in homogenous dispersion:** It can be difficult to develop solid scaffolds for the homogenous dispersion of cells, which can result in variances in cell density and distribution within the construct and compromise model accuracy. One such scaffold is porous polymers.
3. **Reduction in Mechanical Properties:** Compared to the original native tissue, decellularized native tumor tissue might occasionally lose mechanical characteristics such as elasticity, tensile strength, and roughness. This may affect the model's capacity to faithfully reproduce the biomechanical characteristics of the tumor microenvironment(39).
4. **Difficulty in Mass Production:** It can be difficult to mass produce ultralow attachment surfaces, which are useful for creating tumor spheroids, and they may not be uniform between individual spheroids. This may restrict the model's capacity to grow and produce a high volume of consistent constructs(38).
5. **Selection pressure:** The ability of patient-derived tumor xenografts (PDXs) to properly simulate the tumor microenvironment and its evolution is limited by the selection pressure that PDXs can exert, which over time modifies the clonal makeup of the tumor.
6. **Limited Standardization:** One major drawback that can impede the capacity to generalize findings and create widely acknowledged best practices is the absence of defined protocols and the challenge of comparing outcomes from various 3D tumor models(28).
7. **Cost and Complexity:** The creation and application of cutting-edge biomaterials and bioprinting methods can be expensive and complex, which may prevent them from being widely used, especially in environments with limited resources.
8. **Limited Scalability:** The utilization of current bioprinting techniques in some applications, such as the creation of implantable devices or the mass manufacture of tissue constructs, may be restricted due to their inability to scale to enormous numbers.
9. **Limited Regulation of Cell Behavior:** Although biomaterials can affect how cells behave, they might not be able to fully regulate how cells operate. This might make it difficult to pinpoint the precise mechanisms guiding the development of tumors and how they respond to treatments(28).
10. **Contamination Potential:** To maintain the accuracy and dependability of 3D tumor models, contamination risks associated with the use of biomaterials and bioprinting methods must be properly controlled(38).

**Clinical Significance**

Biomaterials play a crucial role in the construction of three-dimensional (3D) tumor models because they can simulate the complex interactions that occur in vivo between stromal cells, cancer cells, and the extracellular matrix (ECM). For example, patient-derived tumor cells have been employed in hydrogel bioprinting to construct patient-specific tumor models, which is crucial for personalized therapy techniques. These models can replicate particular features of the tumor microenvironment (TME), which are important for understanding the development and metastasis of tumors. These features include hypoxia, acidity, and mechanical stress. More complicated biomaterials and fabrication techniques, such as 3D printing and electrospinning, have been developed as a result of recent developments in biomaterials science. These technologies allow for the construction of intricate, hierarchical structures that can imitate the extracellular matrix (ECM) and tumor vasculature(40).

As a result, 3D tumor models are now much more relevant and accurate, which makes them better suited for preclinical testing and applications in customized treatment. Moreover, researchers will be able to noninvasively track the behavior of cancer cells and the TME in realtime through the integration of cutting-edge imaging and analytical techniques such as magnetic resonance imaging (MRI) and optical coherence tomography (OCT), which will provide important insights into tumor biology and treatment responses(41). Overall, biomaterial-assisted 3D tumor models offer a more realistic and physiologically appropriate environment for researching tumor biology and formulating novel therapeutic approaches and have the potential to completely transform cancer research and personalized therapy.

**Conclusion and Future Perspective**

In cancer research and customized therapy, biomaterial-assisted 3D in vitro models show significant promise for overcoming the drawbacks of conventional 2D in vitro models. These models provide a more realistic and physiologically appropriate setting for researching the biology of tumors and creating novel treatment approaches. However, to reach their full potential, a number of obstacles need to be overcome. These difficulties include the requirement for highly repeatable, reasonably priced analytic tools as well as the optimization of scaffold physico-mechanical characteristics to guarantee ideal cell colonization and differentiation. Furthermore, for the creation of effective biomaterial-assisted in vitro models, careful consideration of biomimetic cues is essential.

One of the most significant advantages of hydrogel 3D bioprinting is its potential for personalized medicine. By creating patient-specific tumor models, researchers can develop more effective treatment strategies that take into account the unique genetic and cellular makeup of each individual's cancer. This personalized approach to cancer treatment has the potential to significantly improve patient outcomes and reduce the risk of treatment-related side effects. Researchers can more effectively develop and use biomaterials to produce more precise and useful 3D tumor models by having better knowledge of these characteristics. Three-dimensional (3D) tumor models based on biomaterials and microfluidics have a number of benefits for medication development and cancer research. By combining these state-of-the-art technologies, in vitro models that more closely resemble the intricacies of cancer biology and treatment responses can be produced. This development closes the knowledge gap between conventional 2D cell culture and in vivo research, which will eventually result in more precise and potent cancer therapies.

**References**

1. Habanjar O, Diab-Assaf M, Caldefie-Chezet F, Delort L. 3D Cell Culture Systems: Tumor Application, Advantages, and Disadvantages. Int J Mol Sci [Internet]. 2021 Nov 1 [cited 2024 Jun 22];22(22). Available from: https://pubmed.ncbi.nlm.nih.gov/34830082/

2. Neufeld L, Yeini E, Pozzi S, Satchi-Fainaro R. 3D bioprinted cancer models: from basic biology to drug development. Nature Reviews Cancer 2022 22:12 [Internet]. 2022 Oct 24 [cited 2024 Jun 22];22(12):679–92. Available from: https://www.nature.com/articles/s41568-022-00514-w

3. Li W, Zhou Z, Zhou X, Khoo BL, Gunawan R, Chin YR, et al. 3D Biomimetic Models to Reconstitute Tumor Microenvironment In Vitro: Spheroids, Organoids, and Tumor-on-a-Chip. Adv Healthc Mater [Internet]. 2023 Jul 1 [cited 2024 Jun 22];12(18):2202609. Available from: https://onlinelibrary.wiley.com/doi/full/10.1002/adhm.202202609

4. Augustine R, Kalva SN, Ahmad R, Zahid AA, Hasan S, Nayeem A, et al. 3D Bioprinted cancer models: Revolutionizing personalized cancer therapy. Vol. 14, Translational Oncology. 2021.

5. Huang T, Song X, Xu D, Tiek D, Goenka A, Wu B, et al. Stem cell programs in cancer initiation, progression, and therapy resistance. Theranostics [Internet]. 2020 [cited 2024 Jun 22];10(19):8721–43. Available from:

https://pubmed.ncbi.nlm.nih.gov/32754274/

6. Zhou Y, Tao L, Qiu J, Xu J, Yang X, Zhang Y, et al. Tumor biomarkers for diagnosis, prognosis and targeted therapy. Signal Transduction and Targeted Therapy 2024 9:1 [Internet]. 2024 May 20 [cited 2024 Jun 22];9(1):1–86. Available from: https://www.nature.com/articles/s41392-024-01823-2

7. Gambardella V, Tarazona N, Cejalvo JM, Lombardi P, Huerta M, Roselló S, et al. Personalized medicine: Recent progress in cancer therapy. Vol. 12, Cancers. 2020.

8. Pulumati A, Pulumati A, Dwarakanath BS, Verma A, Papineni RVL. Technological advancements in cancer diagnostics: Improvements and limitations. Cancer Rep [Internet]. 2023 Feb 1 [cited 2024 Jun 23];6(2). Available from:/pmc/articles/PMC9940009/

9. Meirson T, Gil-Henn H, Samson AO. Invasion and metastasis: the elusive hallmark of cancer. Oncogene 2019 39:9 [Internet]. 2019 Nov 19 [cited 2024 Jun 23];39(9):2024–6. Available from: https://www.nature.com/articles/s41388-019-1110-1

10. Xue L, Thatte AS, Mai D, Haley RM, Gong N, Han X, et al. Responsive biomaterials: optimizing control of cancer immunotherapy. Nature Reviews Materials 2023 9:2 [Internet]. 2023 Dec 22 [cited 2024 Jun 22];9(2):100–18. Available from: https://www.nature.com/articles/s41578-023-00617-2

11.Unnikrishnan K, Thomas LV, Ram Kumar RM. Advancement of Scaffold-Based 3D Cellular Models in Cancer Tissue Engineering: An Update. Front Oncol [Internet]. 2021 Oct 25 [cited 2024 Jun 22];11. Available from:/pmc/articles/PMC8573168/

12.Pati F, Jang J, Ha DH, Won Kim S, Rhie JW, Shim JH, et al. Printing three-dimensional tissue analogs with decellularized extracellular matrix bioink. Nat Commun. 2014;5.

13.Dwivedi R, Pandey R, Kumar S, Mehrotra D. Poly hydroxyalkanoates (PHA): Role in bone scaffolds. J Oral Biol Craniofac Res [Internet]. 2020 Jan 1 [cited 2024 Jun 23];10(1):389. Available from:/pmc/articles/PMC6854076/

14.Qiu B, Wu D, Xue M, Ou L, Zheng Y, Xu F, et al. 3D Aligned Nanofiber Scaffold Fabrication with Trench-Guided Electrospinning for Cardiac Tissue Engineering. Langmuir [Internet]. 2024 Mar 5 [cited 2024 Jun 23];40(9):4709–18. Available from: https://pubs.acs.org/doi/abs/10.1021/acs.langmuir.3c03358

15.Cooke ME, Ramirez-GarciaLuna JL, Rangel-Berridi K, Park H, Nazhat SN, Weber MH, et al. 3D Printed Polyurethane Scaffolds for the Repair of Bone Defects. Front Bioeng Biotechnol [Internet]. 2020 Oct 23 [cited 2024 Jun 23];8. Available from:/pmc/articles/PMC7644785/

16.Vitale C, Marzagalli M, Scaglione S, Dondero A, Bottino C, Castriconi R. Tumor Microenvironment and Hydrogel-Based 3D Cancer Models for In Vitro Testing Immunotherapies. Cancers (Basel) [Internet]. 2022 Feb 1 [cited 2024 Jun 23];14(4). Available from:/pmc/articles/PMC8870468/

17.Serrano A, Berthelet J, Naik SH, Merino D. Mastering the use of cellular barcoding to explore cancer heterogeneity. Nature Reviews Cancer 2022 22:11 [Internet]. 2022 Aug 18 [cited 2024 Jun 23];22(11):609–24. Available from: https://www.nature.com/articles/s41568-022-00500-2

18.Tomar A, Uysal-Onganer P, Basnett P, Pati U, Roy I. 3D Disease Modeling of Hard and Soft Cancer Using PHA-Based Scaffolds. Cancers (Basel) [Internet]. 2022 Jul 1 [cited 2024 Jun 23];14(14):3549. Available from:/pmc/articles/PMC9321847/

19.Kim SY, Lee JY, Kim DH, Joo HS, Yun MR, Jung D, et al. Patient-Derived Cells to Guide Targeted Therapy for Advanced Lung Adenocarcinoma. Scientific Reports 2019 9:1 [Internet]. 2019 Dec 27 [cited 2024 Jun 23];9(1):1–12. Available from: https://www.nature.com/articles/s41598-019-56356-4

20.Jiang S, Wang M, He J. A review of biomimetic scaffolds for bone regeneration: Toward a cell-free strategy. Bioeng Transl Med [Internet]. 2021 May 1 [cited 2024 Jun 23];6(2). Available from:/pmc/articles/PMC8126827/

21.Elblová P, Lunova M, Dejneka A, Jirsa · Milan, Lunov O. Impact of mechanical cues on key cell functions and cell-nanoparticle interactions. Discover Nano 2024 19:1 [Internet]. 2024 Jun 22 [cited 2024 Jun 23];19(1):1–31. Available from: https://link.springer.com/article/10.1186/s11671-024-04052-2

22.Karamanos NK, Theocharis AD, Piperigkou Z, Manou D, Passi A, Skandalis SS, et al. A guide to the composition and functions of the extracellular matrix. FEBS J [Internet]. 2021 Dec 1 [cited 2024 Jun 23];288(24):6850–912. Available from: https://pubmed.ncbi.nlm.nih.gov/33605520/

23.Gupta P, Miller A, Olayanju A, Madhuri TK, Velliou E. A Systematic Comparative Assessment of the Response of Ovarian Cancer Cells to the Chemotherapeutic Cisplatin in 3D Models of Various Structural and Biochemical Configurations-Does One Model Type Fit All? Cancers (Basel) [Internet]. 2022 Mar 1 [cited 2024 Jun 23];14(5). Available from: https://pubmed.ncbi.nlm.nih.gov/35267582/

24.Unagolla JM, Jayasuriya AC. Hydrogel-based 3D bioprinting: A comprehensive review on cell-laden hydrogels, bioink formulations, and future perspectives. Appl Mater Today, [Internet]. 2020 Mar 1 [cited 2024 Jun 23];18. Available from:/pmc/articles/PMC7414424/

25.Gnatowski P, Piłat E, Kucińska-Lipka J, Saeb MR, Hamblin MR, Mozafari M. Recent advances in 3D bioprinted tumor models for personalized medicine. Transl Oncol [Internet]. 2023 Nov 1 [cited 2024 Jun 23];37. Available from:/pmc/articles/PMC10440569/

26.Castro F, Leite Pereira C, Helena Macedo M, Almeida A, José Silveira M, Dias S, et al. Advances on colorectal cancer 3D models: The needed translational technology for nanomedicine screening. Adv Drug Deliv Rev. 2021 Aug 1;175:113824.

27.Peiffer QC, de Ruijter M, van Duijn J, Crottet D, Dominic E, Malda J, et al. Melt electrowriting onto anatomically relevant biodegradable substrates: Resurfacing a diarthrodial joint. Mater Des. 2020 Oct 1;195:109025.

28.Contessi Negrini N, Franchi A, Danti S. Biomaterial-Assisted 3D In Vitro Tumor Models: From Organoid toward Cancer Tissue Engineering Approaches. Cancers 2023, Vol 15, Page 1201 [Internet]. 2023 Feb 14 [cited 2024 Jun 23];15(4):1201. Available from: https://www.mdpi.com/2072-6694/15/4/1201/htm

29.Prem Ananth K, Jayram ND. A comprehensive review of 3D printing techniques for biomaterial-based scaffold fabrication in bone tissue engineering. Annals of 3D Printed Medicine. 2024 Feb 1;13:100141.

30.Carvalho MR, Lima D, Reis RL, Correlo VM, Oliveira JM. Evaluating Biomaterial- and Microfluidic-Based 3D Tumor Models. Trends Biotechnol. 2015 Nov 1;33(11):667–78.

31.Parodi I, Di Lisa D, Pastorino L, Scaglione S, Fato MM. 3D Bioprinting as a Powerful Technique for Recreating the Tumor Microenvironment. Gels. 2023 Jun 1;9(6).

32.Shelkey E, Dominijanni A, Forsythe S, Oommen D, Soker S. Modeling of the Tumor Microenvironment in Tumor Organoids. Biomaterial Based Approaches to Study the Tumor Microenvironment. 2022 Dec 7;279–303.

33.Mohandesnezhad S, Monfared MH, Samani S, Farzin A, Poursamar SA, Ai J, et al. 3D-printed bioactive Chitosan/Alginate/Hardystonite scaffold for bone tissue engineering: Synthesis and characterization. J Non Cryst Solids [Internet]. 2023 Jun 1 [cited 2024 Jun 23];609:122261–122261. Available from: https://typeset.io/papers/3d-printed-bioactive-chitosan-alginate-hardystonite-scaffold-3a7tvezu

34.Zhou Y, Pereira G, Tang Y, James M, Zhang M. 3D Porous Scaffold-Based High-Throughput Platform for Cancer Drug Screening. Pharmaceutics [Internet]. 2023 Jun 1 [cited 2024 Jun 23];15(6):1691–1691. Available from: https://typeset.io/papers/3d-porous-scaffold-based-high-throughput-platform-for-cancer-1v1oobd3

35.Abuwatfa WH, Pitt WG, Husseini GA. Scaffold-based 3D cell culture models in cancer research. J Biomed Sci [Internet]. 2024 Dec 1 [cited 2024 Jun 23];31(1):7. Available from:/pmc/articles/PMC10789053/

36.Lv D, Hu Z, Lu L, Lu H, Xu X. Three-dimensional cell culture: A powerful tool in tumor research and drug discovery. Oncol Lett [Internet]. 2017 Dec 1 [cited 2024 Jun 23];14(6):6999. Available from:/pmc/articles/PMC5754907/

37.Kort-Mascort J, Shen ML, Martin E, Flores-Torres S, Pardo LA, Siegel PM, et al. Bioprinted cancer-stromal in vitro models in a decellularized ECM-based bioink exhibit progressive remodeling and maturation. Biomedical Materials (Bristol). 2023;18(4).

38.Kilian K, Fischbach C, Fong ELS. Engineered Biomaterials for Developing the Next Generation of In Vitro Tumor Models. Vol. 12, Advanced Healthcare Materials. 2023.

39.Ma Y, Zhang B, Sun H, Liu D, Zhu Y, Zhu Q, et al. The Dual Effect of 3D-Printed Biological Scaffolds Composed of Diverse Biomaterials in the Treatment of Bone Tumors. Vol. 18, International Journal of Nanomedicine. 2023.

40.Ahmed T. Functional biomaterials for biomimetic 3D in vitro tumor microenvironment modeling. In vitro models. 2023;2(1–2).

41.Guan X, Huang S. Advances in the application of 3D tumor models in precision oncology and drug screening. Vol. 10, Frontiers in Bioengineering and Biotechnology. 2022.

CHAPTER TEN

# FUTURE OF BIOMATERIALS IN DRUG DELIVERY AND CANCER

**Mani Sharma**[a]

[a] CSIR-Indian Institute of Chemical Technology, Tarnaka, Hyderabad, Secunderabad-500007, Telangana , India

**Introduction**

Biomaterials have revolutionized the field of drug delivery, offering versatile platforms for controlled release, targeted delivery, and personalized medicine. This paper provides a comprehensive review of recent advancements and future prospects in biomaterial-based drug delivery systems. We discuss the role of nanotechnology, biodegradable polymers, and multifunctional carriers in enhancing therapeutic efficacy and minimizing side effects. Furthermore, we explore emerging trends such as combination therapies, stimuli-responsive materials, and theranostic platforms, highlighting their potential for transforming the landscape of drug delivery. Through interdisciplinary collaborations and innovative materials design, biomaterials are poised to play a pivotal role in addressing current challenges in drug delivery and advancing towards more effective and patient-centric treatments.

In the realm of biomedical engineering, the convergence of materials science and medicine has unlocked tremendous potential for addressing complex healthcare challenges. One of the most promising frontiers is the utilization of biomaterials for drug delivery and cancer therapy. This interdisciplinary field merges the principles of chemistry, biology, and engineering to develop innovative strategies for targeted drug delivery, personalized medicine, and enhanced therapeutic efficacy. Looking ahead, the future of biomaterials in this domain holds immense promise, driven by advancements in nanotechnology, bioinformatics, and material design.

**Nanotechnology Revolutionizing Drug Delivery**

Nanotechnology has revolutionized drug delivery by offering precise control over the size, shape, and surface properties of nanoparticles. These nanocarriers, typically ranging from 1 to 100 nanometers in size, can encapsulate therapeutic agents such as chemotherapeutic drugs, nucleic acids, or proteins. Their small size facilitates efficient penetration into tissues and cellular uptake, enabling targeted delivery to specific sites within the body. Moreover, surface modification with ligands or antibodies allows for selective binding to receptors overexpressed on cancer cells, minimizing off-target effects and reducing systemic toxicity.

Nanotechnology has emerged as a transformative force in the field of drug delivery, offering unprecedented control over the design, fabrication, and delivery of therapeutic agents. At the nanoscale, materials exhibit unique properties that can be harnessed to overcome traditional limitations of drug administration, such as poor solubility, limited bioavailability, and off-target effects. This chapter explores the future potential of nanotechnology in revolutionizing drug delivery, focusing on key advancements, emerging trends, and challenges in the field.

Nanoparticle-Based Drug Delivery Systems:

Nanoparticle-based drug delivery systems represent one of the most promising applications of nanotechnology in medicine. These systems typically consist of biocompatible materials such as polymers, lipids, or inorganic nanoparticles, engineered to encapsulate and deliver therapeutic agents to specific target sites. Nanoparticles offer several advantages, including prolonged circulation time, enhanced cellular uptake, and the ability to protect encapsulated drugs from degradation. Future advancements in nanoparticle design will focus on improving biocompatibility, stability, and targeting specificity, thereby optimizing therapeutic efficacy and minimizing side effects.

Targeted Drug Delivery:

One of the key advantages of nanotechnology in drug delivery is its ability to achieve targeted delivery of therapeutic agents to specific tissues or cells. By functionalizing nanoparticle surfaces with targeting ligands or antibodies, researchers can direct drug-loaded nanoparticles to diseased tissues while sparing healthy cells. Targeted drug delivery not only enhances therapeutic efficacy but also minimizes off-target effects and reduces systemic toxicity. Future advancements in targeted drug delivery will involve the development of novel targeting strategies, including molecular recognition techniques and biomimetic approaches, to further enhance targeting specificity and therapeutic outcomes.

Multifunctional Nanocarriers:

The future of nanotechnology in drug delivery lies in the development of multifunctional nanocarriers capable of integrating diagnostic, therapeutic, and targeting functionalities into a single platform. These multifunctional nanocarriers, often referred to as theranostic nanoparticles, enable simultaneous imaging and therapy, allowing for real-time monitoring of treatment response and disease progression. By combining diagnostic and therapeutic capabilities, theranostic nanoparticles offer new opportunities for personalized medicine and precision therapy. Future advancements in multifunctional nanocarriers will focus on enhancing integration of diagnostic imaging modalities, improving theranostic performance, and enabling personalized treatment regimens.

Stimuli-Responsive Nanomaterials:

Stimuli-responsive nanomaterials hold promise for achieving precise control over drug release kinetics and spatial distribution in response to specific environmental cues. These nanomaterials can be engineered to undergo changes in structure, morphology, or physicochemical properties in response to external stimuli such as pH, temperature, or enzymatic activity. Stimuli-responsive drug delivery systems offer several advantages, including on-demand drug release, site-specific targeting, and reduced systemic toxicity. Future advancements in stimuli-responsive nanomaterials will focus on expanding the repertoire of stimuli that can be exploited for drug release, improving responsiveness and sensitivity, and optimizing biocompatibility for clinical applications.

Despite the tremendous potential of nanotechnology in drug delivery, several challenges remain to be addressed to translate research findings into clinical applications. These challenges include scaling up production processes, ensuring long-term stability and safety of nanomaterials, and navigating regulatory pathways for approval and commercialization. Furthermore, concerns regarding potential toxicity, immunogenicity, and biocompatibility of nanomaterials require careful evaluation and mitigation strategies. Future research efforts will focus on addressing these challenges through interdisciplinary collaborations, innovative materials design, and rigorous preclinical and clinical evaluation. By harnessing the transformative capabilities of nanotechnology, the future holds immense promise for revolutionizing drug delivery and improving patient outcomes

**Biodegradable Polymers Enhancing Biocompatibility**

Biodegradable polymers have emerged as key components of biomaterial-based drug delivery systems due to their biocompatibility and tunable degradation kinetics. These polymers can be tailored to degrade at controlled rates, releasing encapsulated drugs in a sustained manner over extended periods. Furthermore, their biodegradability eliminates the need for surgical removal post-treatment, minimizing patient discomfort and improving therapeutic outcomes. Biodegradable polymer-based nanoparticles, micelles, and hydrogels offer versatile platforms for delivering a wide range of therapeutics, including small molecules, peptides, and nucleic acids, with enhanced stability and bioavailability.

Biodegradable polymers have emerged as indispensable components in the field of biomaterials, offering unique advantages for enhancing biocompatibility and reducing adverse effects associated with medical implants and drug delivery systems. These polymers, which undergo degradation into biologically compatible byproducts upon exposure to physiological conditions, provide temporary support or delivery vehicles for therapeutic agents while minimizing long-term foreign body reactions. This chapter explores the role of biodegradable polymers in enhancing biocompatibility, focusing on their properties, applications, and future prospects in biomedical engineering.

Properties of Biodegradable Polymers:

Biodegradable polymers exhibit a wide range of properties that make them well-suited for biomedical applications. These polymers can be classified based on their chemical composition, including synthetic polymers such as poly(lactic-co-glycolic acid) (PLGA), poly(caprolactone) (PCL), and poly(ethylene glycol) (PEG), as well as natural polymers like collagen, chitosan, and gelatin. Key properties of biodegradable polymers include tunable degradation kinetics, mechanical strength, biocompatibility, and versatility in fabrication processes. By adjusting polymer composition, molecular weight, and degradation rate, researchers can tailor polymer properties to meet specific application requirements, ranging from tissue engineering scaffolds to drug delivery carriers.

Applications in Tissue Engineering:

Biodegradable polymers play a crucial role in tissue engineering by providing scaffolds for cell growth, proliferation, and tissue regeneration. These scaffolds mimic the extracellular matrix (ECM) of native tissues, providing structural support and biochemical cues for cell attachment, migration, and differentiation. Biodegradable polymer scaffolds can be fabricated using various techniques, including solvent casting, electrospinning, and 3D printing, to create complex structures with controlled porosity, mechanical properties, and degradation kinetics. Furthermore, incorporation of bioactive molecules such as growth factors, cytokines, or drugs into polymer matrices enhances tissue regeneration and accelerates healing processes. Future advancements in tissue engineering will focus on developing multifunctional scaffolds capable of integrating mechanical support, biological signaling, and controlled release of therapeutic agents to promote tissue regeneration in complex biological environments.

Drug Delivery Systems:

Biodegradable polymers serve as versatile carriers for controlled release of therapeutic agents in drug delivery systems. These polymers can encapsulate drugs, proteins, or nucleic acids within biodegradable matrices, providing sustained release over extended periods while minimizing systemic toxicity. By adjusting polymer composition, degradation kinetics, and drug loading capacity, researchers can modulate drug release kinetics and achieve desired therapeutic outcomes. Biodegradable polymer-based drug delivery systems offer several advantages, including improved drug stability, enhanced bioavailability, and reduced dosing frequency. Furthermore, surface modification with targeting ligands or stimuli-responsive moieties enables targeted delivery to specific tissues or cells, minimizing off-target effects and maximizing therapeutic efficacy. Future advancements in biodegradable polymer-based drug delivery systems will focus on improving drug loading efficiency, enhancing targeting specificity, and enabling personalized dosing regimens for precision medicine applications.

Implantable Medical Devices:

Biodegradable polymers have revolutionized the field of implantable medical devices by providing temporary scaffolds or coatings that promote tissue integration and minimize long-term complications. These polymers can be used to fabricate stents, sutures, orthopedic implants, and cardiovascular devices with tailored mechanical properties, degradation kinetics, and biocompatibility. Upon implantation, biodegradable polymers gradually degrade into non-toxic byproducts, eliminating the need for surgical removal and reducing the risk of chronic inflammation or immune responses. Furthermore, biodegradable polymer coatings can be applied to implant surfaces to modulate tissue responses, prevent biofouling, and enhance biocompatibility. Future advancements in implantable medical devices will focus on developing smart materials with dynamic properties that respond to physiological cues, promoting tissue regeneration and integration while minimizing adverse effects.

Despite significant progress, several challenges must be addressed to fully realize the potential of biodegradable polymers in biomedical applications. These challenges include optimizing degradation kinetics, enhancing mechanical properties, and ensuring long-term stability and biocompatibility of polymer-based devices. Furthermore, scalability, regulatory considerations, and cost-effectiveness pose hurdles to clinical translation and widespread adoption of biodegradable polymer technologies. Future research efforts will focus on overcoming these challenges through interdisciplinary collaborations, innovative materials design, and rigorous preclinical and clinical evaluation. By harnessing the unique properties of biodegradable polymers, the future holds immense promise for enhancing biocompatibility and improving patient outcomes in biomedical engineering.

**Personalized Medicine through Biomaterials**

Personalized medicine represents a paradigm shift in healthcare, moving away from a one-size-fits-all approach towards tailored treatments that account for individual variability in genetics, physiology, and lifestyle. Biomaterials play a pivotal role in personalized medicine by enabling precise targeting of therapeutic agents based on the unique molecular profiles of patients. This chapter explores the emerging field of personalized medicine through biomaterials, focusing on key strategies, applications, and future prospects for improving patient outcomes across various disease conditions.The era of personalized medicine is being propelled by biomaterials that enable precise targeting of therapeutic agents based on individual patient characteristics. Advances in bioinformatics and high-throughput screening techniques have facilitated the identification of biomarkers associated with specific diseases, including cancer subtypes. Biomaterial-based drug delivery systems can be engineered to incorporate targeting moieties that recognize these biomarkers, allowing for tailored treatments tailored to the unique molecular profiles of patients. By enabling the delivery of therapeutics to diseased tissues while sparing healthy cells, personalized drug delivery holds the potential to optimize treatment outcomes and minimize adverse effects.

Combination Therapies and Multifunctional Biomaterials:

The future of biomaterials in drug delivery and cancer therapy is characterized by the development of multifunctional platforms capable of delivering combination therapies with synergistic effects. Combinatorial approaches, such as co-delivery of chemotherapy drugs with immunomodulators or gene-editing agents, offer new avenues for overcoming drug resistance and enhancing therapeutic efficacy. Biomaterials can be engineered to encapsulate multiple therapeutic agents within a single carrier, enabling precise spatiotemporal control over drug release kinetics. Moreover, integration of diagnostic imaging modalities into biomaterial-based delivery systems allows for real-time monitoring of treatment response and disease progression, facilitating adaptive therapy regimens.

Understanding Patient Variability:

Central to personalized medicine is the recognition of patient variability in disease susceptibility, progression, and response to treatment. Advances in genomics, proteomics, and metabolomics have enabled the identification of biomarkers associated with specific diseases, allowing for personalized diagnosis, prognosis, and treatment selection. Biomaterials serve as versatile platforms for integrating diagnostic and therapeutic functionalities, enabling real-time monitoring of disease biomarkers and adaptation of treatment regimens based on individual patient responses. By harnessing the power of biomaterials, personalized medicine aims to optimize therapeutic efficacy, minimize adverse effects, and improve patient outcomes through tailored interventions.

Targeted Drug Delivery:

Biomaterial-based drug delivery systems offer a promising approach for achieving targeted delivery of therapeutic agents to diseased tissues while sparing healthy cells. By functionalizing biomaterial carriers with targeting ligands or antibodies, researchers can direct drug-loaded nanoparticles, micelles, or hydrogels to specific cell types or biomarker-expressing tissues. Targeted drug delivery not only enhances therapeutic efficacy but also minimizes off-target effects and reduces systemic toxicity. Furthermore, biomaterial-based carriers can be engineered to respond to specific physiological cues or disease microenvironments, enabling spatiotemporal control over drug release kinetics. Personalized medicine through biomaterials thus enables tailored treatments that address the unique molecular signatures of individual patients, optimizing therapeutic outcomes and minimizing adverse effects.

Implantable Medical Devices:

In addition to drug delivery systems, biomaterials play a crucial role in the development of implantable medical devices for personalized medicine applications. These devices, such as stents, orthopedic implants, and tissue-engineered constructs, can be customized to match the anatomical, mechanical, and biological properties of individual patients. Biomaterial scaffolds provide temporary support for tissue regeneration and integration, promoting healing processes while minimizing long-term complications. Furthermore, biomaterial coatings can be applied to implant surfaces to modulate tissue responses, prevent biofouling, and enhance biocompatibility. By tailoring implantable medical devices to individual patient needs, personalized medicine through biomaterials offers new opportunities for improving surgical outcomes, reducing implant-related complications, and enhancing patient quality of life.

Combination Therapies and Multifunctional Biomaterials

The future of personalized medicine through biomaterials lies in the development of multifunctional platforms capable of delivering combination therapies with synergistic effects. Combinatorial approaches, such as co-delivery of chemotherapy drugs with immunomodulators or gene-editing agents, offer new avenues for overcoming drug resistance and enhancing therapeutic efficacy. Biomaterials can be engineered to encapsulate multiple therapeutic agents within a single carrier, enabling precise spatiotemporal control over drug release kinetics. Moreover, integration of diagnostic imaging modalities into biomaterial-based delivery systems allows for real-time monitoring of treatment response and disease progression, facilitating adaptive therapy regimens. Personalized medicine through biomaterials thus enables tailored combination therapies that address the molecular complexity of individual patients, optimizing treatment outcomes and improving patient survival rates.

Despite the tremendous potential of personalized medicine through biomaterials, several challenges must be addressed to translate research findings into clinical applications. These challenges include optimizing the pharmacokinetics and pharmacodynamics of drug-loaded carriers, enhancing targeting specificity, and ensuring long-term safety and biocompatibility. Furthermore, scalability, regulatory considerations, and cost-effectiveness pose hurdles to clinical translation and widespread adoption of personalized medicine through biomaterials. Future research efforts will focus on overcoming these challenges through interdisciplinary collaborations, innovative materials design, and rigorous preclinical and clinical evaluation. By harnessing the synergistic capabilities of biomaterials, nanotechnology, and personalized medicine, the future holds immense promise for transforming the landscape of healthcare and improving patient outcomes

Combination therapies, involving the simultaneous administration of multiple therapeutic agents with complementary mechanisms of action, have emerged as a promising strategy for improving treatment outcomes across various disease conditions. Multifunctional biomaterials, capable of integrating diagnostic, therapeutic, and targeting functionalities into a single platform, play a pivotal role in enabling effective combination therapies. This chapter explores the rationale behind combination therapies, the design principles of multifunctional biomaterials, and their applications in advancing precision medicine across different biomedical fields.

Rationale for Combination Therapies:

Combination therapies offer several advantages over single-agent treatments, including enhanced therapeutic efficacy, reduced drug resistance, and mitigation of adverse effects. By targeting multiple pathways involved in disease progression, combination therapies can achieve synergistic effects that surpass the efficacy of individual drugs alone. Moreover, combination therapies enable the targeting of heterogeneous cell populations within tumors, minimizing the emergence of drug-resistant clones and improving overall treatment response. Biomaterial-based delivery systems provide an ideal platform for combination therapies, allowing for precise control over drug release kinetics and spatial distribution, thereby maximizing therapeutic outcomes while minimizing systemic toxicity.

Design Principles of Multifunctional Biomaterials:

Multifunctional biomaterials are designed to incorporate multiple functionalities, such as drug delivery, imaging, targeting, and stimulus responsiveness, into a single platform. These biomaterials can be engineered at the nanoscale, microscale, or macroscale, depending on the specific application requirements. Key design considerations include selecting biocompatible materials with tunable properties, optimizing drug loading and release kinetics, and functionalizing biomaterial surfaces with targeting ligands or stimuli-responsive moieties. Furthermore, integration of diagnostic imaging modalities, such as magnetic resonance imaging (MRI) or positron emission tomography (PET), enables real-time monitoring of treatment response and disease progression, facilitating adaptive therapy regimens.

Applications in Cancer Therapy:

Combination therapies and multifunctional biomaterials hold great promise for improving outcomes in cancer therapy, where the complexity and heterogeneity of tumors pose significant challenges to effective treatment. Combinatorial approaches, such as co-delivery of chemotherapy drugs with immunomodulators or targeted therapies, offer new avenues for overcoming drug resistance and enhancing therapeutic efficacy. Multifunctional biomaterial carriers can be engineered to encapsulate multiple therapeutic agents within a single platform, enabling precise spatiotemporal control over drug release kinetics and targeting specificity. Moreover, integration of diagnostic imaging modalities into biomaterial-based delivery systems allows for non-invasive monitoring of treatment response, guiding therapeutic decisions and optimizing patient outcomes.

Applications in Infectious Disease Treatment:

Combination therapies and multifunctional biomaterials also hold promise for improving outcomes in infectious disease treatment, particularly in the context of antimicrobial resistance and persistent infections. Combinatorial approaches, such as combination antibiotic therapy or co-delivery of antibiotics with immunomodulators, offer new strategies for overcoming drug resistance and enhancing antimicrobial efficacy. Multifunctional biomaterial carriers can be engineered to deliver multiple antimicrobial agents with synergistic effects, while also modulating immune responses and promoting tissue regeneration. Furthermore, biomaterial-based delivery systems can be designed to target specific pathogens or infected tissues, minimizing off-target effects and reducing the risk of systemic toxicity.

Despite the tremendous potential of combination therapies and multifunctional biomaterials, several challenges must be addressed to translate research findings into clinical applications. These challenges include optimizing the pharmacokinetics and pharmacodynamics of drug-loaded carriers, enhancing targeting specificity, and ensuring long-term safety and biocompatibility. Furthermore, scalability, regulatory considerations, and cost-effectiveness pose hurdles to clinical translation and widespread adoption of combination therapies and multifunctional biomaterials. Future research efforts will focus on overcoming these challenges through interdisciplinary collaborations, innovative materials design, and rigorous preclinical and clinical evaluation. By harnessing the synergistic capabilities of combination therapies and multifunctional biomaterials, the future holds immense promise for advancing precision medicine and improving patient outcomes across various biomedical fields.

**Future challenges of biomaterials in drug delivery and cancer**

In envisioning the future of biomaterials in drug delivery and cancer therapy, it is imperative to acknowledge and address the challenges that lie ahead. Despite the significant progress made in this field, several obstacles must be overcome to fully realize the potential of biomaterial-based approaches in combating cancer and delivering therapeutics with precision and efficacy.

One of the primary challenges is optimizing the pharmacokinetics and pharmacodynamics of drug-loaded biomaterial carriers. Achieving a balance between controlled release and sustained therapeutic effect while minimizing off-target effects and systemic toxicity remains a complex task. Additionally, the heterogeneity of tumors poses a significant challenge in achieving effective drug delivery to all cancerous cells within a tumor, especially those residing in hypoxic or poorly vascularized regions.

Furthermore, enhancing targeting specificity represents a critical area for future research. While biomaterials can be engineered to selectively target cancer cells through surface modifications or ligand conjugation, achieving uniform distribution and penetration throughout the tumor microenvironment remains a challenge. Overcoming biological barriers such as the extracellular matrix and the blood-brain barrier is essential for ensuring effective drug delivery to tumor cells while minimizing damage to healthy tissues.

Another challenge is ensuring long-term safety and biocompatibility of biomaterial-based drug delivery systems. Biodegradable polymers, while advantageous in facilitating controlled drug release and minimizing the need for device removal, must be carefully designed to avoid adverse inflammatory reactions or immune responses. Additionally, concerns regarding the potential accumulation of degradation byproducts and their impact on systemic physiology necessitate thorough preclinical evaluation and long-term monitoring.

Scalability and regulatory considerations also pose significant challenges to the clinical translation and widespread adoption of biomaterial-based drug delivery systems. Achieving reproducibility and standardization in manufacturing processes while complying with regulatory requirements for safety and efficacy represents a formidable task. Moreover, the cost-effectiveness of biomaterial-based therapies must be carefully evaluated to ensure accessibility and affordability for patients.

Despite these challenges, the future of biomaterials in drug delivery and cancer therapy holds immense promise. Advances in nanotechnology, materials science, and personalized medicine are poised to address these challenges and revolutionize the landscape of cancer treatment. Interdisciplinary collaborations, innovative materials design, and rigorous preclinical and clinical evaluation will be essential in overcoming these obstacles and harnessing the full potential of biomaterial-based approaches for improving patient outcomes in the fight against cancer.

## Reference


1. Zhang, L., Gu, F. X., Chan, J. M., Wang, A. Z., Langer, R. S., & Farokhzad, O. C. (2008). Nanoparticles in medicine: therapeutic applications and developments. Clinical pharmacology & therapeutics, 83(5), 761-769.
2. Hrkach, J., Von Hoff, D., Mukkaram Ali, M., Andrianova, E., Auer, J., Campbell, T., ... & Zarif, L. (2012). Preclinical development and clinical translation of a PSMA-targeted docetaxel nanoparticle with a differentiated pharmacological profile. Science translational medicine, 4(128), 128ra39-128ra39.
3. Davis, M. E., Chen, Z., & Shin, D. M. (2008). Nanoparticle therapeutics: an emerging treatment modality for cancer. Nature Reviews Drug Discovery, 7(9), 771-782.
4. Peer, D., Karp, J. M., Hong, S., Farokhzad, O. C., Margalit, R., & Langer, R. (2007). Nanocarriers as an emerging platform for cancer therapy. Nature nanotechnology, 2(12), 751-760.
5. Cheng, R., Meng, F., Deng, C., Klok, H. A., & Zhong, Z. (2013). Dual and multi-stimuli responsive polymeric nanoparticles for programmed site-specific drug delivery. Biomaterials, 34(14), 3647-3657.
6. Blanco, E., Shen, H., & Ferrari, M. (2015). Principles of nanoparticle design for overcoming biological barriers to drug delivery. Nature biotechnology, 33(9), 941-951.
7. Farokhzad, O. C., & Langer, R. (2009). Impact of nanotechnology on drug delivery. ACS nano, 3(1), 16-20.
8. Petros, R. A., & DeSimone, J. M. (2010). Strategies in the design of nanoparticles for therapeutic applications. Nature Reviews Drug Discovery, 9(8), 615-627.
9. Li, Y., Xiao, K., Luo, J., Xiao, W., Lee, J. S., Gonik, A. M., ... & Lam, K. S. (2011). Well-defined, reversible disulfide cross-linked micelles for on-demand paclitaxel delivery. Biomaterials, 32(27), 6633-6645.
10. Wang, Y., Gao, S., Ye, W. H., Yoon, H. S., Yang, Y. Y., & Coombes, A. G. (2006). Reversibly stabilized multifunctional dextran nanoparticles efficiently deliver doxorubicin into the nuclei of cancer cells. Angewandte Chemie International Edition, 45(44), 6126-6130.
11. Barenholz, Y. C. (2012). Doxil®—the first FDA-approved nano-drug: lessons learned. Journal of controlled release, 160(2), 117-134.
12. Fang, J., Nakamura, H., & Maeda, H. (2011). The EPR effect: Unique features of tumor blood vessels for drug delivery, factors involved, and limitations and augmentation of the effect. Advanced drug delivery reviews, 63(3), 136-151.
13. Dreaden, E. C., Alkilany, A. M., Huang, X., Murphy, C. J., & El-Sayed, M. A. (2012). The golden age: gold nanoparticles for biomedicine. Chemical Society Reviews, 41(7), 2740-2779.
14. Torchilin, V. P. (2011). Multifunctional nanocarriers. Advanced drug delivery reviews, 63(9), 813-816.
15. Park, K. (2013). Facing the truth about nanotechnology in drug delivery. ACS nano, 7(9), 7442-7447.
16. Perry, J. L., Reuter, K. G., Kai, M. P., Herlihy, K. P., Jones, S. W., Luft, J. C., ... & DeSimone, J. M. (2012). PEGylated PRINT nanoparticles: the impact of PEG density on protein binding, macrophage association, biodistribution, and pharmacokinetics. Nano letters, 12(10), 5304-5310.
17. Jokerst, J. V., Lobovkina, T., Zare, R. N., & Gambhir, S. S. (2011). Nanoparticle PEGylation for imaging and therapy. Nanomedicine, 6(4), 715-728.
18. Alexis, F., Pridgen, E., Molnar, L. K., & Farokhzad, O. C. (2008). Factors affecting the clearance and biodistribution of polymeric nanoparticles. Molecular pharmaceutics, 5(4), 505-515.
19. Farokhzad, O. C., Cheng, J., Teply, B. A., Sherifi, I., Jon, S., Kantoff, P. W., ... & Langer, R. (2006). Targeted nanoparticle-aptamer bioconjugates for cancer chemotherapy in vivo. Proceedings of the National Academy of Sciences, 103(16), 6315-6320.
20. Torchilin, V. P. (2011). Multifunctional nanocarriers. Advanced drug delivery reviews, 63(9), 813-816.
21. Ferrari, M. (2005). Cancer nanotechnology: opportunities and challenges. Nature reviews cancer, 5(3), 161-171.

22. Lammers, T., Hennink, W. E., & Storm, G. (2008). Tumour-targeted nanomedicines: principles and practice. British journal of cancer, 99(3), 392-397.
23. O'Brien, M. E. R., Wigler, N., Inbar, M., Rosso, R., Grischke, E., Santoro, A., ... & Casado, A. (2004). Reduced cardiotoxicity and comparable efficacy in a phase III trial of pegylated liposomal doxorubicin HCl (CAELYX™/Doxil®) versus conventional doxorubicin for first-line treatment of metastatic breast cancer. Annals of Oncology, 15(3), 440-449.
24. Maeda, H., Nakamura, H., & Fang, J. (2013). The EPR effect for macromolecular drug delivery to solid tumors: Improvement of tumor uptake, lowering of systemic toxicity, and distinct tumor imaging in vivo. Advanced drug delivery reviews, 65(1), 71-79.
25. Wilhelm, S., Tavares, A. J., Dai, Q., Ohta, S., Audet, J., Dvorak, H. F., & Chan, W. C. W. (2016). Analysis of nanoparticle delivery to tumours. Nature Reviews Materials, 1(5), 16014.
26. Blanco, E., Shen, H., & Ferrari, M. (2015). Principles of nanoparticle design for overcoming biological barriers to drug delivery. Nature biotechnology, 33(9), 941-951.
27. Danhier, F., Feron, O., & Préat, V. (2010). To exploit the tumor microenvironment: Passive and active tumor targeting of nanocarriers for anti-cancer drug delivery. Journal of Controlled Release, 148(2), 135-146.
28. Sengupta, S., Eavarone, D., Capila, I., Zhao, G., Watson, N., Kiziltepe, T., ... & Sasisekharan, R. (2005). Temporal targeting of tumour cells and neovasculature with a nanoscale delivery system. Nature, 436(7050), 568-572.
29. Mura, S., Nicolas, J., & Couvreur, P. (2013). Stimuli-responsive nanocarriers for drug delivery. Nature Materials, 12(11), 991-1003.
30. Shi, J., & Kantoff, P. W. (2011). Wooster. Gene J. Therapy and Oncolytic Virotherapy. Cancer research, 71(15), 4780-4784.
31. Wicki, A., Witzigmann, D., Balasubramanian, V., Huwyler, J., (2015). Nanomedicine in cancer therapy: challenges, opportunities, and clinical applications. Journal of Controlled Release, 200, 138-157.
32. Bae, Y. H., & Park, K. (2011). Targeted drug delivery to tumors: myths, reality and possibility. Journal of controlled release, 153(3), 198-205.
33. Peer, D., Karp, J. M., Hong, S., Farokhzad, O. C., Margalit, R., & Langer, R. (2007). Nanocarriers as an emerging platform for cancer therapy. Nature nanotechnology, 2(12), 751-760.
34. Trédan, O., Galmarini, C. M., Patel, K., & Tannock, I. F. (2007). Drug resistance and the solid tumor microenvironment. Journal of the National Cancer Institute, 99(19), 1441-1454.
35. Blanco, E., Shen, H., & Ferrari, M. (2015). Principles of nanoparticle design for overcoming biological barriers to drug delivery. Nature biotechnology, 33(9), 941-951.
36. Hrkach, J., Von Hoff, D., Ali, M. M., Andrianova, E., Auer, J., Campbell, T., ... & Zarif, L. (2012). Preclinical development and clinical translation of a PSMA-targeted docetaxel nanoparticle with a differentiated pharmacological profile. Science translational medicine, 4(128), 128ra39-128ra39.
37. Shi, J., & Kantoff, P. W. (2011). Wooster. Gene J. Therapy and Oncolytic Virotherapy. Cancer research, 71(15), 4780-4784.
38. Verma, A., Stellacci, F., (2010). Effect of surface properties on nanoparticle-cell interactions. Small, 6(1), 12-21.
39. Bae, Y. H., & Park, K. (2011). Targeted drug delivery to tumors: myths, reality and possibility. Journal of controlled release, 153(3), 198-205.
40. Peer, D., Karp, J. M., Hong, S., Farokhzad, O. C., Margalit, R., & Langer, R. (2007). Nanocarriers as an emerging platform for cancer therapy. Nature nanotechnology, 2(12), 751-760

# Author's Biography And Contribution

## AUTHOR(s) BIOGRAPHY

**Dr. Mani Sharma**, Editor & Author**Email:** mninup2015@gmail.com@gmail.com

Dr. Mani Sharma is a distinguished researcher with over a decade of expertise in the fields of pharmaceutical formulations, nanoparticles, liposomes, and drug delivery systems. His research career, spanning ten years from UKTU, UPTU, AKUMS (R&D), INMAS-DRDO, CSIR-CDRI and CSIR-IICT, has been marked by significant contributions to the development and optimization of advanced drug delivery mechanisms. Dr. Sharma's work primarily focuses on enhancing the bioavailability and efficacy of therapeutic agents through innovative formulation strategies and nanotechnology. His studies have provided crucial insights into the design of nanoparticles and liposomes, aiming to improve targeted drug delivery and minimize side effects.

Dr. Sharma has published research papers, books and chapters extensively in renowned scientific journals, with his research garnering substantial recognition in the scientific community. His Google Scholar profile highlights numerous citations and impactful papers that underline his role in advancing the field. Notable among his contributions are his developments in the encapsulation of drugs within liposomes and nanoparticles, which have paved the way for new therapeutic approaches in treating various diseases. Through his ongoing research, Dr. Sharma continues to push the boundaries of pharmaceutical science, striving to deliver safer and more effective treatments.

**Mr. Abhiram Kumar**, Author**Email:** abhiramkumar123@gmail.com

**Mr. Abhiram Kumar** is a pharmacy post graduate with diverse specializations including molecular pharmacology, nanotherapeutics, and pharmacokinetics, boasts a decade of extensive experience in both the pharmaceutical industry and research institutes. Throughout his academic and professional journey, he has consistently delivered exemplary work, evident through his numerous publications in national and international journals, including book chapters, review articles, and research papers. Presently focusing on cancer therapeutics.

**Mohini Rawat,** Co-author**Email:** mohinirawat299@gmail.com

Mohini Rawat is currently employed as an associate professor in Himalayan Institute of Pharmacy and Research, Atak Farm, Rajawala Dehradun, Uttarakhand. She holds a Master degree in Pharmaceutics from SBS University Dehradun Uttarakhand. She possesses a strong skill set in areas such as Liposomes, Microemulsion, Control release drug delivery system, in-vivo studies and cationic lipid synthesis. Over the past two decades she has contributed significantly to the field through research papers, demonstrating extensive involvement in formulation and development Processes.

**Ms. Anjali Rai,** Co-Author**Email:** raianjali1114@gmail.com

Ms. Anjali Rai has completed post-graduate in Pharmacy (M. Pharm in Pharmacology), delves deeply into understanding the drug-drug interaction, molecular mechanism and adverse drug reaction. Throughout her academic journey, she has been wholeheartedly devoted to propelling the realm of pharmacology forward.

**Mr. Shivang Shukla,** Co-Author**Email:** ShivangShukla20@gmail.com

**Mr. Shivang Shukla** hold master degree in pharmacy (Pharmacology) from Amity University Lucknow, U.P. Throughout his academic and professional journey, hehas published review and research article in national and international journals as a co-author. Currently, he is working on nuro-pharmacology and Cancer biology. He has sound knowledge on tumor microenvironments study.

**Mr.Madhaw Kumar,** Co-Author**Email:** madhawchandrabashu.111@gmail.com

**Mr.Madhaw Kumar** has completed master in pharmaceutics associated with CSIR-CDRI, Lucknow. Presently, He has been instrumental at Goel Institute of Pharmacy and Sciences, Lucknow as an Assistant Professor in the Pharmaceutics department. His research interests are the characterization of pharmaceutical dosages form including transdermal patches, OTF, Solid oral, liquid formulations etc.

**Dr. Neeraj Sharma, Co-authorEmail:** tanveladu2010@gmail.com

**Dr. Neeraj Sharma** is a pharmacy graduate with over 20 years of experience in pharmaceutical R&D. He is currently serving as a Director at a multinational pharmaceutical company.

**Mr. Aamir Anwar, Co-authorEmail:**Aamiranwar57@gmail.com

**Mr. Aamir Anwar** has made significant strides in pharmacy with a robust academic background and professional experience. Currently, he is pursuing a PhD in Pharmacy with a specialization in Pharmacology, focusing on hepatic oncology.

**Mr. Mohd Mursal, Co-authorEmail:** mohdmursal99@gmail.com

**Mr. Mohd Mursal** holds a Master's in Pharmacy specializing in Pharmacology from Integral University and a Bachelor's from AKTU. He has authored review articles and a book chapter, showcasing expertise in pharmacological research. With a commitment to advancing knowledge in the field, Mohd remains dedicated to scholarly pursuits and innovation in pharmaceutical sciences.

**Ms. Alina Khan, Co-authorEmail:**iamalinakhan1999@gmail.com

**Ms. Alina Khan** is an accomplished academic student currently completing her Master's in Toxicology from the Department of Medical Elementology& Toxicology at JamiaHamdard, New Delhi. She holds a Bachelor's degree in Pharmacy from NIET, Pharmacy Institute, Noida, where she laid a strong foundation in pharmaceutical sciences.

**Mr. Sahil Hussain, Co-authorEmail:** sahilhussain.grad@gmail.com

**Mr. Sahil Hussain**, a passionate pharmacist and dedicated research scholar in the field of pharmacology. Actively engaged in unraveling pharmacological mechanisms, he strives to uncover novel insights that can revolutionize treatment paradigms. His work covers critical areas, including drug development, pharmacokinetics, toxicology, and therapeutic interventions.

www.ingramcontent.com/pod-product-compliance
Ingram Content Group UK Ltd.
Pitfield, Milton Keynes, MK11 3LW, UK
UKHW062000290726
14090UKWH00021B/1300